Cross-Curricular Learning 3–14

Education at SAGE

SAGE is a leading international publisher of journals, books, and electronic media for academic, educational, and professional markets.

Our education publishing includes:

- accessible and comprehensive texts for aspiring education professionals and practitioners looking to further their careers through continuing professional development

- inspirational advice and guidance for the classroom

- authoritative state of the art reference from the leading authors in the field

Find out more at: **www.sagepub.co.uk/education**

Cross-Curricular Learning 3–14

Second Edition

Jonathan Barnes

⑤SAGE

Los Angeles | London | New Delhi
Singapore | Washington DC

First edition published in 2007
Reprinted in 2008 and 2009

Second edition published in 2011

SAGE Publications Ltd
1 Oliver's Yard
55 City Road
London EC1Y 1SP

SAGE Publications Inc.
2455 Teller Road
Thousand Oaks, California 91320

SAGE Publications India Pvt Ltd
B 1/I 1 Mohan Cooperative Industrial Area
Mathura Road
New Delhi 110 044

SAGE Publications Asia-Pacific Pte Ltd
33 Pekin Street #02-01
Far East Square
Singapore 048763

Library of Congress Control Number: 2010934341

British Library Cataloguing in Publication data

A catalogue record for this book is available from the British Library

ISBN 978-0-85702-067-3
ISBN 978-0-85702-068-0 (pbk)

Typeset by C&M Digitals (P) Ltd, Chennai, India
Printed in Great Britain by CPI Antony Rowe, Chippenham, Wiltshire
Printed on paper from sustainable resources

MIX
Paper from
responsible sources
FSC
www.fsc.org   FSC® C013604

'...just help them find where they can be creative and fulfilment will follow.'

To

Gerry Tewfik who said these words and inspired many of the principles which underpin this book and to Kay and Bill Barnes my parents, my wife Cherry and my dear sister Jane who have tirelessly encouraged me towards clarity of values and personal creativity.

Contents

prev pg.

About the Author

Jonathan is senior lecturer in Education at Canterbury Christ Church University. He has lifelong interests in music, geography, history, religion and art. These cross-curricular leanings led him first to teach history and geography and the history of art in two Kent secondary schools in the 1970s, then to become a primary class teacher for most of the 1980s. His passion for relevance and engagement in learning led him to devise a ground-breaking interdisciplinary curriculum based wholly on the school locality in the Kent school of which he was head throughout the 1990s.

Since 2000 as a teacher educator, Jonathan has researched links between the 'science of learning', cross-curricular and creative approaches and the well-being of teachers and children. He has taught in India, Germany, Kenya and Malaysia on innovative curriculum projects as well as leading initiatives for Creative Partnerships in Kent, London and throughout England. His interest in making place the focus of curriculum choices continues now in his work for Engaging Places (an English Heritage/Commission for Architecture and the Built Environment website), for A New Direction London and for Future Creative Kent.

Acknowledgements

There is no doubt that monumental thanks go to my wife Cherry who has loved, sustained, inspired and encouraged me throughout a difficult year so crammed with important family events that writing a book seemed impossible. Similarly, my children Ben, Naomi, Esther and Jacob have contributed in ways they are not always fully aware of. They have tolerated my divided attention and listened, always with love and patience, to my overexcited conversation on the topics raised in this book.

Many friends and colleagues have been generous with their time and attention. Stephen Scoffham, particularly, has courageously read chapters and generously commented in fine, informed and intelligent detail. But I must also thank Vanessa Young, Linden West, David Wheway, William Stow, Glen Sharp, Jane Stamps (my inspiring sister), Paul Thompson, Ian Shirley, Robert McCrea, Ken and Matt Miles, Andrew Lambirth, Robert Jarvis, Bryan Hawkins, Grenville Hancox, Teresa Cremin, Tony Booth and Judy Baker who met my fervour for curriculum reform with enthusiasm and added their own wisdom to my thinking. I owe a great deal to them.

I have attempted not to identify individual schools who have helped, because the messages they give can apply across schools in many different locations and settings. The following schools, without their town or county, will know who they are when I thank them for accommodating me on my research. I admire them all for their immense energy, inspiration and hope: Astor Arts College, Bethersden Primary School, Bodsham C of E Primary School, Brockhill Performing Arts College, Brompton Westbrook School, Goodwill Primary School, Hythe Community Infants School, Nightingale Primary School, Ospringe Primary School, St Nicholas School, St Peter's Methodist School, St Stephen's Junior School, The Churchill School, The Coram School, The Priory School and Woolmore Primary School.

Organizations and individuals have also helped in many ways and I have been grateful for moral support and photographic materials from The Scottish Children's Parliament, Room 13, Creative Partnerships, Kent, North London and Bristol, The HEARTS project, Siemens, Canterbury Christ Church University, Simon Adams, Jane Heyes, Tony Ling, Dorothee Thyssen and Priory Sue.

Finally, I thank SAGE Publications for their patient and wise editorial and organizational support.

Introduction

Curriculum freedom is once again on the political agenda. I wrote this book to make a twenty-first-century case for placing cross-curricular experience at the heart of the school curriculum. It attempts to steer a path between the heavy emphasis on separate 'core' and 'foundation' subject disciplines which has characterized primary and secondary education since 1990 and the over-generalizing and usually adult-led tendencies of 1970s-style 'topic work'. The book is intended for head teachers and coordinating teachers planning a securely based, cross-curricular approach to children's learning, teacher education students, educationalists and education tutors. I offer a guiding rationale for cross-curricular teaching and learning, practical suggestions, planning formats, carefully chosen case studies, research evidence and issues for debate.

Innocence and experience

And Priests in black gowns, were walking their rounds, And binding with briars, my joys and desires. (Blake, 1789 [1967])

Our experience of the world is cross-curricular. Everything which surrounds us in the physical world can be seen and understood from multiple perspectives. As adults we tend to see each aspect of the perceptible and imagined universe from a variety of more or less 'experienced' viewpoints, but the 'innocent' eyes of the child have probably always seen a different world to that of their parents and elders. When, as experienced adults, we look at the tree or bramble outside our window, depending on our education and experience we will each 'see' it in slightly different ways; we may 'know' something of its biology or its geographical implications – the part it plays in reducing the impact of pollution or releasing oxygen. We may, like Blake, think of the poetic or symbolic resonances of our bramble, its potential as an art object or the way it enhances or spoils a view. Perhaps a child is more likely to see the same tree as a quiet place for talking, a hiding place, a threat, a magical mine of fascinating moving things, a den or simply one side of a goal. Perhaps the

1

bramble will represent an uncomfortable memory of scratches, a threat or a source of tasty blackberries – the possible associations are endless.

Children may need liberating from an adult-dominated curriculum. Perhaps a 'relentless focus on the basics' (DoE, 2010, website) is not the best way to include and enthuse all children in the aim to build a learning society. One of the threads which bind this book will be the suggestion that it is important for the child to enjoy being a child, to enjoy learning *now* for its own sake and not primarily for some future role they may or may not take on in the adult world. This emphasis on the child's 'here' and 'now' will involve the examination of various research and curricular attempts to discover what is important to children in today's school classes. The concentration on children's lives will result in considering how we as teachers might help to use children's distinctly different viewpoints, as motivation, method and model for their learning. It seems from all we know about children learning, that motivation, self-esteem, personal relevance, authentic challenge and a sense of achievement are all crucial. At the same time, current thinking on emotional well-being and children would suggest that an inner sense of personal happiness is not just a key motivator for now, but also central to future good health and security. What experiences, attitudes and resources can we weave into our curricula that make the generation of positive feelings more likely for each child?

Research

This book is underpinned by a range of research projects involving teachers, student teachers and children aged 3–14. My own research was conducted in five recent projects:

- the Higher Education Arts and Schools (HEARTS) projects funded jointly by the Esmee Fairbairne Trust and the Gulbenkian Foundation (Barnes and Shirley, 2005, 2007)
- the Creative Teaching for Tomorrow (CTFT) project funded by Creative Partnerships and Future Creative (Cremin et al., 2009)
- the TRACK project where primary school children tracked the development of creativity within their own schools (Powell and Barnes, 2008)
- a series of observations in case study schools between July 2005 and May 2010, followed up by email and telephone interviews with key members of staff
- my own PhD thesis on values and resilience in successful teachers (Barnes, 2010b).

In addition to this empirically grounded work which I draw upon throughout the text, I include themed reviews of recent research by others, from which I draw tentative conclusions relevant to the classroom. The research has employed mixed methods, in particular interviews, observations and field notes, and *autoethnography* – thinking about the influence of my own history and character in the development of the values and educational practice I propose.

Interviews

I interviewed school heads and/or heads of curriculum in six of the case study schools about their views on curricula in general and their own school curriculum in detail. In each semi-structured interview, I asked about principles, views on creativity, cross-curricular links and the organization of principles into a curriculum. I also held a series of group interviews with children engaged in cross-curricular activity. Some children were given cameras, and in two cases a video, to capture key moments in their work at school. These images were used to guide conversations which were recorded and transcribed. I also made dated research notes on informal interviews or informal comments from children whilst engaged in cross-curricular activities in school. I interviewed teachers in 10 different schools, teaching 3–14-year-olds in cross-curricular settings. Some of these interviews were fully transcribed and analysed as part of a research study for Future Creative, Kent (Cremin et al., 2009) and in field notes in my research journal. These schools are acknowledged at the beginning of this book.

Many interviews were followed up with email conversations and enquiries, which also formed part of the evidence base for this book.

Observations

I had the privilege of observing many lessons in many different indoor and outdoor settings (Barnes, 1994; Barnes and Hancox, 2004; Dismore et al., 2008; Powell and Barnes, 2008; Engaging Places website). Observations were, with permission, supplemented by photographs, many of which you will see in the text. Notes taken in observations were again analysed for themes and salient examples, which illustrated theoretical positions. Approximately 50 hours were devoted to these observations.

Autoethnography

The interpretations and viewpoints taken are my own. I come from a particular and unique history, like all of us. Take, for example, one moment in my life:

> I am in St Paul's Cathedral, an 11-year-old school choirboy temporarily covering the services for the 'real' choir. Standing at the foot of the odd and fascinating monument to John Donne, I am waiting to process into the choir of the vast cathedral. The light is streaming in through

gold-coloured windows to my right and the overpowering organ music of Olivier Messiaen is crashing and echoing around the colourfully mosaic-ed walls. I am fully aware and proud that minutes later I am to be altering the environment by my sounds and my presence in a daily ceremony once central to my culture.

The experience of joy was so positive, affirming, overpowering, almost transcendental that I have struggled ever since to re-create it in other forms for myself and the children I work with. That moment and many others profoundly influenced my attitude to the combining of subjects in interpreting experience.

Equally powerful was my experience 40 years later as a head teacher: I am in a meeting with a school inspector who tells me that our creative and cross-curricular ideas are 'too risky' and I should only consider continuing them after the Standard Assessment Tests (SATs) results have achieved well above the expectations for our particular school. This painful and unnerving experience galvanized me to action. I decided I was in the wrong job and moved to teacher education.

I cannot fail to keep both (and many, many more) stories in mind as I examine the curricula of schools, and read prospectuses, learned papers and government proposals. The stories in my life profoundly influence the views I take. The views I take have been shaped by the very mind that holds those views. My mind is also part of a culture, indeed many cultures, part of a profession and part of a team of professionals and friends who deeply impact upon my thinking. In writing several versions of my own autobiography for my doctoral thesis, I have become very aware of such layers of influence. Reflexive study has shown that this book is an attempt to make sense of the aspects of my own life which might have a bearing on the curriculum. In research terms, therefore, I have used my fully written-out autobiographies as a further source of research data. This data has been used to maintain an awareness of the sources of my assumptions and sometimes to challenge or seek corroboration of them.

The chapters

Chapter 1 briefly explores some relevant aspects of the twenty-first-century world into which our children have been born. These aspects are highly selective, but chosen because of their implications for education and, particularly, potential plans for the curriculum that children will follow. There can be no escape from the fact that, currently, adults make the decisions, produce the plans and control the direction of learning. That this is as things should be does not seem unreasonable. The experienced adult perhaps might have the advantage of a wiser, longer and wider perspective. But the second thread running through this book is the proposition that adults in school should be easy with a more complex set of roles than simply planner, imparter and assessor of knowledge and 'standards'. Perhaps a key distinction between a trainer and a teacher is that the teacher allows space for individual learners to be different from one another; indeed, such individual differences could be seen as the chief resource of the teacher. There may be times when power relationships in a class are more appropriately shifted towards the children. In a cross-curricular setting, conscious of the child's cultural, spiritual, social, physical, personal and intellectual needs, the teacher may at different times be follower, co-learner, instructor, coach, observer, adviser, assistant, mentor, conscience, Master of Ceremonies (MC), servant or inspiration.

Chapter 2 discusses recent education policy with regard to cross-curricular and creative learning. Chapter 3 examines a fairly detailed set of case studies in ordinary schools which show some of the variety and range of cross-curricular approaches. Chapters 4, 5, 6 and 7 consider the classroom implications of social, neuroscientific, psychological and pedagogical research.

The remainder of the book is devoted to practical guides on implementing a cross-curriculum in your school. The issue of the role of the individual subject disciplines must be discussed, however, before we begin to address the idea of teaching across them.

Discipline or not?

Howard Gardner, educationalist, psychologist and neurologist, and argued by some to be amongst the most influential of Western thinkers on education, said recently that the 'scholarly disciplines' were the most significant invention of the last two millennia. The subject disciplines represent for Gardner, 'the most advanced and best ways to think about issues consequential to human beings' (Gardner, 2004: 138). Yet it is clear from other areas of his writing and research that he also believes, 'any topic of significance can, and should, be represented in a number of different ways in the mind' (Gardner, 2004: 141). Some of the 'intelligences' Gardner postulates correspond closely to particular subject disciplines (musical, naturalistic, linguistic, logical–mathematical), some are closer to what we might call character traits (interpersonal, existential, intra-personal) and some to more physical capabilities (spatial, bodily, kinaesthetic) but all are ways in which we make sense of real-life experience (Gardner, 1999a). Gardner, like Hirsch, his critic (Hirsch, 1999) is a great defender of subject skills and subject knowledge but sees twenty-first-century education as providing: 'the basis for enhanced understanding of our several worlds – the physical world, the biological world, the world of human beings, the world of human artefacts and the world of the self' (Gardner, 1999b: 158). He follows this by a revealing statement about the relative importance of disciplined knowledge and skills:

the acquisition of literacy, the learning of basic facts, the cultivation of basic skills, or the mastery of the ways of thinking of the disciplines ... should be seen as means, not ends in themselves ... literacies, skills and disciplines ought to be pursued as tools that allow us to enhance our understanding of important questions, topics and themes. (Gardner, 1999b: 159)

British writers (for example, Alexander, 2010; Robinson, 2001; Robinson and Aronica, 2010; Wrigley, 2005) argue with equal passion for the breakdown of subject boundaries. Some argue for a competencies-based curriculum to 'open minds' (RSA, 2003), some the development of a curriculum which engenders 'a creative and critical orientation towards experience' (Abbs, 2003: 15), a curriculum which makes sense to pupils rather than teachers (Halpin, 2003: 113), more opportunities for play (David, 1999), less curricular prescription (Alexander, 1998, 2010; Rose, 2009) or an emotionally literate curriculum (Morris and Scott, 2002). The sum of educational advice grows daily.

There are principles, however, which may well reach beyond specific cultural and institutional contexts, and these are examined in Chapter 8. There is no shortage of educational research and general advice on how to enhance the learning experience of a child, but few publications offer usable models within which the ideals of cross-curricular and creative learning may be realized in practice. This book hopes to address such a need in Chapters 9, 10 and 11.

Organization

You will read here an argument for a balance between the unique skills, knowledge and attitudes of each 'traditional' subject and the uniquely motivating effects of cross-curricular and child-centred learning. This book is written now because in the coming five years many self-governing schools and academies will have the opportunity to rethink their curricula. The rapidly growing interest in topic-based, thematic and cross-curricular approaches in primary schools has spread increasingly to Years 7 and 8 classes in secondary school. This interest was growing before the publication of the reports on primary and secondary education by Sir Jim Rose, (2008, 2009) and was strengthened briefly with the abortive *National Curriculum Primary Handbook* (DCSF/QCDA, 2010), but more sustainably in the ongoing influence of Robin Alexander's Cambridge Primary Review (Alexander, 2010). A practical guide for teachers in service and student teachers seems necessary because of concerns that guiding principles should be debated and established and direct guidance offered. I believe that the curriculum should be packed with opportunities for each child to find his or her strengths and activities which provide genuine challenge and multiple prospects for individual achievement. It is hoped that you will find workable examples of how such activities and experiences can be successfully planned and delivered.

The book is divided into chapters with clear foci. You do not have to read the chapters in any particular sequence, but can read them in order of their relevance to you. Each chapter is headed by a question or broadly descriptive title that indicates the theme:

Chapter 1: What should schooling in the twenty-first century look like?

Chapter 2: Cross-curricular policy and practice

Chapter 3: What does good cross-curricular practice look like?

Chapter 4: Social perspectives on the learning journey

Chapter 5: What does neuroscience tell us about cross-curricular learning?

Chapter 6: Psychology and cross-curricular learning

Chapter 7: Cross-curricular pedagogies

Chapter 8: What principles should we apply?

Chapter 9: What themes are suitable for cross-curricular learning?

Chapter 10: How can we assess cross-curricular and creative learning?

Chapter 11: How should we plan for cross-curricular activity?

Chapter 12: Key issues for debate

There are summaries and key questions at the end of each chapter and full lists of references and websites at the end of the book.

You may already have noticed that this book is well illustrated. Most illustrations come from the schools consulted and researched in writing this book. If information, principles, examples and issues are shown visually as well as in text, a different, perhaps deeper and more personal, level of understanding may be gained. There seems little doubt that visual images form an increasingly important part in the world of communication and knowledge, and every advertiser knows that images and objects have a powerful effect upon our minds and imaginations. I argue that we also learn through the feelings and associations that images generate in us. I believe we vastly underestimate the power of the visual in our teaching and learning. By more fully exploiting our species' ability to make fine and wide-ranging visual discriminations, we access areas of knowing beyond words. Each chapter is therefore illustrated with examples of children's work and children working in a variety of contexts. Photographs and diagrams are used as models too, but names of individuals are changed and schools are only identified by their region.

Definitions

It is fairly easy to define the unique qualities of each National Curriculum subject; the National Curriculum document (DfEE/QCA, 1999) provides a clear lead on this for each of the nine subjects of the curriculum, Information and

Communications Technology, and (later) Citizenship, Personal, Social and Health Education and Modern Foreign Languages. The various Special Advisory Councils on Religious Education in Schools (SACREs) in each education authority have made their own definitions of Religious Education. However, definitions of the terminology used in discussions on cross-curricular approaches are often vague and used interchangeably. In this book, the following definitions apply:

The curriculum

The narrow definition is the subjects, topics and emphases chosen (usually by adults) to be the focus of learning in a school. In the context of this book, however, a broader definition, which also includes the 'hidden curriculum' of attitudes, assumptions, environments, relationships and school ethos, is used.

A discipline

The generally accepted skills, knowledge, language and attitudes that characterize a traditional area of learning in a culture. A discipline differs from a subject in that the term 'subject' is generally confined to the knowledge belonging to a particular area of learning. The word discipline or subject-discipline suggests something more demanding – the 'rules', skills, thought processes, values and typical activities that distinguish one domain of learning from another. A discipline is both a broader and more active concept than a subject. Disciplinary learning concentrates upon aspects that are applied in the real world, often in combination with other disciplines. Each discipline is presided over by past luminaries and 'policed' by a field of experts, located in 'subject associations', academies, universities or colleges who judge where the discipline is moving and what constitutes knowledge and standards within it.

For progress within a discipline, traditionally creative advances have needed to be accepted by what Csikszentmihalyi (1997) calls 'the field', the groups of experts culturally accepted as the gatekeepers of the discipline. In this internet era, exclusive concepts like 'expert' and 'field' are under challenge, but at present and in education the dominant and conservative view is that there is an established body of knowledge and skills for each discipline and there are arbiters of good practice within them. Disciplinary understanding is shown when students are able to use the knowledge and 'ways of thinking of a particular subject discipline, appropriately in novel situations' (Boix-Mansilla et al., 2000).

Various subject associations fight tirelessly and effectively for the maintenance of a disciplinary approach to teaching and learning in both secondary and primary schooling. The current emphasis on clear objectives and the carefully planned progression of skills and knowledge in the disciplines, championed by the subject associations, has significantly contributed to best teaching and learning in schools.

Meaningful experiences

A meaningful or what some schools call a 'wow' experience (Ofsted, 2010) is an encounter that emotionally engages and drives a child or children to want to understand and know more. This kind of experience is highly motivating for the recipient. A meaningful experience does not need to be a high-profile event, resource-heavy and weeks in the planning. Effective single-subject teachers daily utilize a wide variety of engaging techniques to motivate, enhance, illustrate and summarize learning. Some of these experiences are so powerful that for a time they fully engage the whole class – they are clearly meaningful. A meaningful experience is simply one which grasps learners' attention at emotional, physical, sensory, social and/or intellectual levels. A story well-read, an interesting visitor from the community, a visit to the school pond or the high street may be made personally meaningful, usually by fully engaging for a while the emotions or the senses. As Gardner reminds us:

> the brain learns best and retains most when the organism is actively involved in exploring physical sites and materials and asking questions to which it actually craves the answers. Merely passive experiences tend to attenuate and have little lasting impact. (Gardner, 1999a: 108)

Teaching

Teaching is the transmission of knowledge, skills and understandings from one source to another. In schools, we imagine that most teaching is done by teachers and other adults, though closer examination might show that sources like technology, environments, peers, accidental experience and personal interests teach as much. Those influencing teacher education (Abbs, 2003; Arthur and Cremin, 2010; Halpin, 2003; Pollard, 2008) frequently remind us that deliberate teaching does not automatically result in learning. Children have to 'agree' to enter into the learning their teacher wants them to achieve and therefore much teaching must involve motivating the child to want to learn.

Thinking

The mental representation of ideas. Good thinking can be considered as the process in which people are mentally engaged in attempts to solve a difficult or challenging task and which results in improvement in a person's intellectual power (Shayer and Adey, 2002).

Learning

The mental and physical internalization of knowledge, skills, language and attitudes. These learned features may then be transferred and used in new contexts and combined with others to solve problems and understand issues. The learning of many life skills may not be related to any discipline, but be part of growing up into a particular set of cultures and communities. Learning arises, perhaps chiefly, from the everyday accidents and incidents of life, but schools specialize in passing on the learning of past generations in a planned and disciplined way. I have proposed that the real world is best understood through the lenses of a number of disciplines and that cross-curricular learning should be a significant part of the curriculum of every school, but there are several different ways of promoting learning across the curriculum.

Cross-curricular learning

When the skills, knowledge and attitudes of a number of different disciplines are applied to a single experience, problem, question, theme or idea, we are working in a cross-curricular way. The experience of learning is considered on a macro level and with the *curriculum* as focus.

Topic-based or thematic curriculum

These terms are used interchangeably to mean a curriculum where at least part of the week is devoted to the study of a particular theme or topic (like water, 'beauty', India or the microscopic life in the school pond) through the eyes of several curriculum subjects. The *stimulus* is the focus.

Creativity

The ability in all humans imaginatively or practically to put two or more ideas together to make a valued new idea.

Creative teaching

Teaching which uses the teacher's own inherent and learned creativity to make learning accessible.

Teaching for creativity

The intention of the teacher is to stimulate and develop the creativity inherent in every child in any subject or experiential context.

Assumptions

It is impossible to write a book on aspects of the school curriculum without making many assumptions. You will become aware of many as you read this book and should apply a critical mind to them. Certain assumptions must be brought into the open from the outset, however. The previous definitions make it clear that, along with many other educationalists, I believe *all children and teachers are potentially creative in some aspect* (see Barnes, 2010b; Craft, 2000, 2005; Csikszentmihalyi, 1997; Perkins, 1992; Sternberg, 1997b, 2003). This is an important assumption because cross-curricular work is often seen as a way of stimulating and nurturing creative thinking. I also believe that *creativity is best stimulated in cross-curricular and authentic contexts.*

It is assumed that *generating thinking is an important role of education.* Professor David Perkins summarized 20 years of research into children's learning in the following memorable phrase: 'Learning is a consequence of thinking' (Perkins, 1992: 34). Although this statement can sound blindingly obvious, when reflected upon in the light of much current practice, it provokes a number of key questions: do schools generally put children's *thinking* at the centre of the learning experience? Is there a difference between politely sitting, listening and following instructions (or not!) and thinking? Are trainee teachers taught to generate thinking in their classes or to pass on a body of knowledge and skills?

This book also assumes that *intelligence is not a single and measurable entity*, that in different times, cultures and settings different behaviours seem to be intelligent. Each psychologist and educationalist will have a slightly or dramatically varying view of intelligence, but few today hold the early twentieth-century view that it is something measured in intelligence tests alone. However we see intelligence – a combined working of several mental processors, our intellectual faculties, our natural mental and physical dispositions, a combination of memory, inherited 'g' factor and individualized creative, practical and analytical strengths – it is only a meaningful concept when it is applied in a relevant cultural setting. We use it when we attend, engage, think or act.

It is assumed that *not all children respond positively to the same style of teaching or the same stimulus*; it is therefore understood that cross-curricular approaches will not suit all children. The good teacher hopes to engage all children, but in Sternberg's words, 'he or she needs the flexibility to teach to different styles of thinking, which means varying teaching style to suit different styles of [student] thought' (Sternberg, 1997a: 115). Engagement *may*, for some individuals, be gained in setting up periods of solitary, academic, convergent and purely cerebral activity, but experience and research (Abbs, 2003; Barnes and Shirley, 2007; Bandura, 1994; Csikszentmihalyi, 2002) suggest it comes more often from a mix of social, practical, personally relevant and creative activity.

The final assumption is more contentious – it is that *education is at least partly about helping children appreciate, enjoy and understand their lives and worlds now*. Geographer Simon Catling has written persuasively of the 'marginalization' of children in both their school environments and their neighbourhoods, and he sees a 'discontinuity between their real lives and the school curriculum' (Catling, 2005: 325). A child's world is clearly very different from an adult's. A Western child's world, which might well include *iPods*, 'blue tooth' connections, satellite television, the internet, video and computer games, social networking sites, mobile phones and digital versatile discs (DVDs), is technologically and geographically more sophisticated than that of many adults that surround them. There are other worlds of the child too: of play, fantasy, playground morality, safe and unsafe places, people or products, unarticulated barriers, taboos, fashion, fast food, loud music, cheap drugs and earlier sexual maturity. These worlds are little seen or understood by many of the adults surrounding them. Indeed, such worlds of children may not even be acknowledged in some primary classrooms. This book is written to suggest ways in which adults can adjust the curriculum so that children's worlds are represented and widened, and their views, concerns and interests allowed for, celebrated and developed. It is suggested that a major route towards a more child-centred education is through creative and cross-curricular responses to real experience.

The history

Cross-curricular learning has a long pedigree. Educators since the beginnings of formal education have been conscious that combined perspectives were required in order to understand aspects of the physical, social or personal world. More than two millennia ago, Plato promoted a mix of story, physical education and music in an early version of Personal, Social and Health Education (PSHE) and citizenship. In his curriculum, Plato combined subjects to serve a higher goal than simple disciplinary instruction: 'Anyone who can produce the best blend of the physical and intellectual sides of education and apply them to the training of character is producing harmony in a far more important sense than any mere musician' (Plato, *The Republic*, 1955: 155).

Cross-curricular pedagogies infer a particular set of values and attitudes. These are often liberal, inclusive, constructivist and perhaps more recently also relativist and intercultural. Plato, who despite many elitist and exclusive ideas on education, called it: 'the initial acquisition of virtue by the child, when the feelings of pleasure and affection, pain and hatred that well up in his soul are channelled in the right courses before he can understand the reason why' (Plato, *The Laws*, 1970: 653b).

Seventeenth- and eighteenth-century pioneers: nature and meaning

Unlike Plato, the seventeenth-century Czech philosopher, Jan Comenius, believed that education was for *all* people and that nature was herself the great teacher. Comenius was an early champion of physical and outdoor education, and saw physical education, playing with ideas, artefacts and materials, and learning by easy stages as essential foundations for education. Sometimes known as the 'father of modern education', he was probably the first to illustrate children's textbooks. But his views on internationalism in education, his belief that teachers should understand the developing mind of the child and his insistence on teaching 'with the greatest enjoyment' and *thoroughly*, put him at the forefront of influences on modern educational thought in Europe. His eloquent and humane approach to learning is captured by the following paragraph from his book *The Great Didactic*, published in 1649:

> The proper education of the young does not consist in stuffing their heads with a mass of words, sentences, and ideas dragged together out of various authors, but in opening up their understanding to the outer world, so that a living stream may flow from their own minds, just as leaves, flowers, and fruit spring from the bud on a tree. (Comenius, 1967: 82)

Jean Jacques Rousseau (1712–78) was also deeply inspired by the natural world. The eighteenth-century 'enlightenment' brought forth, and to an extent rested upon, powerful and romantic philosophies like his. Rousseau was a believer in the inborn good of humanity and was the originator of the idea of 'the noble savage'. Typical of the intellectuals and artists of his time, he was awed and fascinated by nature. He believed that education was needed in order to learn how to live and that the best learning was accomplished very near to the natural world. Rousseau felt that experience was the starting point for learning. He used very physical and sensory images throughout his writing: for example, the metaphor of education as plunging into the cold waters of the Styx, or feeling the warts on the back of the toad to illustrate natural learning. He saw education as a meeting of the natural, the practical and the cultural; as he put it in his education treatise *Émile ou de l'éducation*, of 1762:

> This education comes from nature, from men or from things. The inner growth of our organs and faculties is the education of nature, the use we learn to make of our growth is the education of men, what we gain by our experience of our surroundings is the education of things. (Rousseau, 1762, website, para. 15)

> We are each taught by three masters. If their teaching conflicts, the scholar is ill-educated and will never be at peace with himself; if their teaching agrees, he goes straight to his goal, he lives at peace with himself, he is well educated. (1762, website, para. 16)

First by using the senses, then by making and using artefacts and, finally, by seeking truth in arts, science and religion, Rousseau expressed a progression which was much later taken up by Piaget. But he also had strong views about the adult domination of the curriculum: 'We never know how to put ourselves in the place of children; we do not enter into their ideas; we lend them ours, and, always following our own reasonings, with chains of truths we heap up only follies and error in their heads' (1762, website, para. 577).

Comenius and Rousseau among many thinkers of the seventeenth and eighteenth centuries suggested that education was lifelong, aligned with nature and, by implication, cross-curricular because it relied upon helping the child interpret and understand their day-to-day *experience* of the world. They argued that children should be allowed to be children before they were 'men' and accepted philosopher Locke's view that children were rational beings. Such thoughts on the meaning and purpose of education still underpin many of the arguments of those who defend cross-curricular, experiential and child-centred approaches to learning.

Nineteenth-century pedagogs: play, purpose and perfection

As formal and eventually state-run education developed throughout the Western world in the nineteenth century, Rossueau's educational philosophies were added to by thinkers and teachers such as Johann Pestalozzi (1746–1827) and Friedrich Froebel (1782–1852). Pestalozzi wanted children to learn through activity and arrive at their own answers. The personality was all important and each child needed to be taught with love in the context of direct concrete experience and observation. Froebel's major contribution was the foundation of the 'kindergarten' and his powerful arguments for the importance of play. These early nineteenth-century progressives advocated primary education through practical activity, objects, 'natural' interest and spontaneity. Contemporary traditionalists, on the other hand, encouraged the pragmatic and efficient mass education techniques of textbook and rote learning required by religiously conservative and rapidly industrializing countries. In line with the times, however, even the radical pioneers maintained a religious justification for their ideas:

> I wish to wrest education from the outworn order of doddering old teaching hacks as well as from the new-fangled order of cheap, artificial teaching tricks, and entrust it to the eternal powers of nature herself, to the light which God has kindled and kept alive in the hearts of fathers and mothers, to the interests of parents who desire their children grow up in favour with God and with men. (Pestalozzi, quoted in Silber, 1965: 134)

> The purpose of education is to encourage and guide man as a conscious, thinking and perceiving being in such a way that he becomes a pure and perfect representation of that divine inner law through his own personal choice; education must show him the ways and meanings of attaining that goal. (Froebel, 1826, *Die Menschenerziehung*, p. 2)

Twentieth-century child-centred education

Much modern education theory is still underpinned by the work of Jean Piaget. He and his followers suggested, from the 1920s, that humans go through distinct stages of learning (Piaget, 1954). Passing through periods of sensori-motor exercise and reflex actions, to exploratory activity consisting of either pre-conceptual or intuitive experimentation with tangible things, humans finally arrive at a state of 'formal operations', which relies upon reason, imagination and abstract thinking. At each stage, the child is said to be learning through *accommodation* and *assimilation* – essentially through making and understanding errors. Piaget likened the developing child to a scientist constantly making, testing and revising hypotheses. Piaget's theories still underpin much of our educational and curriculum decision making, though many have recognized that the developmental stages he described need not be tightly ascribed to particular ages but apparently need to be passed through in sequence at *any* age if a new concept is to be fully learned.

Lev Vygotsky's (1962, 1978) and, later, Jerome Bruner's work on the centrality of social intercourse in helping children make sense of the world has also had profound impacts upon schools and curricular organization (Bruner, 1968, 1996). Under their influence, many school sessions have introduced forms of 'scaffolded learning', where 'more knowledgeable others' support the concept formation of the rest. Learning is seen by these psychologists as primarily a social activity: 'making sense is a social process; it is an activity that is always situated in a cultural and historical context' (Bruner and Haste, 1987: 4).

The current context

It has become almost a truism of educational criticism that in these times of perhaps unprecedented change, we need to develop a flexible and learning society. The lifelong learning lobby is well accepted and strong, and organizations such as the Campaign for Learning (website) have much support from a broad spectrum including education, politics and industry. However, *what* is to be learned is very much more debatable. Homespun American philosopher, Eric Hoffer, noted in the middle of the twentieth century that current education may not be relevant: *'In times of change learners inherit the earth, while the learned find themselves beautifully equipped to deal with a world that no longer exists'* (Hoffer, website). But late in the same century, some of Britain's educated elite applauded heartily when Sir Roy Strong argued for a distinctly narrow and culturally exclusive definition of the curriculum:

> It is more important for a young person to be made to wonder at the architecture of something like the Palace of Versailles or glimpse what underlies … a single scene in a Mozart opera than to paint another bad picture or bang a drum in the false interests of self expression. (SCAA, 1997)

This debate rumbles on against a background of massive social, political and technological change, as you will read in Chapters 1 and 2, but it is an essential debate. What we teach, what we require children to know and understand, will without doubt significantly change the minds of the generations that will shape the twenty-first century.

How we teach is equally important. Governments have became newly concerned with individual well-being, partly as a result of alarming statistics on depression (Layard, 2006; Layard and Dunn, 2009; UNICEF, 2007; WHO, 2004, 2008, websites). The new interest in well-being has sparked a number of initiatives directed at a more holistic view of health (see, for example, DHSS, 2004; DoH/DfES, 2005). Education is now seen to play a key role in the physical and mental health of children and the curricular implications are wide.

The curriculum in today's schools is increasingly complex. It is set to become more diverse. Those responsible for schools have to respond to concerns about falling standards in 'basic' as well as 'general' knowledge. Teachers feel they should address public and political perceptions of declines in behaviour and morality. At the same time, parents have become empowered to demand individualized solutions for the barriers their children face. Yet schools often feel starved of the resources, training, support and recognition that would help them meet such demands. As governments have increasingly involved themselves in the minutiae of educational practice, they have been expected to provide general solutions to these challenges – Chapters 2 and 3 discuss the progress of government intervention as well as providing guidance for those in academies and 'free schools' seeking curricular freedom.

CHAPTER 1

What Should Schooling in the Twenty-First Century Look Like?

What you think a school should be like depends on the values you hold. What a school *is* like results from the values of those who dominate it. Values – the fundamental beliefs that guide all action – are particularly reflected in the curriculum a school offers. *Curriculum,* as used throughout this book, is defined very broadly to include not just the subjects taught, but also the choices made within those subjects, the styles and means chosen to teach them, the activities, attitudes, environments, relationships and beliefs which pervade a school. By putting early emphasis on values, I imply that school communities need to clarify their fundamental beliefs before considering their curriculum. In choosing to explore cross-curricular and creative developments in primary and secondary curricula, I claim that these are highly relevant approaches to twenty-first-century learning.

We are constantly reminded of the unprecedented rates of change we are experiencing as we travel through the twenty-first century (for example, Greenfield, 2003, 2009; Puttnam, 2009, website; Robinson, 2001; Robinson and Aronica, 2010). Illustrations of the exponential growth of knowledge, the development of technology, nanotechnology, micro-biology, artificial intelligence and the rest, pepper most books about the future. This is not the place to comment on such predictions, but it is safe to say that the world today's children will inherit will be very, very different from our present one. Almost undoubtedly, our children will have to face the realities of global warming, rising sea levels, pandemics, human cloning, population pressures, increasing terrorism and extremism, water, oil and food shortages, frequent job changes and perhaps economic meltdown. Taking a more optimistic view, our children may witness more concerted international cooperation, just government, longer, healthier lives, a more equitable sharing of the earth's resources and the global development of sciences and technologies to address twenty-first-century challenges. Either way, today's children live in times of rapid and

Illustration 1.1   *Teachers can have a major influence on children's futures. School children from a village in south India*

global transformations which will quite literally change human minds and societies. What our education system can do to address such uncertainties, how we might establish an empowering curriculum that offers hope and purpose as well as knowledge, is the subject of this book.

Preparing for an uncertain future

The future has always been uncertain but rapid advances in global communications have made us hyper-sensitive to the speed and unpredictability of change. The education we currently offer our children may not be good enough to help them thrive in, and live fulfilling lives through, the century. Aside from Information and Communications Technology (ICT), Modern Foreign Languages (MFL), Citizenship and PSHE, the National Curriculum subjects taught in English schools would have been recognizable in a late nineteenth-century school. Whilst the six 'areas of learning' (DCSF/QCDA, 2010) proposed by the Rose Review of Primary Education (2009) expressed a movement towards integrated and values-conscious learning, schools were given little guidance towards making their curricula meaningful and effective for all. After the scrapping of the Rose recommendations, the coalition government of 2010 called for greater degrees of curricular freedom but also for increased emphasis on separate subjects and the core. Governments of all complexions continue to call for schools and their communities to become more involved with each other and education is less centralized, but as local authorities and central government agencies lose their influence, support and guidance on matching curriculum to community is needed. The issues and concerns that dominate the lives of children and communities often seem distant from the curricula they receive.

Meaningful and effective schooling happily resists temporary curriculum change. Successful teachers have always been able to make restrictive curricula relevant to children. Schools have, for example, taken the opportunity offered by Citizenship and PSHE, to propose curricula that address the personal, local and global futures which young people care about (Alexander, 2010; Alexander and Potter, 2005; Leyard and Dunn, 2009; Ofsted, 2010; Page, 2000; Puttnam, 2009, Wrigley, 2005). Geographers and others interested in 'futures education' (the study of views about probable, possible and preferable futures) have championed curricula aimed at helping children think more critically and creatively about the future (for example, Catling and Willey, 2009; Hicks, 2001, 2006; Scoffham, 2010; Slaughter, 1996). Motivated by the desire to empower children, schools have championed ecologically, socially or culturally sensitive issues relevant to their communities. Other schools have revitalized the experience of children through working with organizations like: Creative Partnerships, Creative and Cultural Education (CCE), Capeuk, the Royal Society of Arts (RSA), the Commission for Architecture and the Built Environment (CABE) and The Curriculum Foundation (website).

Today's young people differ in some ways from those of the past. Youngsters contemplating the future in this century seem to expect a very much less utopian prospect than the 'baby boomers' of the 1950s foresaw. Research amongst children in the USA, UK, Sweden and Canada, shows children to be both serious and worried about the future (Catling, 2010; Hicks, 2006). They are pessimistic about societal health, equality, wealth, security, poverty and relationships but, paradoxically, remain generally hopeful about their *own* futures. Children appear to be gloomy about the world's future and particularly worried about issues currently headlined in the news. This shift away from the general optimism of the 1990s (see Bentley, 2006) is evidenced as public policy is increasingly targeted on well-being, health, sustainability, conservation, safety and security.

Contrary to youthful optimism for their personal future, Hicks (2006) shows that boys' views about the *world's* future tend towards the gender-stereotypically violent and destructive, with wars, terrorism, natural disasters and disease dominant. It seems that girls more often imagine a generalized peaceful and idealistic future, but continue to be worried about disease and pollution. These contrasts may be driven by popular culture as much as genetics.

Economy and culture encourage us to live life in the present. Children and adults alike know that today's consumerist public policy will deeply and negatively impact upon our futures but such knowledge scarcely affects our behaviour. Fewer and fewer vote or play an active role in local or national democracy yet more know about its importance. Bentley confronts these paradoxes in expressing radical aims for education. He argues:

> we are searching for means through which individuals can transform themselves through a process of internal discovery and self-actualisation, by participating in the reshaping of the shared context in which they live out their individual lives. (Bentley, 2006)

Confidence and fulfilment are important aims of education. Opportunities for self-actualization (Maslow, 1943) or the development of self-efficacy (Bandura,1994) seem rare for the majority of children and often peripheral to school decisions. Neither liberation of the unique attributes of every child nor the notion of social intelligence (Gardner, 1993; Goleman, 2006) have been systematically addressed across UK schools. Few schools are as values-driven as Makiguchi's *Soka* schools in Japan, which attempt to live out values like justice, fairness and peacemaking, in their curriculum, interpersonal behaviour and relationships with the local and world community (Sharma, 2008). Values and purposes like these, evident in education philosophy and the aims of education for millennia, have in many cases been squeezed out of the curriculum. Reference to the twin aims of nurturing individuality and fostering better social and global relationships are therefore among the themes running through this book.

In addition to their keen interest in aspects of the future, a number of topics have become pressingly relevant to the twenty-first-century child. Key preoccupations seem to be:

- information and communications technology
- global politics/issues
- relationships
- individualism and the sense of self.

These powerfully motivating interests form the starting point of this new look at our school curricula.

Harnessing children's interest in information and communications technology

Nowhere are the rapid changes in the developed and developing world more evident than in the area of ICT. Growing numbers of people in all societies have access to powerful and sophisticated technologies which two decades

Illustration 1.2   *Year 2 boy's view of the future: guns, army, bang bang, bullets, dried up river, dried up stones*

ago were the stuff of science fiction. In 2002 in England, 93 per cent of 11-year-old children reported having at least one computer at home, whilst in the USA the figure was 89.4 per cent (WHO, 2004, website).

Home computers and the internet are heavily used by children aged 9–16. Twice as many boys as girls used the internet to get information in all 35 countries studied by the World Health Organization (WHO, 2008, website; Children's Use of the Internet, 2006, website). Yet a recent survey showed that 40 per cent of 15-year-old girls considered the internet-based social networking site *Facebook* more important to them than family (Techeye 2010, website). The internet has rapidly become a preferred source of

Illustration 1.3 *Year 2 girl's view of the future: wind, fallen trees and bushes, shattered houses*

information for the young, with 50 per cent of parents admitting to little idea of what their children do on the internet (Pew, 2005, website). Large numbers of children regularly use internet 'chat rooms', and social networking sites to contact and make friends and see such technologies as very influential on their lives (BBC News, 2010, website). Some of the worst implications of these easy, anonymous and sometimes unpoliced contacts are well known. Adults' lack of knowledge and control over the medium is illustrated in recent findings documented by the National Children's Homes (*Guardian*, 2006, website).

Illustration 1.4 *Children gather enthusiastically around a computer screen in a village school in south India*

Year 11 pupils at a Dover school were given a free choice of fairy story to update and perform within a single session. They chose to rewrite *Little Red Riding Hood*. After starting their play at the end, but in the traditional manner with Red Riding Hood quizzing a wolf disguised as grandma about her big teeth and hairy arms, the students did a 'time warp' sequence and the audience was catapulted to the beginning of the story. The scene was the chilling context of a twenty-first-century Red Riding Hood sitting alone at her bedroom computer. She was in an internet chat room talking to a paedophile 'wolf' pretending to be her grandmother. (McCrea, 2005)

Currently over 50 per cent of northern European children aged between 5 and 11 have a mobile phone (cell phone), rising to well over 90 per cent for those between 12 and 16. To children, the advantages of mobile phones over other ICT are privacy and control. Children report that for their mobiles, they need no permission, have little supervision and they appreciate the possibilities of constant communication (Childnet International, 2010, website). Some estimates suggest teenagers average up to four hours a week text-messaging their friends.

Children today say they like the internet and mobiles because these give them the greatest independence over what they see and find out (Byron, 2008, website). As interactive and user-centred Web 2.0 applications develop, blogs, wikis, social networking sites and a host of other applications have become commonplace for many children. Children like the ways ICT helps them discover and connect to friends, and they appreciate the way it can help them create and communicate visually and in sound. Around 50 per cent of 13-year-olds in Britain, for example, use the internet or mobiles to communicate with friends *every day* (WHO, 2008, website). Through the internet and mobile technology, children have access to music, sports and world news, advertising and powerful new games; can communicate with television and film stars; vote out an unpopular *Big Brother* resident or catapult an unknown to *X Factor* stardom. Children are also increasingly aware of the dangers of new technologies. Most have dealt with text bullies, unwanted pornography, salespeople and crackpots well before their parents find out about it. Sadly, some do not have the personal resources to cope with such onslaughts and the ghastly results of the abuses of ICT are all too evident from news reports and investigative journalism. There are, however, interesting and positive uses of mobile phone technology which suggest it is an underused feature in our current school curricula (see box).

> A primary school in Harrow maintains their link with a school in Uganda through mobile phone and texting links with the teachers in the Ugandan school. The head teacher reported: 'Rather than holding one-off cultural events, I wanted to promote a deeper understanding of global issues such as interdependence, global citizenship and rights and responsibilities'. Therefore, children write regular letters to their partner school, but significantly they and their teachers now send regular texts with questions which are instantly answered and relevant to the moment. (*TES*, 2005, website)

The monitor screen also continues its major influence on children's lives. In 2001, about 40 per cent of pre-school children in the USA had a television in their bedroom (Pediatrics, 2002, website). In 2004, 90 per cent of UK children between 7 and 14 reported watching television every day, and 93 per cent of the same age group reported watching a video or DVD 'at least once a month' (UK Film Council, 2004, website). As direct and indiscriminate TV watching decreases, the selection of particular programmes through iplayer® and other customer-controlled technologies increases. Most 2010 estimates place the average US or British child as watching about four hours of television per day, 61 per cent of them in their own bedroom – significantly less time than most spend with family. The image of large numbers of children alone in their room using televisions, games consoles, computer monitors and videos for more than 28 hours a week conjures up a rather lonely image. Susan Greenfield has suggested we may already have reached the point where for some families, many of the traditional parental roles – imparting culture, providing a model, resolving conflict, telling stories, sharing knowledge, passing on morals, sayings, advice and wisdom – have been unintentionally delegated to the monitor screen (Greenfield, 2003, 2009).

A Romanian study once attempted to capture the influence of TV. By far, the chief role models of school-aged children were film stars and television personalities (Popenici, 2006). A stirring judgement on our profession was

Illustration 1.5 *Teacher introducing the video camera to 8-year-olds in a class project on the future of the local school environment*

that teachers were amongst the least likely adults to be considered as role models, scoring lower than terrorists. There may be reasons for national variations in such figures but teachers and parents are probably less important, in the short term, to children than they think.

Even the subject of children's toys is not without its implications for education. Aside from the plethora of toys linked to video, television and computer game characters, the new generation of interactive cyber toys respond 'intelligently' to particular types of treatment or 'grow' or change with time or display 'real' facial expressions. The toy RoboSapien® is sold as 'truly a fusion of technology and personality'. Such toys may be argued to create new kinds of moral and ethical dilemmas. Do they and their descendants teach particular values and attitudes to children? Do they come with 'hidden agendas'? If so, what are they and who decides?

Any web search will deliver large numbers of statistics and studies about ICT use amongst children and young people. Some findings should be interpreted with care because of the social/political agendas of their sponsors. But a thorough reading of research in these areas tells a consistent story of large numbers of children spending significantly more hours with ICT than they do at school. The fact that much of this activity may well be solitary or unsupervised is an issue largely for parents, but there are serious implications for schools too.

Schools use ICT too little. Currently, and perhaps understandably, mobile phones are rarely welcome in the classroom. Internet use – particularly the use of interactive and user-centred sites – is less developed in schools than at home despite the ubiquity of interactive whiteboards. The class digital camera, recorder or video may remain little used for lack of time. Television and film is less used now in school than 25 years ago, but *Wii* technology and other Web 2.0 possibilities have not yet become common features of classroom experience.

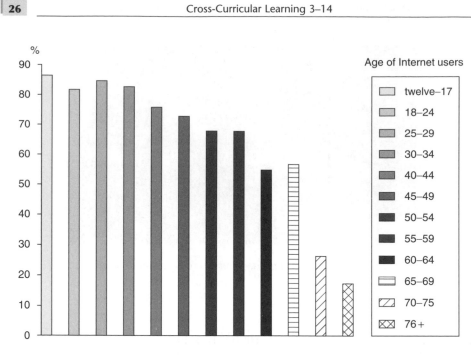

Figure 1.1 Graph to show the age and percentage of internet use in the USA

Such technologies are very much part of the child's world and perhaps schools should systematically consider their use as motivators and means in formal educational settings (Riddle, 2009). Signs of change are already apparent. ICT is argued to deepen understanding and promote new learning more effectively than traditional methods. As a result, many new Academies make the provision of laptop computers or 'tablets' a priority. The BBC's 'Digital Curriculum' covering half the 7–14 curriculum was launched in 2006 and though abandoned in 2008 will undoubtedly be followed by other virtual curricula. Even the power of the mobile phone can be well utilized for educational purposes – texting a précis description, utilizing the camera or recording applications, contacting another school following a similar theme, permission to 'phone a friend' in the playground for help in a class quiz or voting for a school council member by text message might all be used to enliven school learning.

A rural primary school in Suffolk asked groups of six children on fieldwork near the school, to cooperate in using a mobile phone to text succinct (they could only send one message) descriptions concerning a range of contrasting environments near their school to a central group back in the classroom 'headquarters'. The 'HQ team' plotted the incoming summaries against appropriate locations on a base map so that the descriptive journey was already recorded as the 'environmental' teams returned to class.

In considering the power of ICT to influence the lives and thinking of children, we are immediately confronted with questions of value:

- How do these technologies fit with our agreed values?
- How do we develop good and wholesome attitudes through ICT?
- How do we decide what good and wholesome is?
- *Should* schools be extending the time children spend with ICT?

Chapter 3 includes some examples of how schools are beginning to address such issues in cross-curricular contexts.

Supporting children's interest in global themes

Schools have allowed and encouraged political debate for millennia. Easily available and global communications should have made the possibilities for debate even stronger. Almost instant awareness of major events anywhere brings dramatic, violent or tense international situations, threats, images and moral issues almost daily into the homes of most in the developed and developing world. In the past, such trauma would confront an unlucky individual only a few times in a lifetime. Despite the disturbing and challenging nature of many images open to children, there are surprisingly few guidelines or exemplars on how to address current events within the curriculum. Timetables in many schools have become inflexible. Tightly packed daily schedules rarely allow time for discussion or questions on real issues from the local, national or international news. Few British schools found the time or courage to follow the example of an international school in Dar es Salaam which organized a series of civilized and informed debates between children of all faiths and none, within a few days of the attacks of 11 September 2001 in the USA. Similarly, college curricula in Kerala, south India, were flexible enough to accredit the work of hundreds of students who spontaneously ran to the aid of local communities devastated by the Tsunami of Boxing Day 2004. If our curricula have become too crowded for relevance and the unexpected, perhaps children with their interest in global issues are telling us to think again.

Bruner (1968) reminds us that no issues are too complex for children. Emotive subjects like terrorism, war, poverty, HIV/AIDS, pollution, social inequality, disasters or peace treaties, are important to children as well as adults. Successful current events programmes like the Children's British Broadcasting Corporation's (CBBC) daily *Newsround* and its associated website cater for this interest. Such programmes are popular with children; viewer figures (BBC Trust, 2008, website) show that between two and three hundred thousand 5–12 year olds watch *Newsround* every evening. Whilst research (Pew International, 2008, website) shows a decline in young people's news

Illustration 1.6 *Children interviewing a local Member of the European Parliament and the Scottish Children's Commissioner on matters of global importance. Courtesy of Scottish Children's Parliament*

reading over the last few years, the rise in social networking sites like *Facebook* and *Twitter* means that world news comes to them even faster. Increasing viewer figures and donations show that TV/internet campaigns like *Make Poverty History*, the ONE campaign, *Comic Relief* and *Sport Relief* have significantly raised young people's consciousness of and participation in addressing world poverty.

Such initiatives catch the imagination of schools and children perhaps because they demonstrate that ordinary voices can influence seemingly impersonal trends in the global economy (One Org, 2005, website).

Young people are clearly at ease with the digital media. Increasing numbers have an automatic function on their mobile phones informing them instantly of key cricket or football scores or 'breaking news'. Video, internet and television channel facilities on mobiles, Mp3s and *iPod*s are rapidly becoming accessible to children in the rapidly developing countries of Asia and South America too. Each new technology brings the world closer to the child's life, but perhaps in ways which make the events they portray seem less real.

'Green issues' are particularly significant to many children. Topics such as poverty, pollution, deforestation and climate change are regularly highlighted by children's TV, film and curriculum initiatives (e.g. Eco Schools, 2010). TV and internet campaigns supporting water, rainforest and developing world anti-pollution projects, regularly reach ambitious targets from school and individual donations. The David Puttnam documentary, *'We are the people we've been waiting for'* (Puttnam, 2009, website) has been used in many secondary schools to direct young people's existing commitment towards global issues and their place in their education now. Individual schools and clusters have been instrumental in raising awareness of environmental issues nearer home too.

The apparent interest in global issues is not straightforward however. Children's connection with the wider world seems dependent upon what has been highlighted by the television and tabloid news editors. Very few American children knew where Iraq or Afghanistan were before the wars there, and the word 'tsunami' meant little to most children before December 2004. For British children, Haiti and the Mississippi Delta were unheard of before the 2010 tragedies of earthquake and oil spill. Whilst global communications have successfully raised consciousness, place and general geographical knowledge is often poor. A study of world 'place knowledge' amongst 18–20-year-old prospective teachers on a UK teacher education course, showed a serious ignorance about the location of many foreign countries outside Western Europe (Catling, 2004). The same lack of knowledge can apply to environmental or development issues. Unless a child attends a school which has followed up leads such as the United Nations' (UN's) millennium goals (UN, 2000, website) or the Eco Schools programme, or an individual teacher has shared an interest in a particular concern, then children's exposure to crucial aspects of their changing world remains a lottery.

It is not difficult to fire children's interest in the environment. They experience signs of environmental ill-health all around them in dying trees, polluted rivers, fly-tipping, disappearing countryside and asthma. Concerns about the future of environments also arise from children's generic interest in nature, life forms and the outdoors. Students of teaching frequently remark on the good behaviour of children engaged in well-planned fieldwork. Schools with a clear environmental focus to their curriculum capitalize on this interest and use it to generate the feeling that individuals can do something to change the probable future of damaged or threatened environments. The Eco Schools programme (Eco Schools, website) is a good example of a well-supported initiative providing guidance and resources to feed these interests. Suggested and potentially engaging topics, such as litter, waste, energy, water, transport, healthy living and school grounds, however, require a range of very specific subject skills and knowledge to bring them alive for children.

Recognizing the importance of relationships

The popularity of *Facebook* and other social networking sites among young people arises naturally from their interest in relationships. Websites and

Illustration 1.7   *Shared endevour often promotes improved relationships*

magazines devoted to personal, beauty and relationship problems of young people have also grown in recent years (National Literacy Trust, 2005, website). Relationships are important to all, but for the developing psyche of the child they may dominate everything. Each year, the numbers of children who contact the charity ChildLine grows by more than 10 per cent (ChildLine, 2010, website). This UK charity gives support to children who are abused, fearful or worried, and in 2008 supported 700,000 children (NSPCC, 2009, website). The vast majority were between 5 and 15 years old and about a third of cases concerned bullying and interpersonal relationship problems, by far the most common reasons for contacting ChildLine. Concerns about family, peers, friendships, who they can trust and who is caring towards them are central to children's lives (see Illustration 1.7).

The family into which a child is born provides the first and most powerful model of relationships. Most of us recognize that the interrelationships within family go on influencing the trajectory of our lives well beyond childhood. Family support is often the key to a child's learning and development within school. A family member was given as the most important role model by 16 per cent of children in a recent European survey (Popenici, 2006). Yet there may be a mutual suspicion between schools and families, and few schools currently place family centrally in their curriculum. The establishment of multi-agency children's centres and the extension of the school day under the UK Children Act 2004 has had a positive effect on contact between some schools, families and communities. There are several aspects of twenty-first-century life, however, where mistrust seems to be growing.

Recent reports show a growing atmosphere of suspicion in some societies. One large-scale study involving 160,000 children shows, for example, that only 43 per cent of English children aged 11–15 (53 per cent in the USA) could agree with the statement, 'I find my peers kind and helpful'. By contrast, 80 per cent in Switzerland agreed with the same statement (WHO, 2004, website). UNICEF places the UK bottom of a 21-nation league in 'family and peer relationships' (UNICEF, 2007, website). Growing distrust may be evidence of social polarization and increasing suspicion between generations, sub-cultures and communities. The gap between the educational achievement of rich and poor children continues to widen in the UK (BBC News, 2010, website).

Polarization is likely to be increased by schools if they do not recognize and address the gulf between their aims and values and those of their children. Popenici found that in Romania most secondary-aged children saw school as simply instrumental to getting a good job, and that a school's interest in altruism, goodness, education and sincerity was somewhat irrelevant to their lives (Popenici, 2006). If a school community is given genuine opportunity to discuss and agree their values however, they will most often arrive at similar caring and community values (Booth and Ainscow, 2002).

Intercultural and cross-community understanding is seen by many to be crucial to national and international peace and progress in the twenty-first century. Schools can play their part to in fostering such a utopia. Relationships between cultures and sub-cultures have been subject to a number of UK government-sponsored initiatives, especially since the Stephen Lawrence Inquiry (1999, website) and the subsequent Race Relations Act 2000 (Ajegbo, 2007). The QCA site, 'Respect for all: reflecting cultural diversity through the curriculum' (QCA, 2003, website), is a helpful attempt to show teachers how relationships of greater understanding between and across cultures can be developed through the curriculum. A number of websites, for example the DfES-sponsored Global gateway (DfES, 2006c, website), promote international links between schools, where meaningful and unpatronizing contact across continents can be developed.

Wholesome relationships are, of course, important to well-being and inclusion. Children need them to feel secure and ready to learn. We give little formal attention to building, maintaining and understanding relationships in our curricula and yet – as Daniel Goleman (1996, 1999, 2006) and Elizabeth Morris (2005) remind us – 'emotional intelligence' can be more important than other kinds of intelligence. By emotional intelligence, Goleman means the ability to understand and handle one's own emotions (the subject of the next section) and relationships, and how to understand and deal with those of others. Emotional literacy programmes have been very successfully introduced in a number of schools seriously approaching the PSHE and Citizenship curriculum. The recommendations from the now disbanded UK Qualifications and Curriculum Development Agency (QCDA) for Key Stage 2 include:

- taking responsibility
- feeling positive about the self
- participating in decision making
- making real choices
- understanding the different views of others
- developing relationships through work and play
- dealing with inappropriate pressure
- recognizing risks
- resolving differences (QCA, 2002a).

The danger is that these non-compulsory aspects of the primary curriculum are left to chance and excessive pressure on timetables means that such themes are often only dealt with in a cursory and unplanned manner (Layard and Dunn, 2009).

Helping develop a positive sense of self

As far as we know, our sense of self is a defining human characteristic. Self-consciousness is argued to have massive survival and evolutionary advantages (Dawkins, 2003; Morris, 2004) and with it comes awareness of good and bad about our world. The concept of 'self' is, as neuroscientist Antonio Damasio puts it: 'the critical biological function that allows us to know sorrow or know joy, to know suffering or know pleasure, to sense embarrassment or pride, to grieve for lost love or lost life' (Damasio, 2000: 4). Deutscher (2006) sees language as 'the invention that invented us', in that self-talk or thought can be argued to shape both consciousness and identity.

The trend towards prizing and nurturing individuality has resulted in increased interest in cultural and personal identity. The philosophy for children movement (e.g. Fisher, 2008) is also part of this development. Damasio has devoted his career to research in the area of self-consciousness and describes two identifiable selves in our minds: a *core self* and an *autobiographical self*. The core self is that sense of consciousness where objects, sounds and senses around us are not only perceived but understood within our mind to be being perceived at that moment by ourselves. Core consciousness is consciousness in the moment, here and now, 'ceaselessly recreated for each and every object with which the brain interacts' (Damasio, 2000: 17). The auto-biographical self consists of a set of memories of situations which bear centrally and usually invariably upon an individual's life: 'who you were born to, where and when, your likes and dislikes, the way you usually react to a problem or conflict, your name ... your anticipated future' (p. 17). Significant to those involved in education, Damasio draws three key conclusions from work in the field of selfhood. He suggests first that both the core and autobiographical self are interrelated; secondly, that consciousness is inseparable from emotion; and finally, that the sense of self exists to maintain or promote the healthy equilibrium of the body. Deutscher (2010), on the other hand, reminds us of the crucial impact of culture and language on that self.

Four questions of central educational importance emerge from this research:

1 If core consciousness is so totally dependent upon the senses and society, what do we do in our curriculum positively to introduce, develop and enhance experience across all the senses and social groups?

2 If the fully developed sense of self includes a clear sense of autobiographical self, what help are we giving children in school to identify their own *individualized* and special sense of identity confidence and belonging? How are we adding to their own *positive* memories, responses, talents and opinions? (Illustration 1.8)

3 If emotion is so closely linked with consciousness, are we spending enough time and effort in our teacher education on understanding emotion? In the education of children, are we planning for the positive engagement and enhancement of their *feelings*?

4 If self-awareness has developed from language and from nature as a way of promoting, assessing and fine-tuning our health, what are we doing in our curricula *holistically* and positively to involve both mind, body and relationships in the learning process?

It will not have escaped attention that I have used the word 'positive' in each of the four key educational implications of current thinking on self. Many writers attempt to place their scientific conclusions outside any values framework; teachers and the curriculum can have no such luxury. Almost everything teachers do is interpreted in some way as support or denial of some value or another. Each facet of the child's world described so far has implied questions of value. Some kind of morality is always at the heart of what society has required of its teachers and this fact can be used to generate vital discussion and decisions in schools. If we agree, for example, on a desire to work to make the world 'a better place', common sense might suggest that we agree on what better might mean. We might, for example, start by establishing a culture in which a positive sense of self, behaviour, feelings, relationships and

Illustration 1.8 *A 12-year-old introducing David Miliband (UK ex-government minister) to his group presentation on identity. Courtesy Gifted and Talented Summer Academy, Canterbury*

environment are more likely than negative ones. The theme of promoting well-being through the educational choices we make runs through every chapter in this book.

Well-being is as important to our learning as it is to our relationships. A wide body of research (see Chapters 4, 5 and 6) suggests that the inner and underlying sense of what we simply call 'happiness' is the most common foundation for the transferable and lifelong learning we aim for in schools. Happiness is not always easy to come by. After basic needs are catered for, increased wealth does not seem to increase happiness (Layard, 2005, 2006; Young Foundation, 2010). The USA and the UK are amongst the richest countries in the world, but can only manage 26th and 28th rankings in a 35-nation survey of life satisfaction in 11-year-olds. Such figures have concentrated government attention on child well-being (e.g. DfES/OFSTED, 2004, website; DCMS, 2008, website).

Not everyone sees happiness as an appropriate aim for education. Placing each child's and teacher's personal happiness as a necessary background to everything that happens in school is sometimes characterized as the family's job or an erroneous, over-idealistic and unrealistic aim. Detractors cite numerous examples of great but unhappy people, like Van Gogh, Schumann or Sylvia Plath, or perhaps their own painful struggles to suggest that good learning does not always come from 'being happy'. These examples do not necessarily negate the value of aiming at a default position of well-being. Neither does aiming at a generalized state of well-being deny the personal importance of living through, empathizing with, expecting, valuing and using periods of suffering, difficulty and pain.

The famous bipolar creators rarely created anything in their times of deep depression, but rather used their times of positive emotion to process and make sense of their more negative experiences. Few would suggest that we deliberately make children depressed in order that they become more creative. Neither is the depressed state typical of the mind at its most creative (see Csikszentmihalyi, 1997; Layard, 2005). Lasting learning can be painful and stressful, but unless this difficulty is experienced *against a background* of deeper personal security, learning is likely to be associated with negative feelings. A preponderance of negative life experiences seems more likely to result in a relative lack of resilience and self-efficacy (Bandura, 1994; Fredrickson and Tugade, 2004).

Personal happiness is generally and deeply important to us. There is clearly something universally recognizable in the happy face (Ekman, 2004), positively interpreted even by children with neurological barriers to emotion such as severe autism (Howard-Jones and Pickering, 2005). Even very young babies respond positively to a smiling face from any cultural source. Several strands of current research now suggest that a feeling of positive emotion is a prerequisite for high-level efficient and creative learning on social, physical and intellectual levels. Placing emphasis on positive aspects of the child's self and supporting all to feel included may not simply be a more efficient way of teaching them; it beneficially affects body and spirit too. Damasio (2003) offers a refinement to earlier thoughts about the links between consciousness and the body. He suggests that positive emotion, particularly the feeling of joy, signifies a biological state of: 'optimal physiological coordination and smooth running of the operations of life ... [Joy is] not only conducive to survival, but survival with well-being' (p. 137). In other words, when we are happy our body is in the best state for psychological and physical survival. When we are in this positive state, our brain responds by 'feeling' happy in order to help us maintain its current context. Damasio describes an unbroken loop between body and mind – the happy/healthy body promotes a more happy/efficiently working mind and vice versa. If this is the case, then seeking curricular opportunities to create the sense of joy in as many children as possible must be considered a desirable way for

Illustration 1.9 *Enjoyment is not always shown in the smile, but shows itself here in intricacy, concentration and application. Courtesy Gifted and Talented Summer Academy, Canterbury*

them to be and to learn. Teaching with *enjoyment* as a major aim seems to have the potential to serve mind and body, here and now, and also to create in children a positive sense of self which will benefit them well into the future.

These findings mirror those by 'positive psychologists' like Csikszentmihalyi (2002), Fredrickson (2003, 2009), Fredrickson and Branigan (2005) and Seligman (2004), who also propose that positive emotional states are the optimum mental conditions for learning, social and intellectual connection making, discovery, creativity and invention. A particularly accessible hypothesis in this regard is Fredrickson's 'broaden and build' theory of positive emotions. This is examined in Chapter 4.

There also seem to be strong links between happiness and creativity (Csikszentmihalyi, 1997). Veteran 'people watcher', Desmond Morris, has suggested that our feeling of happiness relates to 'the degree to which we find ourselves able to exercise the particularly human skills of creativity, the use of symbols including symbolic language, and family relationships' (Morris, 2004). A recurring theme of this book is the relationship between the self involved in creative activity and the ensuring sense of contentment, achievement, fascination, engagement and joy we often call happiness.

The developing self of the child is also prey to a powerful set of negative influences. Notions of rampant materialism, excessive wealth, risky behaviour, violence, fame and a narrow concept of physical beauty are all too easily assimilated into the hoped-for self. These features of young life are constantly reinforced by toys, advertising, television, film, computer, internet and video images. Human young are probably genetically predisposed to finding joy in these things, but it is also commonly held that such simple pleasures do not bring particularly long-lasting satisfaction. Indeed, studies of lottery winners throughout the world have demonstrated the short-lived nature of happiness from material wealth. Left to their own devices without ICT to distract them, children quickly find enjoyment in physical and social activities. Physical play clearly engages the vast majority of young mammals. A casual observation of children during games sessions and at playtime shows most exhibiting wide grins, sparkling eyes, relaxed faces and joyful conversation – the key signals of happiness. It seems particularly disastrous that school sports and PE are so constrained by time, especially since negative body image and obesity are growing issues in developed societies like the UK and the USA (WHO, 2004, 2008, websites; Young Foundation, 2010).

Schools of the twenty-first century are right to be thinking hard about what implicit and explicit values they wish to teach their pupils. Perhaps the call for more complex and challenging activities in the curriculum results from a feeling that it is in creative, often symbolic, physical activity that lasting human satisfaction is to be found (Morris, 2004). Political demands on schools have sometimes resulted in significant conflicts of values in this regard. In the context of 'back to basics' demands on US education (Hirsch, 1999), Csikszentmihalyi castigated schools and parents for: 'making serious tasks dull and hard and frivolous ones exciting and easy. Schools generally fail to teach how exciting, how mesmerisingly beautiful science or mathematics can be; they teach the routine of literature or history rather than the adventure' (1997: 125). He goes on to give evidence from his own research which suggests that creative individuals in all walks of life go beyond the limitations of genetic or cultural programming to live 'exemplary lives … [which] show how joyful and interesting complex symbolic activity is'. Attitudes to the self – how I learn best, what I find fascinating, satisfying, pleasure-giving, helpful – can be developed through education, but it is probably important that we consider carefully what kind of 'selves' we are helping to create in our classrooms.

How can we know what it is like to be a child in the twenty-first century?

The current concerns of children remind us that it may not be easy being a child in the first quarter of the twenty-first century, anywhere in the world. At one extreme, children suffer disproportionately. In the developing world, five-sixths of the world's children have the least access to scarce resources and

Illustrations 1.10, 1.11, 1.12 *Seek out the facial manifestations of happiness, the smile, the shining eyes, the raised cheekbones and the un-furrowed brow. Photos: Cherry Tewfik*

16,000 of them die each day because of poverty (Bread for the world, 2010, website). Two hundred and fifty million children under 14 work for their survival (UN, 2006, schools website). On the evidence of researchers and current media headlines, many young people in the resource-rich and developed world live a pretty sad and lonely existence too. Poverty of all kinds singles children out for special problems. The United Nations Children's Fund (UNICEF, 2009, website) reminds us that 30 per cent of children in the UK and USA live in poverty described as 'an environment that is damaging to their mental, physical, emotional and spiritual development' (UNICEF, 2005, website). The gap between rich and poor is as significant as poverty itself. Life expectancy correlates exactly with levels of inequality, and children born into low-status, low-income and high levels of stress, start life smaller and significantly more prone to psychological problems and illness (Layard, 2005, 2006; Wilkinson, 2005; Young Foundation, 2010).

Beyond poverty, relative wealth may have brought its own problems. Young people in advanced economies are reported to be increasingly involved in risky behaviour. Several studies demonstrate the rapid growth in behavioural and emotional difficulties amongst the young, and rising rates of teenage alcoholism, early smoking, depression, self-harm and suicide (Collishaw et al., 2004; Layard, 2006, website; Layard and Dunn, 2009). Indeed, Collishaw's report recorded that in the UK behavioural and emotional problems among teenagers have risen by over 70 per cent in the past 25 years. The WHO reports (WHO, 2004, 2008, websites), graphically presented a rise in many of the possible causes of such trends: family breakdown, bullying, loss of trust, lack of success or pleasure in school, stress, loneliness and subjective health problems. Within many categories of health-related behaviour, young people in England (not necessarily in the UK as a whole) and the USA were shown to be amongst the least happy in the Western world. There may be a sensationalist element to some newspaper headlines and opinion polls about young people's health, but it is more difficult to argue with international organizations with a well-established research methodology and, hopefully, less culturally biased views.

The most important way of finding out about what concerns children is by asking them. The pupil voice movement is still in its infancy in the UK and USA but increasingly schools are listening. In *The School I'd Like*, Catherine Burke and Ian Grosvenor asked children their views on school (Burke and Grosvenor, 2003) and life in general (Davey et al., 2010). The collected children's statements plead for a very different school environment to the one which many adults may *think* children would like. Here are a few provocative suggestions for the schools of the future:

- Children will learn more about the future than the past.
- Adults will listen to them and not dismiss their opinions.
- Children will be free to be children.

Illustrations 1.13, 1.14, 1.15   *Each child shows engagement in a different way, but it is recognizable across time and culture. Photos: Cherry Tewfik*

- Children will not be 'treated as herds of identical animals wanting to be civilized before we are let loose upon the world. It will be recognized that it's our world too'.
- Playgrounds would have 'something to play with'.
- 'Power will be evenly spread throughout the school'.
- 'More time should be devoted to art, design and technology'.
- The curriculum will be 'concerned with fulfilment'.

Several case studies from this book will outline projects where children have taken the lead in successfully defining and achieving what they wanted to learn and make in environments where the 'locus of control' was passed to them. These may still seem radical more than 200 years after Rousseau's idealized and naturally good, 'noble savage' approach to the education of the child (see Introduction).

Less radical but very much in line with a 'reconstructionist' education ideology, the UK government and government agencies are now acting on the Children Act's *Every Child Matters* (HM Government, 2004). This Act, seen by some as far-reaching and bold, is constructed around five outcomes which arose from consultations with children about their hopes and needs from the adult-controlled worlds of the health, social and education services. These common outcomes, against which all government agencies working with children are judged, are to:

- be healthy
- stay safe
- enjoy and achieve
- make a positive contribution
- achieve economic well-being.

A newly articulated emphasis on feelings, security and well-being is evident in this list. Similar stress is also evident in a number of other UK government directives. Ofsted's 'framework for inspection' (Ofsted, 2004, s. 4: 25) required schools to self-evaluate efforts made towards enhancing the 'personal development and well-being' of all learners. Similarly, the Healthy Schools Status document (DH/DfES, 2005, and website) holds as one of its key areas of activity 'the emotional health and well-being' of children. Under new administration since May 2010, the 'smaller' UK government continues to see itself as enabling children:

to overcome disadvantage and deprivation so they can fulfill their innate talents and take control of their own destiny ... [and affirming a] belief in the power of human agency to give meaning, structure and hope to every life. (Gove, 2010b, website)

It now seems clear that national education systems in the developed world and beyond are charged not just with the education and socialization of children, but also the active promotion of their personal emotional security, health and well-being. Schools are designed to reach every child – they are the only agencies in a position fully to enact such policies and philosophies. In the next chapter, we examine some schools' attempts to address the central issues for children of the twenty-first century.

Summary

The twenty-first century has challenges like every other century. Aside from the obvious implications of overpopulation, there are three major differences to the challenges of this century: the much more rapid *pace* of change (Figure 1.2), their perceived often *negative* character in the minds of modern children and their *global* characteristics.

The changes and challenges in our world, and consequently our minds, cannot be kept local; our global economy, instant communications and global pollution have meant that whatever happens in one place quickly affects every other. If they want, ordinary people, particularly teachers and children, are now in a position to exert some influence over the interrelated

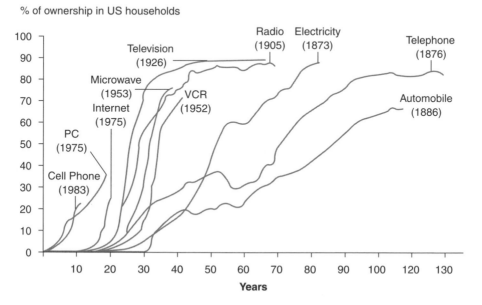

Figure 1.2 How long it takes new technologies to reach a mass market. Where cell phones, internet and personal computers penetrated 20 per cent of the US market in less than 20 years, it took the car and the telephone 50 years to achieve the same take-up

future of this world, but to do so effectively we need to be very clear about what we value most. The answers to questions of value should underpin all our education decisions. So far, we have selected and examined five key areas of special interest to children:

- the future (which is taken to include environmental as well as personal concerns)
- ICT
- global politics
- relationships
- the self.

Research and experience in these areas also suggests that a number of related statements can be made which might impact upon a curriculum designed to liberate those children from the combined threats of materialism, fear, exclusion and lack of self-fulfilment. Each of the following statements rest on arguments for a more cross-curricular, creative, meaningful and child-centred approach:

1 *Security about the future is an essential prerequisite for the happy child.* A curriculum which addresses children's anxiety about the personal and global future (as well as insecurities about the self and relationships) is crucial if we agree that school activities should be relevant to their lives.

2 *A sense of personal control over aspects of their daily life is central to children's motivation for learning.* A concentration on developing emotional literacy, the constructive use of ICT and establishment of personally meaningful, curricular experiences to interpret and examine is more likely to generate personal engagement among children.

3 *It is possible for ordinary individuals to make a positive impact upon global and environmental issues.* It is suggested that cross-curricular themes that touch upon children's culturally or genetically determined interests in any area are more likely to generate involvement.

4 *Opportunities to build and deepen positive relationships with others are embraced by children.* We should seek a curriculum, teaching methods, community links and classroom organization which offer a range of activities to promote and utilize such relationships.

5 *The child's positive self-image is fundamental to a healthy mind and body.* Education should therefore be physically active and individualized as far as possible and aim to promote a personal sense of achievement and resilience and to discover the strengths of each individual.

Education in the UK and USA is now in a position where *government policy* on health, education and social services could be seen to be broadly in line with *theoretical/professional* opinion on priorities for children. Key words which arise from both areas each relate to feelings:

- health
- security
- enjoyment
- positivity
- well-being.

Each of these concepts and each of the five key areas of special interest to children are dependent upon judgements of value. Each school and community should found its curriculum upon the values they agree to share. I believe such decisions and actions would significantly and positively impact on the character of twenty-first-century life.

Key questions for discussion

- Do you think that the 2000s are pessimistic times?
- What do you think schools can do about integrating family learning into the curriculum and structures of the school?
- What can the playground tell us about children's learning? How could this be integrated into the curriculum?
- What are the pluses and minuses of ICT in the lives of children?
- How can we make relationships a more central part of our curriculum?
- How can we ensure times of happiness and positivity for every child?
- What can the school do about the health of the child?

Further reading

Alexander, T. (2001) *Citizenship Schools: A Practical Guide to Education for Citizenship and Personal Development*. London: Campaign for Learning/UNICEF.
Greenfield, S. (2003) *Tomorrow's People*. London: Penguin.
Robinson, K. and Aronica, L. (2010) *The Element: How Finding Your Passion Changes Everything*. London: Continuum.

CHAPTER 2

Cross-Curricular Policy and Practice

Cross-curricular approaches to learning have a long history. They are implicit in ancient Greek and medieval Chinese views of education where drama, music, philosophy and literature were expected to be combined. The two Western curriculum subjects we call music and dance are seen as one and the same thing in some African cultures (Blacking, 1974). Experiences, chosen to be understood through a number of different subject disciplines, exemplify the educational philosophies and recommendations of seventeenth-, eighteenth- and early nineteenth-century philosopher/educationalists like Comenius, Rousseau, Pestalozzi and Froebel. Associated in the twentieth century with ideas of 'child-centred' learning, what we would now call cross-curricular or thematic learning was championed by twentieth-century 'progressives'.

Twentieth-century cross-curricular thinking

Rooted in the history of Western education, the concept of 'child-centred' education spread through early twentieth-century educational thinkers like John Dewey (1859–1952) in the USA and Rudolf Steiner (1861–1925) in Europe. Dewey's 'democratic' approach was founded on concepts of freedom and the provisional nature of knowledge. He argued that children should be deeply and personally involved in the creation of knowledge through problem solving and experiment, and that community would be enriched by individuals whose personal experience had been enlarged through education. Education was rarely seen as an individualistic activity; in his writing and lectures, Dewey was often at pains to stress the importance of the group:

> I believe that the only true education comes through the stimulation of the child's powers by the demands of the social situations in which he finds himself. Through these demands he is stimulated to act as a member of a unity, to emerge from his original narrowness of action and feeling,

and to conceive of himself from the standpoint of the welfare of the group to which he belongs. Through the responses which others make to his own activities he comes to know what these mean in social terms. The value which they have is reflected back into them. (Dewey, 1897: 77–80)

Steiner's ideas were more spiritual and personal – he believed like Rousseau in the innate wisdom of the human. In proposals for his 'Waldorf schools', Steiner (1919) gave a detailed outline of a developmentally based curriculum strongly infused with the arts. The Waldorf curriculum is both subject-based and thematic – the theme is the development of selfhood. It is designed to mirror and guide the child's unfolding dexterity, consciousness, creativity and imagination. Its classical aims – to cultivate responsibility for the earth and other people and prepare children for the challenges of the future – are met through a curriculum designed to be personally engaging, spiritually conscious, experience-based and responsive to the physical world of nature. A Steiner curriculum often uses separated subjects, but also provides regular opportunities to put subject learning into cross-subject contexts like plays, building projects, exhibitions, displays, walks in the countryside and seasonal celebrations.

The 1931 Hadow Report (UK Board of Education, 1931) took up Dewey's ideas in the UK. Even in its time, its proposals were radical. Hadow reflected 'progressive' child-centred philosophies in suggesting that learning, especially in the primary curriculum, should be seen in terms of 'activity and experience rather than knowledge to be acquired and facts to be stored' (UK Board of Education, 1931, para. 75). *Knowing* and *doing* were in some ways seen as synonymous with each other, and purposeful activity suited to the child's specific environment needed to be planned in accordance with the varying nature of children. Unfortunately, as Alexander (2010) reminds us, Hadow's emphasis on activity resulted in the unintended and unhelpful polarization between experience and knowledge which has clouded the debate over cross-curricular learning ever since.

Although the Hadow Report was hailed as a triumph for progressive, constructivist education, the spirit of its recommendations was not fully advanced until the Plowden Report (DES, 1967). This influential report complied evidence from professional, academic and interest groups to argue that:

> Rigid division of the curriculum into subjects tends to interrupt children's trains of thought and of interest and to hinder them from realising the common elements in problem solving ... some work at least, should cut across subject divisions at all stages of the primary school. (DES, 1967, para. 535, p. 197)

In its chapter on 'Children learning in school' (DES, 1967, para. 202, p. 189), Plowden cited a roll-call of eighteenth-, nineteenth- and twentieth-century progressives to bolster its case. In addition to the twentieth-century educationalists already mentioned, Maria Montessori, Rachel Macmillan, Susan Isaacs, Jean Piaget and Jerome Bruner – names which still feature in the education debate today – were called upon to defend 'active learning' – experience-led, 'discovery' approaches in primary education and beyond.

Much of the discovery approach was underpinned by the work of psychologist Jean Piaget (1954) discussed in Chapter 6. Piaget's influence on US and Western European education to an extent, fed individualistic interpretations of child development, whereas the (then) newly translated research of a Russian Lev Vygotsky highlighted the social aspects of learning. Whilst Piaget's stages of development envisaged what Bruner called a 'lone scientist', Vygotsky was clear that the social context was fundamental to language, concept formation and learning (Vygotsky, 1962). Vygotsky observed that learning occurred in similar playful, genuinely exploratory contexts to those observed by Piaget, but Vygotsky believed concepts were more easily formed and understood and that learning was more permanent when the learner thought, spoke and discovered with others. Thus, much educational thought in the 1960s and 1970s linked group work, mixed ability, even mixed ages with cross-curricular activity. In truth, few schools of the 1960s or 1970s ventured very far down the Plowden path and most primary pedagogy remained steadfastly didactic (Alexander et al., 1992, paras 19 and 20).

Only nine years after Lady Plowden's recommendations, British Prime Minister James Callaghan made his 'Ruskin College' speech (Callaghan, 1976) calling for a 'Great Debate' on education and expressing the unease felt by parents and employers regarding: 'the new informal methods of teaching, which seem to produce excellent results when they are in well-qualified hands but are much more dubious when they are not'. To be fair, this was a concern already expressed by Plowden in considering the implications of its recommendations. Callaghan's speech and rapid progress towards a national curriculum effectively stifled the development of cross-curricular teaching and learning in all but the most confident British schools. The 1988 Education Reform Act significantly added to the power of the Secretary of State to interfere in the fine detail of schooling, and for the first time introduced a legal entitlement to a set of separated subjects taught to a statutory and finely detailed programme called the National Curriculum.

The National Curriculum

The English National Curriculum (DES, 1989; DfEE, 1999) subdivided primary children's learning into 10 subjects (11 with RE and 12 after 2010 when Modern Foreign Language was added). These subjects were divided into a 'core' of English, mathematics and science, and 'foundation' (the rest). Sex education, Citizenship and Personal Health and Social Education (PSHE) were also added by 2009 but remained outside the foundation category and their nature depended upon key Stage and school policy. At all times, the core was to be given privileged status in terms of time, inspection, public reporting, statutory tests and school league tables to report results. Most schools quickly settled into a routine of English and maths every morning and the other subjects distributed across the week with science given a little more time than the other subjects. Increased time was given to mathematics and English after 1997 when the National Literacy Strategy (NLS) and the National Numeracy Strategy (NNS) were introduced into primary schools. Extra time was made available for the strategies to become established, by relaxing legal requirements to report on the 'Foundation Subjects' (Office for Standards in Education (Ofsted, 1998). NLS and NNS were not statutory, but league tables and a punitive inspection regime ensured that very few schools dared disregard the detailed interference in pedagogy these strategies represented. The arrival of the strategies had an almost immediate and negative effect upon the teaching of the foundation subjects and science, in terms of ever-diminishing local authority support, rapidly declining quality of teaching and shortened time for learning in them. Cross-curricular teaching almost disappeared between 1997 and 2003.

Cross-curricular approaches were mentioned in the revisions of the English National Curriculum for Key Stages 1–3, in the mid 1990s, but were relegated to tiny, grey print and in the margins of the pure subject orders. Broader amalgamations of subjects and experience-led learning remained alive, partly under the influence of Storyline® (Storyline, 2010, website) and the Scottish 5–14 curriculum where history, geography and modern studies were taught under the heading of the 'Social Subjects' (SOED, 1993). Each subject shared identical skills descriptors. Cross-curricular approaches occupied an even more central position in Scotland's *Curriculum for Excellence* (Scottish Executive, 2004). In Northern Ireland's *Common Curriculum* (1991), the themes 'The Environment and Society' and 'Creative and Expressive Studies' were used to apply the separate subjects and later 'Cultural Heritage' and 'Education for Mutual Understanding' became required cross-curricular themes for both primary and secondary pupils.

Whilst cross-curricular pedagogies were developing in Scotland, Northern Ireland and to a lesser extent Wales, in England the Qualifications and Curriculum Agency (QCA, 1998a) was busy bolstering subject divisions by publishing detailed schemes of work for Key Stage 1, 2 and 3 for each of 12 subjects. Whilst only intended as guidance, the QCA schemes quickly became seen as an alternative national curriculum for many English schools. Public and political pressure ensured however that in each of the four nations of the United Kingdom, mathematics and English had the lion's share of primary and secondary curriculum time. Only the Curriculum Guidance for the Foundation Stage (CGFS) (DfEE, 1999) retained a cross-curricular rationale.

The National Advisory Council on Creative and Cultural Education (NACCCE, 1999) responded to the inequality of subject provision in England by recommending parity of *all* subjects in the curriculum. Whilst a revised and slimmed down National Curriculum was republished (DfEE, 1999), the recommendation of subject parity was ignored by government. Indeed, the term 'foundation subjects' was replaced in some official documents by the some-what demeaning term 'non-core' in 2000. From 1999 onwards, Physical Education (PE) hours were reduced, school fields were sold, school concerts and plays became less frequent and the arts were said to be 'disappearing' from school and college curricula (Rogers, 1999, 2003). The 'Standards' for Qualified Teacher Status (QTS) from this period require trainee teachers only to 'have *sufficient* understanding of a *range* of work' *across* history *or* geography, art/design *or* design/technology and the *performing* arts (Teacher Training Agency (TTA), 2003). This directive on teacher education surreptitiously replaced music and other individual arts disciplines as a requirement for QTS, and thereby lowered the status of geography, history and design/technology too. As a result, local authority foundation subject courses declined, and subject advisers either lost their jobs or were forced to combine subject roles. At the same time, out-of-school visits, field trips, swimming, library visits and other activities dwindled (Barnes, 2001; Bell, 2004; Rogers, 2003). Opportunities for quality cross-curricular work could be argued to have been squeezed out of the English curriculum for lack of time and declining subject expertise.

Cross-curricular approaches were not entirely absent from the early twenty-first-century UK curriculum, however. As social and political pressures pushed schools to take on functions traditionally met by families, social and health services (HMG, 2004), the curriculum itself became even more complex. Interest in the non-statutory Citizenship and PSHE rose as international comparisons rated the UK low on child happiness, and physical, social and mental health scales (see WHO, 2004, website). Inspections and education authority advice devoted more time to the National Curriculum's cross-curricular thinking skills, like creative thinking (see DfES, 2006b, website). Ofsted required inspection reports and school self-assessments on child well-being for the first time in this period and detailed advice was given to schools on the Social, Emotional Aspects of Learning (SEAL 2006, website; DfES, 2005, website). Reports and advice from Ofsted often linked child emotional, intellectual and social well-being with creative and cross-curricular approaches to the curriculum (see Ofsted, 2002, 2009a, 2009b, 2010). Connections between the cross-curriculum and children's sustained engagement were also made by the Department of Health's 'Healthy Schools' campaign (DoH/DfES, 2005) and the Department for Culture Media and Sport's support for Creative Partnerships.

The United Nations Convention on the Rights of the Child (UNICEF, 1989, website), to which the UK signed up, has curricular implications too. In subsequent academic writing, reports, commissions, surveys and evaluations on schools and schooling, children's views were asked for, sometimes for the first time. A message supporting a more open, flexible experience and child-relevant curriculum was commonly conveyed by such consultations (see Alexander, 2010; Burke and Grosvenor, 2003; Layard and Dunn, 2009; Powell and Barnes, 2008, for example). Pupil voice has become a feature of school organization and young people's opinions on curriculum and pedagogy are now taken seriously in many schools (Ruddock and MacIntyre, 2007). In almost every consultation, pressures for both curriculum simplification and increased relevance came from both children and their teachers.

The UK Labour government reviewed the secondary (QCDA, 2007, website) and then the primary curriculum (Rose, 2009) in attempts to rationalize and reduce this overcrowded and complex curriculum. Key Stage 3 curricula remained subject-based but teachers were given considerably more flexibility over curriculum content and coverage. For primary schools, Rose tackled curriculum overload by suggesting the thematic approaches outlined below. The Rose Review, though barred from examining assessment and league tables, was set up as a rival review to the Cambridge Review. This review, funded by the Esmee Fairbairn Foundation from 2006 onwards, published its report four years later (Alexander, 2010). Alexander's review has already had significant impacts upon Initial Teacher Education programmes.

The Rose and Alexander Reviews

The problem of an overcrowded yet narrowed primary curriculum was a starting point for both major reviews published in 2009/10. Rose represented the views of many when stating:

> The availability of time and its management will continue to pose considerable problems unless a better fit of curriculum content to the capacity of primary schools can be achieved. The National Curriculum ... is overcrowded, leaving teachers with insufficient time to enable children to engage adequately with every subject required by law. (Rose, 2009, para. 2.3)

At the same time, Rose reported the concerns of many of its respondents who saw the primary curriculum as:

> narrowed by the Key Stage 2 National Curriculum tests, the focus of Ofsted inspections and the National Strategies ... [and that] as a result of these external pressures the principle of an entitlement to a broad and balanced curriculum is, in effect, denied to many children. (Rose, 2009, para. 2.4)

The following points gathered from wide-ranging consultations directed Rose's decisions on curriculum:

- a reduction in content with greater flexibility and less prescription
- a clear set of culturally derived aims and values
- the securing of high achievement in literacy, numeracy and ICT
- explicit opportunities for children to benefit from subject teaching and cross-curricular studies that cover the principal areas of our history, culture and achievement and the wider world
- explicit opportunities throughout to foster children's personal development and good attitudes to learning. (Rose, 2009, para. 2.12)

The Rose Interim and Final Reports (Rose, 2008, 2009) proposed both increased subject rigour and thematic approaches. These reports suggested that effective learning could occur between subjects and in mixtures of subjects but also that standards in the individual subjects must be improved through being separately taught. This was in line with Ofsted (2010) which simultaneously confirmed that raising standards in individual subjects was in no way compromised by good-quality creative and cross-curricular work. In a sample of good and outstanding schools covering four key stages, Ofsted stated that teachers:

> felt confident in encouraging pupils to make connections across traditional boundaries, speculate constructively, maintain an open mind while exploring a wide range of options, and reflect critically on ideas and outcomes. This [Ofsted comments] had a perceptible and positive impact on pupils' personal development, and their preparation for life beyond school. (Ofsted, 2010: 4)

Ofsted confirmed that in successful schools applying cross-curricular initiatives, 'the distinctiveness of individual subjects was not diminished' (Ofsted, 2010: 11).

Rose proposed that this mix of subject rigour and motivating cross-curricular approaches could be organized under six 'areas of learning':

- understanding the arts
- understanding English, communication and languages
- scientific and technological understanding
- understanding mathematics
- understanding physical development, health and well-being
- historical, geographical and social understanding.

The hastily published and distributed *National Curriculum Primary Handbook*, based on Rose's review (DCSF/QCDA, 2010), picked out 'cross-curricular studies' as a strand in its common format for all programmes of learning. However, one of the first moves of the new government of May 2010 was to reject Rose's recommendations and return primary schools to the national curriculum of 1999 awaiting a curriculum revision in 2012.

A balance of disciplinary skills and cross-curricular themes also character-ized the more nuanced, widely consultative and academically based Cambridge Review chaired by Alexander (2010). The UK coalition government placed flexible and community-based curricula, improved access to the poorest chil-dren in society and subject or theme-based academies at the core of their education policy. Having ditched the Rose Review, the Secretary of State for Education turned to the 'best work' from the Alexander Review (*TES*, 2010, website), though initially he failed to indicate what the best work was. The 2010 government also made clear its attachment to subject-based teaching, raising standards, 'a relentless focus on the basics', didactic methods and a particular approach to the teaching of reading – somewhat contradicting its rhetoric of 'flexibility' (DoE, 2010, website).

Alexander addresses such contradictions by tracing the roots of public policy on curriculum and identifying the main problems facing primary and early secondary schooling today. The Report places considerable emphasis on the aims and values of education and curriculum, the dangers of politicization, loss of professional and local autonomy and the 'pernicious dichotomy' (2010: 243) between a broad and balanced curriculum and high standards in the basics. It combines **aims** of education and **domains** of learning to propose a curriculum flexible enough to serve a wide variety of communities and localities.

It will be noted immediately that Alexander's eight domains are not far from Rose's 'areas of learning' or the 'curriculum areas' in Scotland's Curriculum for Excellence. The addition of faith/belief and ethics/citizenship introduces an important values component to the curriculum itself. The omission of ICT and personal development emphasizes their cross-curricular nature over the sense that they are 'subjects' in their own right. The cross-curricular tone of Alexander's proposal is clear. Domains like 'place and time' and 'arts and creativity' clearly expect connections between geography and history and art, music and drama (and significantly, creativity across the range of non-artistic subjects). But equally, the headings, physical/emotional health, language, oracy and literacy, citizenship and ethics and science/technology also imply approaches which cut across traditional subject boundaries – oracy, emotional health and citizenship may be explored in any context and across contexts.

Throughout the Alexander report, it is stressed that schools and communi-ties should decide upon the interpretation and application of aims and the ways the domains are taught. The 'community curriculum' should, according to Alexander, take 30 per cent of teaching time. Schools in turn should decide upon the programmes of study they follow in applying the 70 per cent devoted to the national curriculum.

Aims of education (working towards ...)		Domains of learning
1. personal well-being		Arts and creativity
2. personal engagement		Citizenship/ethics
3. personal empowerment		
4. personal autonomy		Faith and belief
5. respect and reciprocity for others		Language, oracy and literacy
6. interdependence and sustainability		
7. local, national and global citizenship		Mathematics
8. participation in culture and community		Physical/emotional health
9. knowing, understanding, making sense		
10. fostering skill		Place and time
11. exciting the imagination		Science/technology
12. enacting dialogue		

Figure 2.1 Aims and domain of the curriculum according to Alexander, 2010

In stressing what a domain *is not,* Alexander highlights the problems inherent in cross-curricular pedagogies of the past. The domains his report proposes are not:

- a slot in the school's weekly timetable
- an invitation to low-grade topic work in which thematic serendipity counts for more than knowledge and skill (Alexander, 2010: 265–6).

In stating what domains *are,* Alexander also helps build a case for revisiting (with caution) cross-curricular approaches. The collections of concepts chosen to represent domains, he argues, have 'an identifiable and essential core of knowledge and skill', the capacity to fulfil one or more educational aims, and can be justified as serving the developmental, cultural and future needs of the child. In the light of Alexander's recommendations and those of Rose, Dearing, Plowden and Hadow before him, I outline what I see as good-quality cross-curricular teaching and learning.

What is good cross-curricular teaching and learning?

I argue that cross-curricular learning occurs when the skills, knowledge and attitudes of a number of different disciplines are applied to a single theme, problem, idea or experience. The term cross-curricular applied to both teaching and learning suggests considering education at a macro level, with the *curriculum* as the focus, but cross-curricular approaches may also have micro implications involving the style of pedagogy, classroom organization and interactions. Cross-curricular methods can be effective in teaching and reaching ethical solutions, building individual and group motivation, sustaining interest and raising standards – this I see as good practice. Cross-curricular approaches can also be made ineffective by trivalizing, confusing, misleading, constructing new misconceptions and also by failing to provide a moral context for learning – this I would call poor practice.

Both Alexander and Rose clearly addressed the issue of values in their reviews and reports. Rose made 'Aims, values and purposes' the first section in his primary handbook (QCDA, 2010: 3–5). As well as detailed discussion of values, Alexander recommends 'ethics' to be part of the curriculum and calls education, 'a fundamentally moral affair' (Alexander, 2010: 16). Aims, values and purposes may differ between communities served by a curriculum, but the curriculum must stand on agreed, clear, values-based foundations if it is to be considered 'good' in a moral sense. It must also be good in a professional sense (see also DfES, 2004b, website). If teachers want, in Alexander's words, to 'excite the imagination, provoke dialogue, foster skills and encourage the child to explore, understand and make sense' (2010: 257–8), they must value subject knowledge. This does not mean that teachers should know everything about each of the traditional subjects – rather, that they should be familiar with the distinctive lens each subject provides on the same reality. The detail of the unique and specialized language, skill set, disposition and core knowledge of each subject should be understood by at least one staff member in every school. Teachers must expect to be comfortable with regularly sharing that knowledge with their colleagues (see also DfES, 2006a, website). Good cross-curricular pedagogy should also be relevant, with teachers courting and valuing the contribution of the local community in building knowledge as part of a continual programme of personal and professional development. In short, teachers should 'be able to give a coherent justification citing evidence, pedagogical principle [and] educational aim for all their choices in school (Alexander, 2010: 308).

Effective cross-curricular practice, like all pedagogy, also requires excellence in the science, art and craft of teaching (Pollard, 2010). Cross-curricular approaches must be research-informed which is why Chapters 4, 5, 6 and 7 in this book are devoted to the evidence from psychological, social scientific, neuroscientific and pedagogical enquiry. Working between and across subject boundaries also requires what Pollard (2010: 5) sees as a 'responsive, creative, and intuitive' approach able to maximize on the unexpected reactions of children encountering real problems and using the skills and knowledge of several subjects to solve them. All teaching requires the 'mastery of a full repertoire of pedagogical skills and practices' (p. 5), but cross-curricular teaching specifically requires high levels of ability to work with Pollard's skills list A:

Pedagogical skills list A

- Construct or use scenarios that require the perspectives of several subjects
- Value and use diversity of response and insight
- Follow children's lead
- Find entry points to learning to match the individual
- Link ideas from different subject areas
- Be a co-learner.

Well used, the pedagogical skills in list A will generate motivation, creative thinking and sustain interest, but may not on their own raise standards in individual subjects. To create the challenge necessary to build new knowledge and skills, the good cross-curricular teacher also needs to use several of the skills in skills list B:

Pedagogical skills list B

- Direct children's enthusiasm towards the acquisition of pre-planned, *whole-class subject goals* in two or more subjects
- Direct children's enthusiasm towards *individual subject progression goals* in two or more subjects
- Plan shared meaningful multi-sensory experiences to generate *focused* enquiry and challenge
- Teach *specific* skills and knowledge across a range of subjects as required by children
- Teach *specific* skills and knowledge across a range of subjects
- Empower children to use newly learned skills and knowledge to solve problems, address issues or understand cross-curricular themes
- Plan integral assessment opportunities within each unit of work.

List B is a demanding skill set which usually requires more than one mind, so the final pedagogical skills important to cross-curricular work are the ability to use the skills of list C:

Pedagogical skills list C

- Work in teams with other teachers to promote progression in children's learning
- Work with practitioners from the community outside school to promote progression in children's learning
- Work with children to generate plans, ideas and solutions.

Poor cross-curricular teaching results in fragile, untransferrable and difficult-to-articulate learning. If our aim is to generate both enjoyment *and* excellence in terms which can be assessed and, to a degree, measured, then combinations of skills from each of lists A, B and C are needed. Too much cross-curricular teaching in the past concentrated only on list A. List B is of equal importance – the teacher should *teach* as well as promote learning in all cross-curricular contexts. Practically speaking and because learning for both teachers and children is a social affair, list C reminds us that schools should be collegiate institutions working with the widest community.

Cross-curricular pedagogy is not simple because there are a number of contrasting cross-curricular contexts, all of which have different pedagogical and learning aims.

A cross-curricular taxonomy

The best cross-curricular projects combine the promotion of creative thinking with the maintenance of disciplinary rigour and challenge. It needs to be stressed from the outset that whilst 12 different subject disciplines *may* be applied to a single theme, research suggests that subject progression and integrity is best ensured by limiting the subjects involved in cross-curricular work to two or three (Barnes and Shirley, 2007; Jacobs, 2004; Roth, 2000). In offering a classification of cross-curricular approaches, I recognize a range of differing aims and purposes. I use data from a series of recorded lesson observations made over the past five years and my own experience, and from this analysis I have identified five distinct types of cross-curricular teaching and learning:

- hierarchical
- multi-disciplinary
- inter-disciplinary
- opportunistic
- double focus.

Hierarchical cross-curricular teaching and learning

Hierarchical cross-curricular methods aim at achieving progress in one discipline by using aspects of another. This is probably the most common context in which cross-curricular thinking and learning takes place. A class rendition of *Greensleeves* might introduce the Tudors, a painting of a face might be art's contribution to a Modern Languages lesson or a map might be used to help children understand coordinates in mathematics. In each case, a skill in one

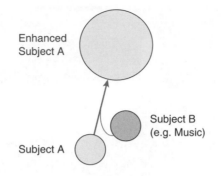

Figure. 2.2 Hierarchical cross-curricular learning. Learning in the 'superior' subject (Subject A, for example English) is enhanced with help from an 'inferior' subject (in this case Music) which is not necessarily developed by its combination

subject supports learning considered more important in another. Effective and lasting learning in one subject is often provoked by calling upon another, as many of us who learned times tables by chanting or rapping remember. However, in hierarchical cross-curricular teaching and learning, there is no pretence that knowledge, skills and understanding in the 'inferior' subject are being improved – one subject is simply a tool to enliven learning in the superior subject. The danger is that in thematic curricula such as that envisaged by Rose (2009), some disciplines like music, art, dance, geography, design/ technology and drama may have become cast forever in this subservient and submissive role.

The arts subjects are often used in hierarchical cross-curricular contexts. Traditionally, the arts involve participation on emotional and physical as well as intellectual levels. The arts are often argued to generate a sense of belonging, motivation and satisfaction (see Evans and Philpott, 2009; Roberts, 2006). Used in hierarchically weaker contexts, new arts skills, knowledge and attitudes may not be learned, though wider elements like communication, emotional literacy, motivation and enjoyment may actually be enhanced.

Many would argue that, practically speaking, representation as the inferior partner in a learning hierarchy is the easiest way to include some disciplines in an overcrowded curriculum. Those who feel insecure in their ability to teach the fundamental modes of thought of a particular discipline, may find it less threatening to place their 'weaker' subjects in this position, but hierarchical methods can also be highly motivating and extend learning to more pupils. If music, or art or PE, or geographical understanding is the 'way in' to language, mathematics, science or ICT for a particular group of children, then hierarchical approaches may be seen as more inclusive and motivating than 'straight' subject teaching. Often however, little progress is made in the 'inferior' subject.

Illustration 2.1   *Technology (in this case the use of class digital cameras) used to enhance skills in language*

Case study 1

Three student teachers visiting a class in a rural school in India, used the song *Heads, Shoulders, Knees and Toes* to teach Tamil children the English terms for parts of the body and then translated the song into Tamil with the help of the children. The lesson ended with the three students singing *Heads, Shoulders … * to the class in Tamil.

Multi-disciplinary cross-curricular teaching and learning

Multi-disciplinary cross-curricular approaches aim at using a single experience or theme to develop higher levels of understanding and performance in more than one discipline. In my experience, the most effective multi-disciplinary projects arise from powerful and emotionally significant experiences that are shared by both children and teachers (Barnes and Hancox, 2004; Barnes and Shirley, 2005, 2007; Scoffham and Barnes, 2009). In multi-disciplinary approaches, the disciplines are introduced and developed *separately* to throw light on an experience, theme, problem or question. Whilst a meaningful experience and subsequent subject learning may be shared, in multi-disciplinary teaching and learning the teacher will have no intention of combining them. Student teachers find linking separate subject learning to themes in this way (suggested in the English National

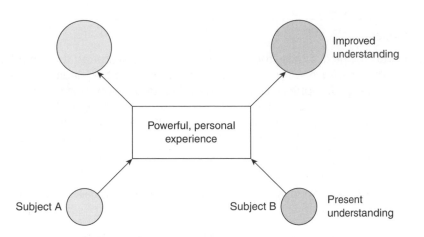

Figure 2.3 Multi-disciplinary cross-curricular learning. Discrete learning in two or three subjects is enhanced by arising from a shared meaningful experience

Curriculum and more fully developed in the Scottish Curriculum for Excellence) is manageable for them and enjoyable for their children. Multi-disciplinary approaches can also treat all disciplines as equal. However, the most effective multi-disciplinary work in schools depends upon high degrees of planning, confidence and teacher knowledge (see Ofsted, 2010; Roth, 2000). This approach is seen by many as the most appropriate cross-curricular approach for novice teachers since it does not involve the planning of complex interrelationships between the disciplines. It is also easier to assess and ensure progression.

Case study 2: A journey in dance

In an east London primary school, Year 4 pupils took a short journey through a nature reserve with a 'journey stick' (a 15 cm strip of card with a band of double-sided sticky tape attached). Children were directed to collect six tiny objects which caught their eye on their journey. Returning to class, each child made a sketch map of their journey, using recently taught geographical skills in map making. They used keys and symbols to represent where they found each of their objects. Their maps were discussed and displayed in the classroom.

Separately, the children were given a PE challenge. In groups of five, they gathered ideas for a shape to represent each of six different places. On site, each group was asked to construct those shapes with their bodies and record them using the class camera. Back at school, the groups used printouts of their photographs to discuss and refine their shapes and eventually reconstruct them for the rest of the class. The teacher advised on stability, contrast and safety. Pairs of groups were then asked to copy each other's shapes and work out ways of morphing one shape into the next. The teacher then taught a range of simple linking movements so that the groups could transform one

(Continued)

(Continued)

shape into the next. Finally, the six groups were placed around the school field and the class performed the progress of their journey in the medium of dance.

Children's geographical learning was founded upon previously taught skills of map making and their dance learning on structure and transformation was part of an ongoing programme of PE. Teachers reported that the experience took children to higher standards than expected in both subjects.

(Website: http://www.engagingplaces.org.uk/teaching+and+learning/art69235)

Illustration 2.2   *Physical and social skills at the beach*

Inter-disciplinary cross-curricular teaching and learning

Inter-disciplinary cross-curricular methods aim at progression in two or more subjects, together with the promotion of creative thinking and connection making between the subjects involved. The prefix *inter* indicates joining, sharing or combining. Inter-disciplinary learning occurs when the disciplines are combined to explain, understand or express a particular experience or idea or to solve a problem. Different disciplines offer differing interpretations of the same event or problem just as different people bring different insights to them. Inter-disciplinary approaches often result in some kind of collaborative response – a presentation, or group solution, performance or product. Student teachers report that this method of cross-curricular teaching generates particularly creative responses and encourages creative approaches to teaching.

The fusion of knowledge and skills between disciplines is common in the arts and advertising. Music, for example, is part of popular culture – TV, film, video games, promotional or advertising videos, websites and DVDs. Though music may seem 'in the background', it is often composed in highly sophisticated ways, fully exploiting the established skills and knowledge of the discipline, so as to satisfy the intended listener. Composers use musical structures and clichés to enhance the emotional power of images and words crafted by experts in the disciplines of art or film making. The music is less comprehensible without the image and the images less affecting without the music; both have equal and complementary status. Examples of such combinations of disciplines are growing with the successes of the Creative Partnerships scheme in the UK (www.creative-partnerships.com/), but they are still not a common curriculum feature in British schools.

Combining subjects in an inter-disciplinary mode is more challenging than multi-disciplinary teaching. This approach requires not only confidence in both disciplines used but also a speculative, flexible teaching style. In a successful project, the combination of several sets of disciplinary skills

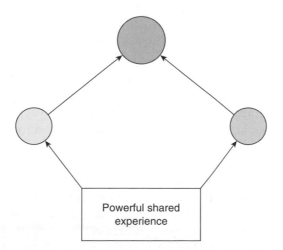

Figure 2.4   Inter-disciplinary learning. Learning in two subjects is taken forward as a result of a shared learning experience and then brought together in a presentation or application to a shared problem

Illustration 2.3 *Teachers perform their Haiku on a staff development day combining drama and music skills and knowledge*

will build on the initial meaningful experience and construct something entirely new. Thus, an exhibition, a museum collection, game, play, dance, composition, map, poster, debate or film might result from the fusion of two perspectives. Ideally, understanding in the separate subjects increases as a result of the new insights generated by the combination. We know from research that this is not always the case. Studies (Barnes and Shirley, 2005, 2007; Roth, 2000) have shown that applying two, three or four subjects to the same theme can produce a 'bland broth' of half-understood ideas and new misconceptions. Inter-disciplinary teaching and learning can easily result in less clarity about what a subject entails, therefore the cross-curricular teacher needs to be confident in subject knowledge, clear about learning intentions and plan genuine challenges for each subject to be successful in taking learning forward. As Ofsted observed in its survey of creative schools:

> Occasionally, teachers failed to grasp that creative learning was not simply a question of allowing pupils to follow their interests; careful planning was needed for enquiry, debate, speculation, experimentation, review and presentation to be productive ... Lack of confidence ... sometimes growing from insecure subject knowledge, led to a more didactic approach ... which then encouraged greater dependency from pupils. (Ofsted, 2010: 26)

Case study 3: Movement Haikus

Each student in a Year 7/8 group in Canterbury wrote their own Haiku (a Japanese poetry form consisting at its simplest of three lines: five syllables, seven syllables and five syllables) arising from a trip to the cathedral. In groups of five or six, they shared their Haikus and chose one which they agreed could best be transformed into a series of tableaux. The group then used their bodies to construct three still scenes, each expressing a line in the chosen Haiku. They then worked on improvising movement links between the three freeze-frames. They performed their Haikus in silence as the rest of the class observed and wrote peer evaluations.

Planned learning intentions linked to and extending previous learning in both English and PE were clearly understood by all children. The authentic challenge of non-verbally expressing their experience in the cathedral led them to achieve at levels well above the teacher's expectations.

Opportunistic cross-curricular teaching

Opportunistic cross-curricular teaching aims at allowing children to dictate the depth and direction of disciplinary learning in a number of subjects related to a shared theme or experience. The world beyond the classroom is cross-curricular. Every environment, each situation, each idea or concept can be looked at from numerous points of view. Learning may therefore arise from any open

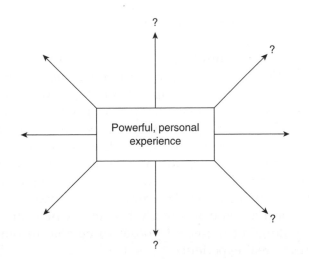

Figure. 2.5 Opportunistic cross-curricular teaching. The teacher exploits unpredictable and child-led learning opportunities arising from a powerful and shared experience

and enquiring interaction with the world. The experienced and creative primary teacher is relaxed about building upon chance happenings in class and generating deep and transferrable learning in any subject (see Austin, 2007; Cremin et al., 2009). Opportunistic approaches to promoting cross-curricular learning are child-led, unpredictable and include an element of risk. This does not mean that the teacher is a mere facilitator or observer – direct teaching and rigorous planning often underpin the best opportunistic learning.

Sometimes for the teacher, children's responses come unplanned and unexpected. A confident teacher will capture these moments and build them into opportunities to develop understanding. On the other hand, the teacher may carefully design a series of 'focusing exercises' – small-scale activities which support the child or children in having a 'present tense' and sensory interaction with a place, object or person(s) – and watch to see how children respond and what questions arise. Teachers clearly require good subject knowledge to be able to exploit the unexpected in this way. They must also feel empowered to follow the lead given by children, knowing that they have the support of colleagues and school leaders. In the current 'high accountability' structures, it may not be easy for teachers to feel this degree of professional trust.

Opportunistic cross-curricular learning, however, has been a successful feature of many projects sponsored by organizations like Creative Partnerships over the past five years in England (see Roberts, 2006; see also Creativity, Culture and Education, 2010, website; DCMS, 2008, website; HC, 2007; Ofsted, 2010). Partly as a result of the UN Convention on the Rights of the Child (UNICEF, 1989, website), the child's voice has become more prominent in planning the curriculum – opportunistic methods are thus discussed more often. But whilst the pupil voice movement gathers pace, restrictive and over-assessed curricula also appear even more dominant (see Alexander, 2010). In the UK, non-specialist primary teachers are trained in specific approaches to the teaching of reading and mathematics but their preparation for the teaching of other subjects is often left to chance (Rogers, 2003). This has implications for both teacher education and opportunistic methods of teaching. Novice teachers need opportunities to play with ideas in the disciplines themselves before generating genuine and personally relevant questions within the disciplines. Only through personally experiencing the framing of core questions and answering real questions within a discipline, can a teacher successfully plan progression in a child's learning in that subject. This argues for a broad and balanced education for both primary and secondary teachers, where they can develop confidence in a range of subjects in order to be able to build upon children's responses to real experience.

Illustration 2.4   *Nursery children visit the local park (see case study 5, Chapter 3)*

Illustration 2.5   *Nursery children in south India play with materials and pattern*

Case study 4

A whole primary school community was taken to a modern financial centre in London. After a series of focus exercises where they were helped to become sensorally aware of the place through smell, touch, sight, sound and feelings, they were left in groups to collect ideas about the place to present to the rest of the school. Groups decided on a wide range of inventive and unusual presentations which were shared with the school in following weeks. Presentations included huge cane and paper sculptures, recorded sound trails, 'smell maps', an art exhibition, a taste lesson – none of which were planned but all of which were supported by teachers and assistants. (See www.engagingplaces.org.uk/network/art66179)

Double-focus cross-curricular teaching

Double-focus cross-curricular teaching attempts to promote a balance between experience-based and disciplinary opportunities for learning. A curriculum consisting of both separate subject teaching and regular opportunities to put that subject teaching into combined action, needs two pedagogical foci. This mode of curriculum organization centres equally upon teaching and learner and involves the total curriculum of a school.

Illustration 2.6   *Creativity generates a sense of achievement*

In my definition of double-focus teaching, each discipline is of equal importance. Where a curriculum offers all disciplines equally, the chances of every child finding a route into learning that suits them, increases dramatically. Traditionally, we have valued some subjects so highly that failure in them signifies failure in education generally. In the USA and Europe, children might be first-class musicians, map readers, sportspeople, naturalists, peacemakers, artists or aesthetes, but if they find serious difficulties in the national language and mathematics they are said to have Special Educational Needs. In the UK, all too often such children lose their precious music, geography, PE, science or art lessons to English or maths booster classes. A double-focus approach suggests the belief that improvements in the core subjects are better secured when the child feels a sense of achievement and progress in any subject that can be developed into a personal strength or passion (see Robinson and Aronica, 2010). The good teacher works to ensure progression at the appropriate level in each subject for each child, but curriculum planning also provides regular chances for the creative application of newly learned subject skills.

The second focus in a double-focus curriculum is on a regular series of cross-curricular events. Each year group shares at least six meaningful experiences each year. These events are intended to provide short, planned opportunities to put learning in two or three subjects into action in an authentic and challenging situation. Children may learn through hierarchical, multi-disciplinary, inter-disciplinary or opportunistic methods of teaching. The events or challenges are followed up with focused subject teaching related to the experience but also to give opportunities for assessment.

When children apply new learning to new situations, they expose the degree of their understanding. In applying learning and planning solutions using the skills of geography, D/T, PE, RE, MFL, history, art, music, mathematics, PSHE and citizenship or science, children inevitably and richly use language. Cross-curricular working generates persuasive and technical language, the shaping of language into reports, plays, poems, stories or labels and the extension of language in arguments, debates, presentations and supporting others. Equally, the ease with which children use ICT means that, given the resources, cross-curricular presentations will imaginatively use cameras, websites, synthesized and recorded sound and a range of visual presentation packages. English and ICT are well served by all cross-curricular approaches.

Neither are cross-curricular approaches confined to cross-curricular themes or activity. It is expected that cross-curricular, experimental and creative references will be made during the normal course of separate subject teaching.

Case study 5

A primary school linked to the Room 13 (website) project in Poptahof, Delft, Holland has two major curriculum foci: sustainability in the environment and

(Continued)

(Continued)

music. The standard curriculum of language, mathematics, science, history, geography and music continues throughout the year using exciting and principled methods but when children have finished their work or can persuade their teacher that they may leave the class to work elsewhere, they are given a ticket to go to Room 13. Here a professional musician/composer is based to help the children in groups and singly to apply their classroom knowledge to real projects. In Room 13, they work on authentic communal compositions and improvisations, exploring the possibilities of sound and how they can be combined. Many of these compositions arise from themes involving the ecology of the surrounding area and recently, for example, students composed the soundtrack for a book festival where their music arose from a story about aliens.

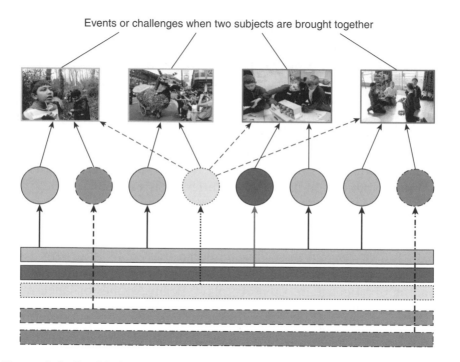

Figure 2.6 Double focus cross-curricular learning. Learning in each curriculum subject continues separately throughout the year but is regularly joined with one or two others and applied to a shared experience

Summary

Cross-curricular approaches have been part of education for millennia. In recent centuries, they have become associated with progressive education, perhaps because of the protective attitudes of those who police the individual subject disciplines, perhaps in England because of a puritan sense that having fun whilst learning is somewhat suspect. As we face a future of exponential and unpredictable change, we need cross-curricular methods which encourage group solutions, collaborative learning, creative combinations and the development of independent learners. The generation of such confident, imaginative and adaptable learners may be the route towards the happy population and flexible workforce most analysts suggest we need.

There are at least five different ways of organizing cross-curricular teaching and learning:

- hierarchical
- multi-disciplinary
- inter-disciplinary
- opportunistic
- double focus.

Each of them have different aims and strengths, but to be effective means of learning all cross-curricular learning should rest on the following principles:

1 Use powerful and meaningful sensory experiences to motivate learning.
2 Use only two or three subjects to interpret or build upon such experiences.
3 Expect English and ICT to be integral parts of all cross-curricular teaching and learning.
4 Plan specific and progressive learning targets in each subject represented.
5 Assess the success of learning by arranging for children to apply their learning in some way.
6 Work hard at all times to increase teacher subject knowledge.

Key questions for discussion

- What topics have you seen operating successfully in a cross-curricular way?
- What kind of cross-curricular teaching and learning have you observed in schools? Give examples.
- How can we adequately assess two or three subjects within a cross-curricular module?
- What are the advantages of cross-curricular learning?
- Should subjects like music be justified in the curriculum because they have 'a hugely positive effect on numeracy and language skills (Gove, 2010b, website) www.education.gov.uk/inthenews/pressnotices/a0064925/education-se

Further reading

Alexander, R. (2010) *Children, Their World, Their Education: The Report of the Cambridge Primary Review*. London: Routledge.

Robinson, K. and Aronica, L. (2010) *The Element: How Finding Your Passion Changes Everything*. London: Penguin.

CHAPTER 3

What Does Good Cross-Curricular Practice Look Like?

The variability between us is surely humankind's greatest resource. Individual uniqueness does not apply simply to our DNA, irises or fingerprints, but to the almost infinite range of potential links making up each human's intelligence and personality. There is an immeasurable variety of possible connections between neurons controlling our senses, memory, physical and emotional responses, and those which process our conscious, rational and intellectual responses. Such a wealth of possibilities suggests that we each experience the world around us in subtly (and not so subtly) different ways. I believe that effective cross-curricular approaches mirror and maximize on this valuable diversity, but it would be foolish to give the impression that there could be a single or even a finite range of answers to the question, 'What does good cross-curricular practice look like?' Good practice in curriculum arrangement and approach is likely to be as diverse as any other aspect of human organization.

Aside from the consciousness of our mental diversity, a second wonder is that humans can communicate so effectively. Considering the potential for some of the billions of neural connections to misfire, it seems little short of miraculous that we ever establish shared perception. The teacher's job is to construct such understandings – mutually acceptable views of aspects of our world. Curricula are designed to support teachers in building minds by providing the intellectual and social settings for learning, but they vary in effectiveness and appropriateness.

Any curriculum that energizes, motivates, provokes and sustains high-quality, useful learning is doing a good job, regardless of whether or not it requires children to work across subjects. This book is *not* written to suggest that all teaching and learning should be cross-curricular. I claim rather that cross-curricular methods are a means of promoting learning that are highly motivating for some, even most, children.

The case studies

I have chosen seven case studies to illustrate a range of successful cross-curricular learning opportunities. Each case study has generated evidence of inclusive, creative thinking and deep learning on the part of the children and adults involved. Each sprung from strong and detailed planning, depended upon meaningful and shared experience and followed or resulted from focused subject application, real and relevant activity, and frequent formative assessment. The case studies include examples of multi-disciplinary, inter-disciplinary and opportunistic modes of learning and double-focus approaches to the school curriculum:

- two cross-curricular terms covering the entire curriculum for a 3–11 nursery/primary school (double focus)
- a cross-curricular module with a cross-phase group of Year 6/7 children (inter-disciplinary)
- a primary school following the Royal Society of Arts (RSA) competences curriculum (double focus)
- a two-day project for Year 4 pupils on 'our lane' (multi-disciplinary)
- a child-led term based on walks in the park with nursery children (opportunistic)
- a two-day session for Year 5 children working with an artist in school (inter-disciplinary)
- a combined arts project with adults and Year 7/8 children (opportunistic).

These seven studies are in no way an exhaustive set of examples. *Whenever* teachers and children apply learning in more than one subject to a problem, experience, issue or theme, cross-curricular practice is happening. When deep, transferrable, useful learning occurs as a result, good cross-curricular practice is happening.

In each example, the required cross-curricular and creative thinking did not just 'happen' – it was the result of thought, planning and usually of secure teacher knowledge. Objectives were met because teachers and other adults involved were constantly aware of them during planning and whilst children were working. Many case study schools brought in outside experts to take learning forward. Several teachers noted that their children were able cheerfully to accept pinpointed criticism and stretching targets from non-teacher experts in ways they would not have done from their regular teachers (see also Brice Heath and Wolf, 2005). The case study evidence confirms that partnership with members of the local community is not simply good for citizenship education but has wider learning benefits (Ofsted, 2010). Whether the expert was a carer, the mayor, an imam, nurse, artist, town planner or a great-grandmother, his or her knowledge helped raise standards of achievement, promoted the

Illustration 3.1 *Children studying full-sized reproductions of paintings in their school hall*

sense of belonging to a living, changing community and provided authoritative, rigorous alternatives to standardized assessments.

Creative curricula

Many schools are experimenting with what they call 'the creative curriculum'. There is no generally accepted definition or guide to such a curriculum, but very often cross-curricular approaches are associated with promoting creativity. Craft (2000) helpfully calls creativity, 'possibility' thinking, and a curriculum designed to help children make connections between different areas of learning in finding possible answers to real questions is likely to be creative. Indeed, in some schools, for example those using the International Primary Curriculum (IPC, 2006, website), they appear to have chosen a curriculum specifically intended to promote it. Arthur Koestler's (1964) insight that creativity is a result of 'bisociation' seems relevant here. Bisociation means the (usually unexpected) meeting of two distinctly different planes of thought. Sternberg (2003) picked up this idea as one of nine types of creativity and calling the bisociative type, 'integration', where creative input integrates two formerly diverse ways of thinking. We may, for example, be analysing in some detail the decorative markings on a Victorian teapot while carrying out an investigation in history, and something makes us think of the markings as reminiscent of music. This unpredicted link between applied pattern and music may result in an imaginative, original and valued musical composition. The chances of making unusual juxtapositions of ideas, approaches and knowledge are high but appropriately unpredictable, in a curriculum where different viewpoints exist side by side and unexpected links are expected (see Ofsted, 2002).

Case study 1: Two cross-curricular terms covering the entire curriculum for a 3–11 nursery/primary school – an example of double-focus cross-curricular activity

This school works with A New Direction (AND website), an organization dedicated to supporting the development of creativity in schools by promoting links between them, their community and local creative practitioners. Working specifically with schools in disadvantaged communities in London, AND hopes to bring positive, dynamic change to curricula, pedagogies and lives to its partner schools. The school has 300 pupils (3–11) and serves a deprived area of east London with a high percentage of first-and second-generation immigrants. More than 75 per cent of its children receive free school meals, whilst 90 per cent have English as a second language. The AND project in this school was based around a simple question: 'Where do we find the creative us?' This was a question which included both staff and children and its answer was to be found over two terms of curriculum work involving the whole school.

Planning with three creative practitioners, the school decided on a radical approach. Three major whole-school outings in the local area were to become the engine of curriculum and pedagogical change. The three trips and related activities would first be experienced by the teachers and assistants themselves and then a few days later the whole school would make the same trip. They chose three contrasting places to visit over the two terms:

- Canary Wharf
- a nature reserve developed from an abandoned Victorian cemetery
- (a tour of) the streets around the school (a visit to a local gallery of modern art had to be postponed).

The three visits shared a similar format and were built upon eight key principles:

- All should see themselves as learners (parents, lunchtime supervisors, governors were all represented as well as teachers, TAs and children).
- Children should be paired in differing age groups (a nursery child paired with a Year 6 child, reception with Year 5 and so on).
- Groups should be composed of three pairs of children and an adult.

(Continued)

(Continued)

- All focusing activities at the sites were to be sensory (using touch, smell, taste, sight, hearing).
- Adults had to participate alongside children.
- All activities were to be open-ended (having no particular end in mind).
- Adults were to stress the 'present tense' experiential nature of the activities.
- The visits would go ahead whatever the weather.

Illustration 3.2   A wow moment at Canary Wharf

'Wow' experiences and focusing exercises

Creative practitioners and staff agreed on the importance of meaningful experience in generating the desire to become involved in learning. So the whole-school trip was a crucial kick-start to each unit of work. A shared experience became a 'wow' experience, partly because of the locations, the large scale of the exercise and the unusual pairings. The places visited, though very near the school, were unfamiliar to well over half the pupils. The teachers and children had never experienced a whole-school outing before and it was very unusual for the Year 6 class to spend extended time with those in the nursery. The initial impact of each familiar yet unfamiliar environment was strong, children often expressed this in 'wow's and excited talk, but interest was sustained and deepened by a powerful series of focus exercises.

Focus exercises are sensory activities intended to be fully inclusive and help all learners experience aspects of a place, theme, object or person in fine detail. In each place, focused listening, careful looking, sensitive smelling and accurate seeing were encouraged through these open-ended exercises (see text box below for a sample of these exercises). They were open-ended because there was no initial objective other than to fully experience the sight, sound, smell or view of usually unnoticed features of the place visited. Children in their unfamiliar groupings entered into these exercises with gusto and real involvement. The social and sensory aspects of the learning process were fully exploited through them, but they also generated questions, thoughts and conversations which went well beyond the exercises themselves.

Following up experience

The big and little experiences of each day energized and motivated the children of all ages. Significantly, the experiences also excited the teachers. Back at school in the following weeks, class teachers picked up the excitement of the day and built a wide range of subject-based responses around them. Early years children talked enthusiastically about what they saw, smelt and heard with the aid of a video taken by a Teaching Assistant. They developed their newly extended vocabulary concerning where sounds came from, by doing more listening exercises around the school. Year 4 made a richly illustrated, three-week science project based upon the children's fascination with decay, re-growth and the minute creatures they found in the nature reserve. They also followed up the *spatialization* exercise with a series of group musical compositions based around four contrasting soundscapes found on the same visit. Year 1 also made a musical trail describing their journey from school to Canary Wharf in a series of sound pictures linked by a foot-tramping *Rondo* theme. The emotional maps of the nature trail led to a Year 6 group suggesting 'emotionally mapping' the school and then the neighbourhood. The children of all ages identified as particularly 'gifted and talented' made sculptures and environments based upon abstractions taken from either the made environments of Canary Wharf or the natural environment of the nature reserve. Children in Year 3 changed their smell trail into a 'taste trail', first of all being taught about the science of taste and then using blindfold sampling of stilton, mango, lime, coffee, 'raw' chocolate and other strong tasting foods to consolidate their learning. Later, they constructed a mapped treasure hunt based on taste identification and challenged another class to find their way to the treasure (chocolate of course!). Each of these provide further examples of multi-disciplinary

---

Outside School Focus Exercises

1. **'Key word' photo**
   Everyone is given a viewfinder with a different *key word* written on it (e.g. red, sad, lonely, awesome, dangerous, etc.). Using your viewfinder to frame it, look around for details (small ones are usually best) which visually illustrate or summarize that key word. Capture your decision in a photo and also include the key word on your viewfinder in the photo. This will remind you of the theme. (Thanks to Catherine Greig)

2. **Spatialization**
   Draw a circle to represent a bird's eye view of your head, put some ears at three o'clock and nine o'clock and a nose at 12.00. Listen carefully for sounds around you. Decide the location of the separate sounds and the direction of movement if the sound is moving (like an aeroplane or a car). Mark the location of each sound in the appropriate area around the diagram of your head. (Thanks to Robert Jarvis)

3. **Big picture**
   On a large sheet of paper (A1 or A2), each of four people draw a big impression of the skyline in front of them. One person should draw the skyline looking north, one east, one south and one west. You should use bold, colourful felt-tip pens. The four team members should then join their drawings to make a continuous collaborative image of 360° of the skyline.

4. **Texture rubbing and words**
   Find a place where two different materials and/or textures meet. Feel the join between them and then talk about the different textures which meet there. Make a rubbing of the join and a little of each material and annotate the rubbing with words describing the two textures. (Thanks to Stirling Clark)

5. **Colour match**
   Use coloured paint swatches to find natural and made matches in the environment. Peel off the double-sided sticky tape and attach as many examples of each colour to its corresponding paint colour as possible.

6. **Mapping**
   Make a map of a little journey you have taken showing significant landmarks (buildings, plants, shadows, furniture and unexpected things which strike you as important). Use your map in one of the following ways:

   (a) **emotional maps:** how do you feel in each place? Mark on your map with words or colours the emotions you feel in different places. For example, which place makes you feel small, lonely, excited, frightened, cold, happy, sad, etc.?

   (b) **sound maps:** what are the dominant sounds in different areas of your map? Draw symbols or write words which capture the locations of different sounds in the environment.

   (c) **smell maps:** what smells can you identify in this place? Mark on the boundaries between different dominating smells. For example, where is there a more natural woody, vegetation smell? How are the smells near the water different? (Thanks to Stephen Scoffham)

Figure 3.1   Some focus exercises to use in the locality of the school

cross-curricular responses – there was no intention to integrate learning in a number of subjects, classes simply responded in different subject ways to the same experience. Whilst subject-based activities related to the visits continued to occupy each class for three or four weeks, the remainder of the curriculum time was devoted to an unrelated programme of learning in the remaining subjects.

Illustration 3.3   *Using word frames*

Case study 2: A cross-curricular module with a cross-phase group of Year 6/7 children

The transition between Year 6 and Year 7 is a difficult one for children. Primary education practice and the pedagogies and curricula of secondary are often seen, even by teachers, as very different from each other. Two schools in the same locality wanted to work to break down these barriers and chose a cross-curricular language project to launch their new relationship. Both schools had identified their learning of modern foreign languages (mfl) as a target for improvement, in terms of motivation as well as outcome. Working with a team of music, English and mfl specialists, the schools developed a short inter-disciplinary module intended creatively to combine the three subjects and classes of Year 6 and Year 7 children. Their work was to be shared with and responded to by two parallel schools in France.

Motivation

Time, organization and money did not allow for a large-scale 'wow' experience to set the module going, but a series of focus exercises was chosen to engage

	Canary Wharf	Nature trail	Tour of streets around the school
Nursery			
Reception	Words: labelled photographs: 30 dark things, 20 red things, 45 cold things, 12 scary things, etc.	Collections – made and natural, colours	
Year 1	Musical journey – composition project		Shapes project – graphs of the most common mathematical shapes found in the locality
Year 2		Art gallery project – paintings of the woodland canopy and close-ups of natural detail collected in drawings and digital images	Designing and making 'Snow world' environments and learning about the history of the seventeenth-century winter markets on the Thames
Year 3	Taste trail – science of taste and geography plan-making project		
Year 4		Growth and decay – a science project on the life cycle of the minibeasts collected on the nature trail and the science of decay	
Year 5			Illustrated stories to be read to Reception children, based upon five personally collected items from the streets and gardens around the school
Year 6		Emotional mapping – geography mapping skills and knowledge, direction	
Gifted and talented cross-phase group	A geometric 'made' environment using forms, patterns and textures found in Canary Wharf – applying design/technology skills and mathematical knowledge		

Figure 3.2 A sample of class follow-up sessions for each year group after their three visits in the school locality

---

School and School Grounds Focus Exercises

7. **Key word viewfinders:** working in groups of four, use four coloured viewfinder frames to find five or six things around the school which express the meaning of each of the words printed on them. After discussing selection and composition, photograph the thing making sure that both the key word is readable and the subject is clear. (Thanks to Catherine Greig)
8. **Fridge magnet poems:** fold a piece of A4 paper into 16 rectangles by folding in half four times. Unfold the paper to reveal the 16 rectangles and then go on a private walk anywhere in the school or school grounds you are allowed. As you walk, write down single words (in English) to capture your feelings, observations, thoughts until you have 16 words. Return to class and gently tear the sheet into 16 separate word rectangles. Arrange your words into a meaningful poem – you can add extra ands, and buts or other short linking words if you like and leave out any words you don't really want to use. (Thanks to Rosanna Raymond)
9. **Spatialization:** as in Figure 3.1.

Figure 3.3   Some focus exercises to use in school grounds and buildings

the classes and give them a reason to want to express themselves in another language. The exercises were intended to help the children find English words to describe the detail and unique qualities of their school environment. These exercises can be done inside or outside school.

The chosen focus exercises are language-based and stimulated a great deal of agitated and enthusiastic talk. The teachers found that setting time limits – 10 minutes for the key words and the poems and 15 minutes for the spatialization helped focus minds more productively. Opportunities to work alone back in the classroom, as in the poem exercise, were particularly valued by some children. Many Year 7 children reported that they felt very motivated by these activities: 'It was great to get out and do real stuff', said one. 'I can't explain it, but when we were doing the exercises I felt really excited and wanted to do much more of it. I 'specially liked it when we were working in pairs on the key words, we kept sparking off new ideas from each other', said another.

Following up

The focus exercises provided motivation and a series of small-scale shared experiences for the children in both classes. When questioned, the vast majority of the class said they felt 'excited', 'energetic', 'happy', 'enthusiastic', 'interested' and 'questioning'. Teachers confirmed pupils' high levels of engagement by applying the Ferre Laevers Leuven Involvement Scale (see Chapter 6). Children's enthusiasm carried through the follow-up sessions which used music or geography skills hierarchically to take learning in French forward.

The pupils in Year 7 were given a degree of freedom in deciding on the relevance of the focus exercises for their learning in French. Several groups repeated the 'key words' idea in French, writing their own French 'emotional vocabulary' provided by the teacher, onto viewfinders. After taking 10 pictures, they used them to make a PowerPoint presentation on the meaning of French words like '*tranquille*'. Other groups used the poem idea and made up French poems from collections of 16 French words from a walk around the school. Motivation to complete and improve the follow-up activities was provided by the teacher introducing the class to a class in Boulogne via a Skype® link up. Some French children introduced themselves and then asked the English children to send them information about their school via email. Richly illustrated French poems and PowerPoints about their school were sent by email by the end of the second day of work.

The Year 6 class used similar focus exercises. Children constructed a series of 'I like …. ' poems about their school. The music specialist then taught the children how to use *Audiomulch*®, a computer programme which transforms recoded sounds digitally, and the children made electronic background music to their poems to illustrate their likes – creatively combining music skills and language skills in one 'product'.

Case study 3: A primary school following the Royal Society of Arts (RSA) competences curriculum

This school serves part of a garrison town and has a highly mobile population, with 60 per cent of its children likely to move into or away from the school in any year. The school describes its reasons for following curriculum guidance from the Royal Society of Arts rather than that of the Qualifications and Curriculum Development Agency as follows:

> Our views have been influenced by international, national, local and school based research and monitoring. We know that methods used in The Foundation Stage have been successful and believe that extending this approach and ethos will have a similarly positive effect on children as they progress through the school. We know that our school has unique characteristics, such as high mobility, and these were highlighted by OFSTED. We have responded to what we know about the school by preparing an appropriate model for teaching the curriculum. As part of this, we believe that building the RSA Competences for Learning into our curriculum will help our children to learn more effectively. (School prospectus, 2010)

The school launched one of the earliest primary versions of the RSA's competences-based curriculum called 'Opening Minds'. The RSA curriculum centres around developing five competences:

(Continued)

(Continued)

- learning
- citizenship
- relating to people
- managing situations
- managing information.

Each competence is chosen to cover an essential and generic aspect of modern life. Schools delivering the RSA curriculum decide upon curriculum themes which will generate development of the competences in a variety of experiential, learning and subject contexts. Working towards mastery of the RSA competences would result, they suggest, in internalizing essential and highly transferable life skills which will be meaningful to children whatever changes come about in twenty-first-century society. In the context of children's preoccupations and worries about the future, outlined in Chapter 1, such a curriculum appears potentially both relevant and timely.

The school has made its own detailed and levelled descriptors (levels 1–5) for each of these competences, but with no or little reference to subject content. Staff, parents and children have made many thoughtful and well-discussed decisions about curriculum. Their curriculum policy contains the following aims:

- For children to produce high-quality outcomes across all curriculum subjects – to bring out the best in everyone.
- To have a time-effective, relevant curriculum with real-life and cross-curricular links.
- To educate children and staff in the broadest sense of the word's meaning – 'to lead out'.
- To focus on children and how they learn best as a priority.
- To ensure children have appropriate access to learning activities that promote physical, moral, social, spiritual, cultural, academic and creative development.
- To encourage children's understanding and tolerance of the world in which they live and its peoples.

To achieve these aims, the school divided the curriculum subjects into what they term *'knowledge subjects'* (Geography, History, Science and Religious Education), each of which form the 'lead' subject for a term. The identification of knowledge subjects gives teachers a clear lead to be teaching knowledge and encouraging children to use it in different settings. What the school

What the competences mean

Learning

Children will understand how to learn and manage their own lifelong learning, they will learn systematically to think, to have explored and extended their own talents and have opportunities to develop a love of learning for its own sake. They will achieve high personal standards in literacy, numeracy and spatial understanding and be able to handle ICT with confidence and understanding.

Citizenship

Children will have developed an understanding of ethics and values and have experience of contributing to society. They will understand how the institutions of society work and their relationship to it. They will understand and value the importance of diversity, both nationally and globally, and will consider the global and social implications of technology. They will also learn to manage aspects of their own lives.

Relationships

Children will understand how to relate to people in a variety of contexts. They will have experience of operating in teams and understand how to help develop other people. They will develop a range of techniques for communicating in different ways and have an understanding of managing themselves and others emotionally. They will know techniques for managing stress and conflict.

Situations

Children will learn to manage time, change, success and disappointment. They will understand what it is to be entrepreneurial and how to take and use initiative. They will learn how to take and manage risks and uncertainties.

Information

Children will develop a range of techniques for assessing and differentiating information and will learn to be analytical. They will understand the importance of reflection and critical judgement and know how, when and where to apply it.

Figure 3.4   The RSA Opening Minds, competences-led curriculum

calls the *'process subjects'* (Maths, English, Design and Technology, Music, MFL, Art and PE) feature throughout the year. Here teachers concentrate more on the teaching of skills and opportunities for children to put those skills into practice in real projects. In consultation with the children, the curriculum designers decided that a literacy and numeracy 'hour' was too long and that the daily sessions should be cut to half an hour. Other English and mathematics and all science was to be subsumed in topic-based work and at other times throughout the week. Science is a term's focus three times a year, and English and mathematics have extra weighting to reflect their 'core' status. Look, for example, at Figure 3.5 to see the way the subjects are shared throughout the week during Key Stage 2.

Illustration 3.4 *Children planning their presentation*

This double-focus curriculum is divided into topics within which each year group chooses a strong and emotionally engaging shared 'event' as the focus for each of six terms. For every class, the event and 'lead' subject define teaching decisions for a six-week block. So a Year 1 or 2 group, for example, worked from (or towards) the following happenings:

- a trip to the seaside (with a history focus on how we used to live)
- a Christmas nativity play (with a science focus on light)
- an art exhibition (RE)
- an Easter fun day (with a science focus on new life)
- 'a day trip to India' (with a geography focus on a distant locality)
- the opening of a wildlife garden (with a science focus on biodiversity).

In this curriculum, 65–70 per cent of all subject-based work falls within the cross-curricular theme. Teachers are encouraged to use texts and examples in the remaining 30–35 per cent, which also relate to either a main or RE theme. Throughout the school, learning is interrelated and contextualized – the learning makes sense to the learners. Subject leaders support their colleagues by using the National Curriculum Attainment targets (DfEE/QCA, 1999) for their subject to construct progressions of skills, knowledge and attitudes. Teachers then use this levelled description to plan extra challenge or provide added skills.

Key Stage 2 total	23.75 hrs	
Literacy	Hours per week	Percentage of time
Discrete teaching of writing	1	4.2
Cross-curricular writing	1	4.2
Guided reading	1.25	5.3
Handwriting	0.25	1.1
Word and sentence work	2.5	10.5
Reading by/with teacher	1	4.2
Total	**7**	**29.5**
Numeracy		
Oral mental work	1	4.2
Number	2.5	10.5
Cross-curricular maths	1.5	6.3
Total	**5**	**21.0**
Other subjects		
Science	1.75	7.4
History and/or Geography	2	8.4
Art and/or Design and Technology	2	8.4
Music	1	4.2
Physical Education	2	8.4
Religious Education	1	4.2
Information Communication Technology	0.5	2.1
Personal Education	0.75	3.2
Modern Foreign Language	0.75	3.2
Total	**11.75**	**49.5**
Final Total	**23.75**	**100.0**

Figure 3.5   Key Stage 2 subject balance in a typical week

Case study 4: A two-day project for Year 4 pupils on 'What is a community?'

A Year 4 teacher wanted to contribute to a two-day unit of work as part of the Engaging Places (2010, website) project. The website, maintained by English Heritage and The Commission for Architecture and the Built Environment (CABE), aims to support schools in using aspects of the built environment as resources for learning. Providing a network of organizations able and willing to work with schools on built environment projects and a wide range of case

(Continued)

Half/Term Curriculum Overview

Whole School Topic Plan

National Curriculum Years 1/2

RE – Christianity/symbols and objects

Term 1	Term 2	Term 3	Term 4	Term 5	Term 6
HISTORY Special People (Changes in lifestyles) (SCIENCE – OURSELVES 1)	**SCIENCE** LIGHT	**RE** Islam (SCIENCE – SOUND)	**SCIENCE** MATERIALS (CHANGES)	**GEOGRAPHY** Contrasting locality [UK] (SCIENCE – INVESTIGATION UNIT)	**SCIENCE** LIVING THINGS IN THEIR ENVIRONMENT

RE – Christianity/symbols and objects

Term 1	Term 2	Term 3	Term 4	Term 5	Term 6
GEOGRAPHY Our School and Neighbourhood (SCIENCE – OURSELVES 2)	**SCIENCE** MATERIALS (GROUPING)	**HISTORY** Special Events (Changes in lifestyle) (SCIENCE – ELECTRICITY)	**SCIENCE** FORCES	**RE** Judaism (SCIENCE – INVESTIGATION UNIT)	**SCIENCE** GREEN PLANTS

National Curriculum Years 3/4

RE – Christianity/religious responses to current issues

Term 1	Term 2	Term 3	Term 4	Term 5	Term 6
GEOGRAPHY Locality in a Less Economically Developed Country (SCIENCE – HABITATS)	**SCIENCE** LIGHT	**SCIENCE** MATERIALS – THERMAL	**RE** Islam (SCIENCE – SOUND)	**HISTORY** Tudors (local study) (SCIENCE – INVESTIGATION UNIT)	**SCIENCE** TEETH & HEALTHY EATING

RE – Christianity/symbols and objects

Term 1	Term 2	Term 3	Term 4	Term 5	Term 6
SCIENCE MATERIALS – ROCKS & SOILS	**GEOGRAPHY** UK Locality (SCIENCE – MICRO ORGANISMS)	**SCIENCE** FORCES	**RE** Judaism (SCIENCE – FORCES CONT.)	**SCIENCE** GREEN PLANTS	**HISTORY** Victorians or Britain Since 1930 (local study) (SCIENCE – ELECTRICITY)

National Curriculum Years 5/6

RE – Christianity/religious responses to current issues

Term 1	Term 2	Term 3	Term 4	Term 5	Term 6
SCIENCE MATERIALS – CHANGES	**GEOGRAPHY]** UK Locality (SCIENCE – GREEN PLANTS)	**RE** Sikhism (SCIENCE – LIGHT)	**HISTORY** Romans, Anglo Saxons and Vikings (local study) (SCIENCE – SOUND)	**SCIENCE** EARTH, SUN AND MOON	**HISTORY** World Study – Egyptians (SCIENCE – INVESTIGATION UNIT)

RE Christianity/symbols and objects

Term 1	Term 2	Term 3	Term 4	Term 5	Term 6
SCIENCE MATERIALS – DISSOLVING	**GEOGRAPHY** Locality in a Less Economically Developed Country (SCIENCE – ELECTRICITY)	**HISTORY** European – Greece (SCIENCE – HEART RATE AND KEEPING HEALTHY)	**SCIENCE** FORCES	**RE** Hinduism (SCIENCE – INVESTIGATION UNIT)	**GEOGRAPHY** Changing Environment (SCIENCE – LIVING THINGS IN THEIR ENVIRONMENT)

Figure 3.6 Yearly topic grid for knowledge subjects

Illustration 3.5 *Intense faces and focussed body language often characterize collaborative projects. Photo: Ian Bottle*

(Continued)

studies, lesson plans and support materials, Engaging Places aims to be a 'one-stop shop' for all wishing to use real places as a focus for learning. The two-day unit of work is an example of multi-disciplinary cross-curricular teaching and learning in the context of a wider and values-based curriculum.

The wider aim of the school is to help all children feel they belong to the local community. This was in the teacher's mind when she decided that the question that would bind their cross-curricular work, would be: 'how is our street a community?' The class teacher set about helping the children answer this question in an oblique way: she asked a town planner, a geographer, a musician and a scientist to come in for the two days to work with her children. She asked these adults how their subject expertise would help them answer the class's question and then to lead the children towards finding answers along scientific, design, musical and geographical lines. The class was divided into four groups of seven and each worked with one of the adults:

- The music group took a 'sound walk' with the musician who wanted to show that musical compositions could construct a 'sonic sense of place'.
- The design/technology group talked with the town planner about the traffic dangers of their street at school opening and closing times. He wanted to help the children discover that they could do something as citizens to influence local government decisions.

(Continued)

(Continued)

- The scientists worked with the scientific advisor to a big company to find out if they could 'live lives any greener'.
- The geography option concerned discovering the uniqueness of their place, by taking a walk from top to bottom of the lane in which their school stood, and mapping together what was special about it.

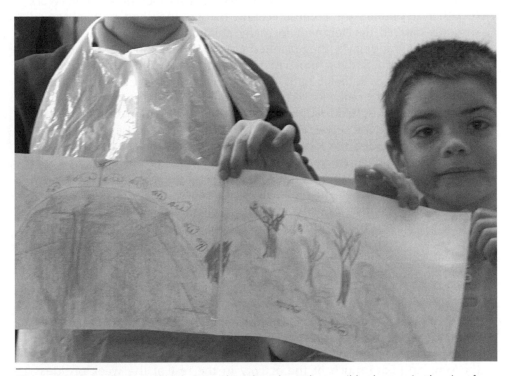

Illustration 3.6 *Six-year-olds showing thoughts about the possible changes in the view from a classroom window in 5o years time. (Left hand side, present; right hand side future)*

The town planner (a friend of the teacher) showed the children how to use copies of a small-scale map to plan changes to a built environment. Children pooled and discussed the changes they felt would be needed to make the school lane safer. They arrived at four practical proposals: speed bumps, a one-way system, a safe crossing point and parking restrictions on a particularly dangerous stretch of the lane. A fifth suggestion, a school bus, was taken up by the scientist's group as they made detailed proposals for a 'green (electric) bus', supported by the scientist who told them about electric engines and their design implications. The scientist also had to help them with the practicalities of a calming fish tank the children wanted for the bus passengers.

The town planning group built a scale model of their proposals on to a base map of the school lane, carefully photographed each aspect and with the planner's help, composed a letter of proposals to the local district council. This decision supported the development of important PSHE targets for the class (for more details, see Engaging Places, 2010, website).

Case study 5: A child-led term based on walks in the park with nursery children

A speech therapist and a nursery leader in Liverpool decided to work together to address the communication barriers they had both observed through delayed development in many children. Emulating practice they had seen in Scandinavia, they planned a series of walks from the nursery to a Victorian park near the school with the aim of stimulating conversation and questions. Each walk took a path through a wood and out the other side to a meadow with a strange locked tower at one end and views across to a set of ornate mansions. With minimal adult leading, the children began to make up stories about the tower and the large decorated houses. The leaders eventually persuaded the local museum to open up the tower and on the fourth walk, the children were able to enter it and add to their stories about what it might have been used for. A museum curator brought a stuffed owl to show them one of the many creatures that currently occupied the tower.

The simple action of six walks in different directions through the park was enough to transform the atmosphere and the learning of the whole group. The walks, which happened rain or shine, took the whole morning and involved collections, woodland sculptures, den building, bird watching, tree, flower and butterfly identification, games and songs. The teachers, parents and helpers noted however that the chief benefit of these open-ended walks was the vast amount of talk they generated: real questions, imaginative solutions, genuine interactions and opportunities to help extend each child's language world at every turn.

The nursery school decided to timetable such walks weekly throughout the year and base much of the activity in the rest of the week on ideas, things and stories the children had brought back with them.

Case study 6: Two afternoon sessions for Year 5 children working with an artist

Case study 6 took place in a primary school in an economically deprived and ethnically mixed part of London; more than 60 per cent of its children had English as their second or third language and about 75 per cent were eligible for free school meals. External inspection and internal personal/professional development had identified two main aims for curriculum progress:

(Continued)

(Continued)

- to improve the standard of English literacy
- to improve the sense of community within the school.

Courageously, the school decided to take an unconventional route towards these two objectives – with a grant from Creative Partnerships, they employed an artist and a curriculum designer to work with children and staff on rethinking the curriculum. This case study records what happened in two sessions in a Year 5 class of 25 children representing 19 different languages. Many could not speak any English when they arrived at school. Analysis of these lessons formed the starting point for staff discussions and decisions about their curriculum for the coming year.

The observed class and their teacher worked with a Maori/Samoan artist for two afternoons. Coming from a culture outside all of theirs, the artist introduced herself by describing her *Tatau* (the Samoan word from which we get 'tattoo'). She described how personal and culturally important each image was to her and the meaning of some of the marks on her hands, arms and legs. After responding to many questions about her country, she suggested that the children might like to draw round their hands and design their own meaningful *tatau* which would symbolically show what was really, really important to them. Children were immediately keen to do this and the artist reminded children that the symbols should not be random but be attached to some kind of story to do with important things in their lives. After some 20 minutes of eager drawing, she said that if children wanted to they could write the story which linked their symbols, in poem form or as a story. After an hour, she called all 25 children into a circle, sat down with them and asked them to share what they had done. All children listened respectfully and attentively to the often moving and very heartfelt stories of the others. One boy who had drawn a flag and a heart and mountains and four dots said this when his turn came round:

> You will not know this flag, it is the flag of my country Kurdistan, this is where I and my mother and father and sisters come from, they are the dots, there are lots of mountains there, I have drawn the heart because I have love for my enemies as well as my friends.

Another, streetwise and mature nine-year-old Romanian, stood up and recited:

I love my mum and I love my dad
I love my grandma too

I like my cat when she's not scratching
I like coca cola but its not matching
I like my chicken but its not hatching

I love my mum and I love my dad
I love my mum and I love my dad.

(Continued)

(Continued)

All were deeply engaged by this simple exercise in celebrating both personal identity and the building of a respectful and diverse community.

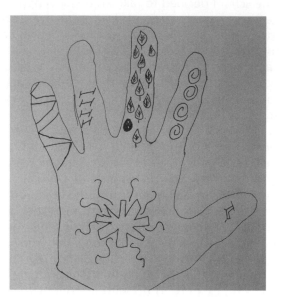

Illustration 3.7   A tatau-ed hand

Illustration 3.8   Arranging found words in a poem

(Continued)

(Continued)

The following day, the artist collected the symbols the children had designed and copied them onto the whiteboard. They discussed how these aspects of life that were so important to them might somehow be brought together and nurtured – under the influence of the previous day's session on Samoa, someone suggested an ideal Pacific Island where everyone lived peacefully together. One group thought the island could be turned into music and at that the whole class became energized. Under the artist's and class teacher's gentle guidance, groups began to compose a spiral-shaped score of Pacific Island music which used their symbols as graphic notation. Thus, the class creatively fused major progression in music learning (composing for the first time from a non-musical starting point, and using a spiral form as a musical structure), geography (detailed understanding of key features of a coral and volcanic island environment) and significantly developed their speaking and listening skills. This was inter-disciplinary in that creative fusion was both the aim and the outcome of these lessons, but also assessable subject progress was made in three subjects.

Case study 7: The Higher Education Arts and Schools (HEARTS) project (a Year 7/8 and ITE cross-arts project)

This project formed part of a teacher education programme, and exemplifies many of the personal and learning benefits for both teacher and pupil when they are involved in activities which seem to be mutually relevant.

The HEARTS project (Barnes, 2005b, 2006; Barnes and Shirley, 2007; NFER, 2007, website) was designed to investigate the power of the arts to enhance the learning of university tutors, trainee teachers and school children. It consisted of a series of practical encounters where cross-arts activities were used to answer profound questions and detailed investigations about environments. The project consisted of three discrete but linked experiences.

Experience 1: A mystery journey in a tiny steam train

Students and pupils were crammed into a half-gauge railway train with carriages just big enough to take four children and two students. Each group of six was given a sealed envelope to be opened as the train started its 50-minute journey. The letter in the sealed envelope simply gave an instruction:

> *Write a rap based upon the rhythms you can hear on the train and the sights you can see from it. Be ready to perform it on the station when you arrive.*

Neither the university students nor pupils were expecting this task and none were music specialists. In almost every one of the 15 groups of six, the school children took the lead. Students reported that the pupils '... just seemed more confident with open-ended challenges'. The pupils noticed the *tid-dly, tid-dly, tid-dly, taa, tid-dly, tid-dly, tid-dly, taa*, often interrupted by other rhythms as

(Continued)

(Continued)

Illustration 3.9 *Children and student teachers were placed together in the tiny carriages of a half-gauge railway to construct 'raps' about the journey*

wheels moved across points and crossings. They also noted the interruptions of whistles and frequent loud puffs of steam from the engine. As they looked from the carriage windows, the pupils recorded the things they saw: 'rubbishy gardens', 'miles of wires', 'traffic waiting', 'pylons, pylons, pylons', wrote one group. By half-way, the students had begun to catch up with the pupils and were making their own contributions. Students and pupils together started to make up their raps and write them down, some had repeated choruses which would hold them together, and some groups had discussed in detail how their raps were going to be presented to the audience of fellow travellers. One group punctuated their pithy take on what they saw as a spoiled landscape viewed from the train, with this repeated refrain:

> This is my time
> This is my place
> This is my en-vir-on-ment
> This is my rhyme

Experience 2: a beach on a drizzly November day

The 90 learners arrived at a forlorn and empty beach in light rain and strong winds. Aside from health and safety warnings, the student teachers had only

(Continued)

(Continued)

been given two instructions for their day: avoid using the words 'you' or 'I', and allow the children to take control of activities as soon as possible. Each group of six students and pupils were simply left with a set of focusing tasks and asked to 'capture the essence' of their place for a short presentation to their peers when they returned to school the next day.

Focusing exercises

9. **A sense of touch:** each member of the group is to go into their own space and sit or stand alone. Feel walls, pebbles, plants, fence, etc. nearest you. Jot down fragments of sentences which describe the fine detail of the physical sensations in the fingers as you feel the immediate environment.
10. **Haiku:** each person in the group is to write a three-line haiku (five syllables, then seven, then five syllables only) that captures the essence of a tiny detail of the place they are in. A haiku often starts with a sensitive description in the first two lines and in the last-five syllable line, the thoughts 'flip' to a 'higher' or more profound association.
11. **Snapshot view:** divide into pairs. In each pair, one of the partners closes their eyes and is led very carefully by their open-eyed partner. When the open-eyed partner sees an unusual or interesting image, they position their friend in the optimum viewing position and then squeeze the hand of their partner. The partner then opens their eyes for the length of the hand squeeze. Do this five times and then swap roles.
12. **One shot only:** each member of the group is allowed one still photograph only (so it has to be a good one). Discuss shots with the whole group but each individual must take a photograph.
13. **A dramatic happening:** plan a dramatic modern (or future) event which could only have happened in your place. Act it out. Summarize the story in three freeze-frame montages. Discuss and draw/plan/note what you would absolutely *have* to construct on your school stage if you wanted to act the scene out back at school. For example, would the light need to be coming from a certain side? Would there have to be a step here, an arch there? Would the arch have to be low/pointed/stone/crumbly? Etc.
14. **Say it in one:** each group has to produce five 'one-shot movies' lasting one minute. Each person will have the opportunity to make a movie. It should be a planned and continuous shot taken by one member but the shot should be discussed by the whole group.

(With thanks to Robert Jarvis for many of these ideas)

Figure 3.7 Excercises to widen and develop sensory and emotional engagement at the beginning of a project

Experience 3: adults and children working together

After a day together, students and children brought their collected data and impressions back to school. They worked on creative ways of bringing several aspects together and presenting them, and finally performed them to the rest of the year cohort. The 15 presentations could not have been more

(Continued)

(Continued)

Illustration 3.10   *Dungeness power station from the beach*

varied – they included two dramas, an art exhibition, a musical composition accompanying a silent film, a puppet show with characters made from pebbles, a dance where nature battled with humankind, a dramatically presented ghost story with music, a sculpture garden and a seven-minute documentary.

Students made detailed records of their impressions and observations, and wrote them up as part of an assignment. Several themes of general interest to those thinking of cross-arts work in schools emerged. Students noted many common outcomes from their three experiences. In each case, students remarked on the impact of placing control in the children's hands for significant periods. All remarked on the effective use of the arts to interpret and communicate the essence of a place. The following themes were commonly highlighted in student's assignments:

- Children's imagination was consistently recorded as being beyond that of the students themselves.
- The focus activities generated a great deal of genuine questioning.
- Children seemed so highly engaged that behaviour never became an issue.
- The atmosphere seemed very relaxed.
- The children displayed facial expressions of happiness and contentedness.
- The cooperation and friendliness of the children involved in the project were frequently remarked upon.
- The sense of pupil control significantly enhanced engagement.

(Continued)

- Children responded well to the open-ended nature of the project.
- The normal barriers between teacher and pupil were significantly broken down.
- Both children and students reported that they had learned significant arts and ICT skills and lots of unexpected place and science knowledge.
- A number of students commented that this activity had been the most enjoyable aspect of their whole course.

In a context where such positive outcomes are so evident, there remain serious pitfalls. University tutors assessing the students' work noted the following:

- Having stepped out of the role of teacher, many students forgot to step back in. Students were happy to see well-motivated, well-behaved, active and link-making children working on the project, but did not use the opportunity to help the children 'raise their game'. They did not step in to offer new challenges, teach new and relevant skills at a higher level or question pupils about ways they could improve their products.
- Having attended a crash course on creative teaching and learning, some students left with the idea that it was going to be easy to generate creativity in their classrooms. Some failed to understand that creativity does not 'just happen' when children are left to their own devices, but it needs serious preparation and discussion amongst teachers, and probably a clear framework to develop within.

Summary

- Each study illustrates different forms of local and child-centred relevance.
- There is no optimum timescale for good cross-curricular practice; a day, a week, a term, two terms and a whole-school curriculum are each represented.
- The fewer the curriculum subjects represented within a single theme, the more teachers are able to help raise subject standards and ensure curriculum progression and coverage.
- Each study relied upon and promoted maximum physical and emotional involvement in an authentic setting.
- Each study generated creative links across the curriculum.
- Each study integrated working adults as experts from the wider community.
- Activities and themes held equal fascination for both the adults and children involved.
- Each activity required and was founded upon detailed and lengthy planning in order to ensure progression and curriculum coverage.

- Every study was reported by teachers to have generated a high degree of focus, motivation and exemplary behaviour on the part of the children (and adults).

Key questions for discussion

- Can you identify the difference between interdisciplinary and multi-disciplinary cross-curricular activities?
- What kind of teacher do you think would be most at home with opportunistic methods of cross-curricular teaching?
- Are the kind of activities outlined in the case studies and focus exercises feasible for novice teachers? Give your reasons.

Further reading

Brice Heath, S. and Wolf, S. (2004) *Visual Learning in the Community School*. London: Arts Council.
Csikszentmihalyi, M. (2003) *Good Business*. New York: Hodder and Stoughton.
Wilson, A. (ed.) (2005) *Creativity in the Primary Classroom*. Exeter: Learning Matters.
Wyse, D. and Rowson, P. (2008) *The Really Useful Creativity Book*. London: Routledge.

CHAPTER 4

Social Perspectives on the Learning Journey

Humans are social creatures. Family, friendships, communities, cultures and, relatively recently, language (Mithen, 2005) evolved out of human sociability. Since the development of language, humans have shown an exceptional ability to communicate within and between social groupings and to make creative connections between ideas, things, places and people. Most communities have invented some kind of schooling to pass these connections on to future generations and extend the possibilities of their ideas. In the West and for the past century or so, those who study human groups and the social nature of creativity, discovery and invention have been called social scientists.

Understandings of social learning expressed by Vygotsky (1962, 1978) arose from a Marxist ideology which saw the social as the all-powerful force for good or evil. Education for Vygotsky was the route through which social reconstruction would happen, and therefore research into the social nature of learning was essential. In translation, Vygotsky's ideas were also highly influential within capitalist and hierarchical societies. His theories about how children learned were taken up by educationalists like Bruner (1968) whose prosaic term 'scaffolding' replaced Vygotsky's 'Zone of Proximal Development' to describe the way in which more experienced others support our learning. The influential psychologist, Bandura (1994), developed his social learning theory showing that those modelling learning behaviours on observation of others were more successful in retaining and transferring knowledge. Lave and Wenger (1991) emphasized the influence of the place where learning happens and Bourdieu (1984) the culture within which it takes place, whilst Bernstein (1971, 1996) showed the power of language to include or exclude the learner. In this century, such ideas have been developed by Vera John-Steiner, whose work (2006; John-Steiner et al., 2008) on interactionist approaches has shifted understandings of creativity as well as literacy and numeracy. Even more broadly, writers like Alexander (2010), Bawden (2006, website), Goleman (2006), Noddings (2003), Pollard (1996, 2008), Rogoff (2003) and Wenger (1999) have highlighted the essential role of others in all learning. Neuroscientists have more recently joined the debate. Usha Goswami, for example, stated that the social nature of learning can now be 'safely concluded' (Goswami and Bryant, 2007).

If the observations of this cross-disciplinary range of scientists and thinkers are accurate, then as teachers we should reflect carefully on the social as well as physical environments we influence. Whilst we cannot plan for each child's unique experience of others, the generalized environment we *do* control can be constructed so that interactions we would call positive are more likely than negative ones.

Children can make choices too. Pinker's (2002) view of children as 'partners in human relationships' and not 'lumps of putty to be shaped', reminds us of the importance of developing less hierarchical social relationships and listening to the child's voice. If 'positive', 'constructive' or 'good' experiences for children are to outweigh negative ones, then social values like collaboration, sharing, fairness and kindness must be championed in schools. Noddings (2003) reminds us, however, that without the support of safe, relevant, nourishing surroundings, respectful systems, positive curricula and personal friendships, such values are difficult to sustain. Schools, education administrators and novice teachers miss a vital ingredient of successful learning if they fail to address the issue of social learning.

Social learning

Bruner (1960) proposed that curricula and classrooms should be arranged to maximize on children's tendency to learn socially. He also noted that language shared between learners is essential to the extension and consolidation of learning. These thoughts led him to devise a curriculum and rearrange classrooms in ways which challenged more traditional arrangements in schools in the USA and UK. Bruner's curriculum, *Man: a Course of Study* (see MACOS (2010) website), rested upon three powerful questions – each holding an implied social element:

- What is uniquely human about human beings?
- How did they get that way?
- How could they be made more so? (MACOS, 2010, website)

Bruner also supplied the intriguing idea of the 'spiral curriculum'. Its underlying principle is that children should '… revisit … basic ideas repeatedly, building upon them until they grasp the full formal apparatus that goes with them' (Bruner, 1960: 13). He made the surprising suggestion that children in collaborative groups could handle 'difficult' subjects like values, philosophy and science, given appropriate language, structure, motivation, opportunity for intuition and others to scaffold the learning. This proposition was expressed succinctly:

We begin with the hypothesis that any subject can be taught effectively in some intellectually honest form to any child at any stage of development. (p. 33)

Relevance and activity were also crucial to learning and often such relevance is defined and sustained by peer group and contagious enthusiasm. Bruner put it this way:

motives for learning must be kept from going passive ... they must be based as much as possible upon the arousal of interest in what there is be learned, and they must be kept broad and diverse in expression. (p. 80)

Recent UK government education, creativity and cultural initiatives have been built around the idea of social learning activity. Group investigations are recommended, for example, in the science national curriculum and group compositions in the music orders (DfEE, 1999). More recently, we have had the *Sing-Up!* and *Youth Music* programmes (Sing up and Youth Music websites, 2010), the *Learning Outside The Classroom* manifesto (DfES, 2006d, website), the *Cultural Offer* and the integrated approaches recommended by Rose (Alexander, 2010; Rose, 2009) which champion groups of different sizes and composition. Schools remain cautious. Teachers are highly conscious of the parallel and undiminished development of impersonal targets, compliance cultures and competition between schools which are often best served by whole-class or personalized teaching and learning. The social characteristics of learning do not diminish under such pressures, however, they are simply less mentioned.

Social learning has many faces. Of particular interest to teachers are the following groupings outside family, which affect learning and the wider curriculum:

- friendships
- learning groups
- community
- culture.

Friendships

Having good friends is a key component in subjective feelings of happiness (Diener and Seligman, 2002; Layard and Dunn, 2009; Ryff, 1989). Friendship may also be crucial to the development of values (Barnes, 2010b) for both adults and children.

Friends and teachers are often the first non-family subjects of attachment behaviour (see Bowlby, 1997, but also Fisher and Williams, 2004). In adulthood, attachment of this kind may be shown in 'shared life projects' or the

Avery – pierdy

union of souls, even the 'union of minds'. Friendships provide a safety net and support system. The risks, disappointments, sadnesses and accidents of life are often softened by friends, who typically sustain with kindness, generosity and care. Whilst childhood friendships may be more fickle and short lived, they are nonetheless central features of playground and classroom life. Some teachers encourage and use friendships to build comfort, confidence and clarity, whilst others outlaw friendship groupings, fearing disruption and lack of concentration. The evidence of my own research suggests that we should consider supporting the development of friendships between all members of the school community as a high priority (Barnes, 2010b).

Today's interest in friendship also fashionably reinforces enhanced interest in personality and individuality which has developed throughout the second half of the twentieth and into the twenty-first century. Over-emphasis on individuality may weaken determination to improve conditions for communities and neutralize conceptions of equality (see James, 2009), but again my evidence suggests that in helping to buttress fundamental values, friends can strengthen the best in us (see Noddings, 2003; Pahl, 2000; Sternberg, 2008). Clearly, some friendships are neither constructive nor positive and a balanced approach to the treatment of friendships needs to be agreed in school communities. Experience has led me to believe that adults and children talking and working together can successfully develop and sustain such a balance in school settings.

Learning groups

Traditionally, UK and US schools have organized children in tightly defined age cohorts, usually with one group per education year. Despite experiments with 'family grouping' in some primary schools in the 1970s, the belief that children should learn with their age mates has prevailed. Small primary schools may of necessity have classes composed of two or three year groups, but this is generally considered a financial, not an educational necessity. Regardless of sustained attacks, social learning has consistently been shown by research and teacher experience effectively to promote learning in the majority of children. Rose and Alexander recommended group and paired learning situations in their respective reports, though their earlier report (Alexander et al., 1992) was used to argue against group work and for more whole-class teaching. The answer regarding size of learning group, as so often is the case, is a balance between different groupings, each favouring different minds and different situations.

Research in education systems outside Western cultures shows, however, that strict peer group learning is not universal. Rogoff (2003) challenges assumptions that children always learn best in homogenous groups. She shows how in many traditional societies children learn successfully in groups of all sizes and ages, in pairs and singly with adult mentors, relatives and elders.

In critiquing the 'production-line' tendencies of Western education systems, Rogoff stresses the importance of dialogue. She exposes the dangers inherent in age segregation and separating children from family culture, contrasting these unchallenged divisions with the cross-generational learning common in less 'modern' societies.

From a Western perspective, Wenger also suggests stronger intergenerational dialogue. To build successful communities schools, he suggests, should:

> maximise rather than avoid interactions among the generations in ways that interlock their stakes in histories of practice ... teachers, parents and other educators constitute learning resources, not only in their ... roles, but also ... through their own membership in communities of practice ... it is desirable to increase opportunities for relationships with adults just being adults, while down playing the institutional aspects of their role as educators. What students need in developing their own identities is contact with a variety of adults who are willing to invite them into their adulthood. (Wenger, 1998: 276–7)

Adults tend to learn best in groups too. Unfortunately, protected time is rarely given to teachers and school managers to reflect on their work and discuss both personal and professional developments in learning. On a course specifically designed to create space for those conversations, headteachers and the leaders of creative industries met to reflect on learning itself. The results of just six extended conversations between participants with a shared interest in creativity and a shared high level of responsibility, were that each participant significantly changed practice in their institutions towards greater reliance on reflection, conversations and supportive learning groups (Dismore et al., 2008).

Community

Platitudinous statements, such as 'the school is a community of learners' mask the fact that affirmative communities do not arise automatically. A community can simply be a group of people sharing the same geographical location. For a community to be personally meaningful, its members must feel a sense of belonging to it. The linguistically linked words common, communication and commonality help define an effective community.

Examples like case study 6 (in Chapter 3) remind us that schools may be the places where hopeful futures are constructed. Schools may become cohesive cultures in themselves, offering a model of a sustainable and supportive community, and some Creative Partnerships programmes have aimed at exactly this. This was certainly Freire's (1994) dream and many schools throughout the country have shown that children can lead the way in creating tolerant, cohesive and moral communities from diverse and sometimes even divergent populations. In this way, a community can take on the characteristics of a culture.

The Education Act of 2006 called for schools to be involved in building 'community cohesion' (HMG, 2006: 24). Cohesion in any organization is characterized by the quality and inclusiveness of its contacts and its responses to diversity. Cohesive communities do not ignore tensions and conflicts but use them creatively to enrich and energize. In educational contexts, this involves large measures of trust not always evident in school or ITE hierarchies (Ajegbo, 2007: 34), perhaps because of punitive inspection regimes. The curriculum can provide a solution – if both teachers and pupils are frequently in a position to share what Wenger called 'experiences that allow them to take charge of their own learning' (1998: 272). Such an ideal brings us back to values. Sharing, conversation, knowledge and understanding may all be put to dreadful or joyless purposes – organizations must decide to what purpose their community cohesion is put. The culture we feel part of will influence these values.

Culture

A culture is defined as the shared patterns of behaviour and thought which hold a group of people together. People can identify with the same culture but live very distant from each other. Culture involves a sense of shared history, shared aesthetic understandings, shared stories, pastimes, tastes, beliefs and traditions. Cultures may be big or small and individuals can belong to several at once, for example feeling British, Asian, working class, a Liverpool supporter and a keen cyclist.

Cultures literally shape our minds. Working at the boundaries of neuroscience and psychology, Csikszentmihalyi observed that the 'normal state of the mind is chaos' and that we order such chaos by 'inventing' culture (Csikszentmihalyi, 1997). From a similar perspective, Gardner argued that the culture in which we live begins impacting upon us 'shortly after conception' (1999b). But language and other means of direct communication make the impact of culture far stronger. Sociologist Basil Bernstein demonstrated the ways in which language differed between different sub-cultures and went on to show how the type of language used by each sub-culture affected the life chances, health, aspirations and death of its members. He showed how different 'codes' of language, at first (1971) divided into 'restricted' and 'elaborated', served to include individuals in certain cultures and exclude them from others. This theory had significant implications for schools which were seen as usually operating elaborated codes (lots of words, complex linguistic structures, detailed explanations) which could conflict with the restricted codes (few words, short sentences, fewer explanations) dominant in the homes of many children. Success at school, according to Bernstein, was defined by the degree to which the language code of the child agreed with the language code of the school. Extending his work on different styles of language use, Bernstein came to believe that all modes of communication influenced the level of the child's achievement in school. He observed:

> different modalities of communication [are] differently valued by the school and differently effective in it because of the school's values, modes of practice and relations with different communities. (Bernstein, 1996: 91)

If cultures, communication and the aim of cultural cohesion are this significant, then one might expect Initial Teacher Education (ITE) to focus heavily upon it, but it does not. Few newly qualified teachers have studied the sociology of education. Few have the opportunity to consider the relevance of social context in their lesson planning. As a result, few children experience what the Ajegbo report (2007) called an education which seems to them, 'contextualised and relevant' (2007: 19).

Adults in education rarely examine their own or others' cultures. They are often unaware of the impact of their own socialization and the impact of their own culture on their thinking. With Scoffham, I have explored how providing opportunities for ITE students to view their culture from outside, can impact on their personal and teaching lives and thoughts (Scoffham and Barnes, 2009). Observing personal thinking and behaviour from a different perspective, where 'one's own assumptions [are] temporarily suspended to consider others' (Rogoff, 2003: 12), can be a transformational experience. The view from another culture provides opportunities to learn from other ways of seeing. It seems no coincidence that personal, cultural and creative advances have often occurred at the meeting point of cultures. Making a point relevant to addressing the sub-cultures in every classroom, Rogoff argues:

> if judgements of value are necessary, as they often are, they [are] much better informed if they are suspended long enough to gain some understanding of the patterns involved in one's own familiar ways as well as in the sometimes surprising ways of others. (Rogoff, 2003: 12–14)

Observing that 'People who have experienced variation are much more likely to be aware of their own cultural ways' (p. 87), Rogoff reinforces Freire's case that the teacher must be both respectful and open to all cultures and actively involved in building new and shared ones.

Socio-political concepts affecting learning

Learning is clearly affected by complex interactions outside directly social ones. Psychological, inherited and environmental factors deeply influence learning. Schools have become used to considering such factors in making curriculum and pedagogical decisions. Social and political issues may not be so frequently considered and yet a range of key socio-political concepts *should*

frame many decisions made in schools. The relative strength of applied social values, such as equality, fairness, trust and inclusion, characterize a school's ethos and often define the degree of success at both individual and academic levels. Whilst social considerations colour the judgements we make in schools, they are rarely discussed at staff meetings, in-service training or the education of new teachers. Successful schools, according to Ofsted (2009a, 2009b), however, are successful in living and communicating their values.

Values are social constructions; we do not develop them alone. Sociologists like Bourdieu (1984) argue that every individual carries a measure of social and cultural capital invested in them by the social group(s) to which they belong. If a child's social capital, its approach to relationships, authority, disappointment, fun and self chime with the expectations of the school then they are more likely to succeed. Equally, the child's *cultural capital*, their received attitudes to the arts, design, language, pastimes, curriculum, learning, will often predict their future in education. Bourdieu saw that schools and teachers represented a particular, predictable and relatively narrow set of social and cultural standards, and as such were open to challenge. As societies in the UK and USA become increasingly disparate, the acceptance of such narrow cultural and social measures seems increasingly difficult to sustain.

Teachers must be sensitive to the cultures of the children they teach. Such sensitivity has curriculum and pedagogical implications, but as more and more teachers become practitioner researchers, their cultural sensitivity should be applied to themselves. In this context, Bourdieu stressed the importance of developing a *reflexive* approach to research. The reflexive teacher examines the social and cultural biases in their own make-up before making judgements on the learning and attitudes of children.

Equality

Positive life experience will often spawn optimistic views on friendliness and other values like trust and equality, but other lives may generate more sceptical responses. In either case, many societies pay at least 'lip service' to the ideals of fairness and inclusion. The UN's 'Convention for the rights of the child', their Millennium Goals and national education statements, such as those in the Primary National Curriculum (QCDA, 2010) proposed by the outgoing Labour government, expressed egalitarian aims quite explicitly.

The purpose of a statutory curriculum is to establish entitlement for all children, regardless of social background, culture, race, gender, difference in ability and disabilities, to develop and apply the knowledge, skills and understanding that will help them become successful learners, confident individuals and responsible citizens. (DCSF/QCDA, 2010: 5)

... including ... pupils with special educational needs, pupils from all social and cultural backgrounds, pupils from different ethnic groups, including travellers, refugees and asylum seekers and those from diverse linguistic backgrounds. Teachers should plan their approaches to teaching and learning so that pupils can take part in lessons fully and effectively ... taking specific action to respond to pupils diverse needs by:

1 creating effective learning environments
2 securing their motivation and concentration
3 providing equality of opportunity ... (2010: 8)

Such ideals do not go unchallenged, however. Some would see such statements as rhetorical and unrealistic – they are not seen in the everyday lives of millions of the most disadvantaged in society. There are credible suggestions that the UK/US form of 'selfish capitalism' has made it impossible for schools to change social divisions and suspicious attitudes which have become deeply entrenched in our societies (James, 2008, 2009). There is little doubt that trust between peers in both the UK and USA (WHO, 2008, website and Chapter 12 in this book) is relatively low and that relationships between adults and children are often strained (UNICEF, 2007), but such observations should not smother hope. Schools remain the only institutions set up to change society, but unless teachers and pupils agree on what that society should be like, then the prospects for constructive change are slim.

Other critics of progressive education policy see egalitarian ideals as indicative of a failed social reconstructionist approach to education, and suggest that schools are the wrong places to attempt to right personal wrongs (Furedi, 2009; Hayes and Ecclestone, 2008; Hirsch, 1999). Their criticism extends to the 'social work' and therapeutic roles many schools have taken on as they try to create environments conducive to the motivation and concentration of children suffering from physical, emotional, spiritual, social and interpersonal ill health. But improving the lot of the underprivileged has been a central aim of education for centuries – and for many the economic well-being of the country is only a meaningful aspiration if the country is a wholesome and inclusive place to live in.

Fairness

What we see as fair will vary according to the way in which we have been socialized. Implicit in the arguments for inclusion is the idea that every human is of equal worth. In terms of the organization of schools and their curricula, a belief in equality and inclusion should result in attitudes and practices which treat each child as precious. As teachers become reflective practitioners, many social scientists argue that they should become increasingly aware of the biases and assumptions which lead them, often unintentionally, to value one child over another.

ITE students have become used to detecting obvious unfairness like gender or racially motivated bias, but fewer are aware of their preference towards thinking or intelligence 'styles' (Sternberg, 1997a, 1997b) which match their own. Sternberg has shown how teachers who favour a creative style of showing intelligence, often overlook pupils showing it in practical or analytical ways. Analytical teachers similarly can easily miss intelligent solutions shown by creatively minded pupils.

Inclusion

Inclusion in an education context, according to Booth, is 'concerned with reducing all exclusionary pressures' in education cultures (Booth, 2003). In *The Index for Inclusion* (Booth and Ainscow, 2002), he offers 'a resource to support the inclusive development of schools'. Used throughout the UK and extensively in 40 other countries, this resource makes values central and requires them to be lived in practice. Its opening section on 'creating inclusive cultures' suggests that schools develop:

> shared inclusive values that are conveyed to all new staff, students, governors and parents/carers. The principles and values in inclusive school cultures, guide decisions about policies and moment to moment practices in classrooms, so that school development becomes a continuous process. (Booth and Ainscow, 2002: 8)

Educators considering establishing inclusive cultures are challenged by three 'indicators' of inclusive values:

1 Staff and students treat one another as human beings as well as occupants of a 'role' (2002: 52).

2 Staff seek to remove barriers to learning and participation in all aspects of the school (p. 53).

3 The school strives to minimize all forms of discrimination (p. 54).

In the *Index for Inclusion*, schools are invited to consider a range of questions under each indicator. These questions offer opportunities for friendly, meaningful and rich conversation, different in every group and community. The discussions, Booth claims, will assist the process of developing improvements in the learning and teaching environment. Progress on the path to inclusion and participation is measured by the degree to which conversations, discussions and opportunities for self-examination are genuine. Schools cannot address such huge issues in a vacuum. With up to one in three children in the UK currently living in poverty (Barnado's, 2010, website) and nationalism on the rise, Potts (2003) suggests we can only move towards inclusion and participation by addressing the poverty and perceptions of difference which exclude. But Bourdieu reminds us that the products of our cultures can also exclude.

Illustration 4.1   *Children learning to communicate with their teacher in a south Indian school*

The products of human cultures

Human creations, whether tangible or conceptual, express our different cultures. Philosopher Karl Popper (1978) called the ideas, values, traditions, artefacts and structures that surround us, the third of three contemporaneous worlds we inhabit. Popper's world one is natural and physical and world two is the world of the mind. We cannot avoid influencing and being influenced by the products of human cultures. Those aspects of culture that are most readily accessed by our senses have a particularly strong impact upon children. Our schools are packed with expressions of world three and they can either promote or obstruct learning.

Localities, schools and classrooms

School buildings and neighbourhoods are resources in themselves. They bring together the aspirations and skills of a wide range of subject disciplines and they form the most familiar backdrop to young learners' lives. Beyond hosting the occasional geography field trip, these free, safe and very local resources are rarely well used. A school building is the product of a combination of mathematical, scientific, technological, artistic, geographical, linguistic, historical and social skills and knowledge, yet genuine surveys of the school fabric, forces, functions, materials or plans rarely form part of the primary child's experience of school. Some of the case studies in Chapter 3 illustrate how schools could use these highly accessible and valued resources across the curriculum.

Places and objects

Artefacts and boundaries are human creations. Differences between specially prized objects and places characterize cultures. Places and objects can also be the medium through which 'deep learning' (Marton and Saljo, 1976) happens. Deep learning is learning which is transferable and can be applied in different situations. Perkins (1992) describes such learning as the 'active use of knowledge', and argues for a curriculum to promote thoughtful learning. He coins the term 'mindware' (website: www.newhorizons.org/future/ Creating_the_Future/crfut_perkins.html) to describe the objects around us: pencils, computers, counters, historical artefacts, landscapes or buildings and so on, which in some way extend our minds and help us think more deeply. Concentrating on understanding and metacognition, and acknowledging the distributed/socially constructed nature of intelligence, Perkins champions 'Educational settings where students learn by way of thinking about and

Illustration 4.2   *Children working in an artist's studio. Photo: Ian Bottle*

with what they are learning, no matter what the subject matter is' (Perkins, 1992: 185). He argues for active learning and 'expert-like understanding' (Andrade and Perkins, 1998) and frequently describes how things, people and places are effective catalysts for such learning.

In a UK context, the *Learning Outside the Classroom* manifesto (DfES, 2006d, website) provides significant 'permission' for shared exploration of places. The manifesto picks up Perkins' argument, that real problems, real places, real implications, relevant skills and knowledge promote transferable, practical and useful understanding. Part of the reality of these activities is that they are shared and usually social.

Children respond positively to collaborative work outside the classroom. For many, the process of enquiry begins in settings which children feel are their own. The recent 'Engaging Places' programme (website) attempts to help teachers support children in experiencing built and open places beyond school as part of their learning environment. Whilst much has been written about learning beyond the classroom by geographers, until recently (Austin, 2007; CABE, 2010, website; Catling, 2010) it has been given little attention by other subject practitioners.

Places and objects, when enthusiastically and knowledgeably used, can become the motivation, focus, purpose and product of learning in any subject of the curriculum. Because it is probably true that 'no objects that surround us are without their emotional tag' (Damasio, 2003: 55), every child brings a slightly different perspective to learning experiences which use real things and locations. It is possible to counter the excluding properties of certain places and artefacts through education. English Heritage pioneered this approach to learning in the 1990s with its 'Teachers' Guide to ...' series of books (English Heritage, 1990, 1999), and their championing of the cross-curricular use of buildings and collections has been taken up by many museums and great houses across the UK (Attingham Trust, 2004). The major impact has been that many more children and adults see great buildings and local architecture as 'their own' (DCMS/English Heritage, 2000).

Summary

Learning is a social activity. Research and experience suggest that the friendships, learning groups and classes that characterize the school should reflect the social nature of learning. Schools are generated by and exist within communities, cohesive or not, and at their most successful they respond to priorities and values emerging from those communities. Schools often form a social and symbolic hub within their community and as such continue to exemplify and lead on social values. Cultures differ from communities in that by definition they include common ways of thinking and acting which transcend time and place. Schools are entrusted with a significant role in the transmission of culture from one generation to another. Modern nations, being composed of many cultures and sub-cultures each endowed with their own social and cultural capital, present schools with new challenges. In the culturally diverse social context of today, the details of culture championed by schools are open to debate and negotiation. Each school must individually examine and agree the social and cultural capital they seek to develop in children – therefore no two schools in the twenty-first century should be alike.

Values are social constructions too. Cultures are defined by the values they hold and display. Values involve fundamental beliefs which power and direct action in the world. Related values like equality, inclusion and fairness are frequently but often rhetorically championed by schools and their success can be judged by the correspondence between rhetoric and deed. Societies also construct the objects and environments that surround their members and these vary in importance and influence between cultures and sub-cultures. Values, environments and artefacts can exclude as well as include and it is up to schools, within an agreed value set, to offer a curriculum that offers the widest range of inclusive environments, resources and cultural activities to support the learning of its children.

Key questions for discussion

- How inclusive are the different social groups in your school?
- How does your curriculum reflect and make use of the social nature of learning?
- What do you think should be the role of friendships (a) between children and (b) between adults, in school?

Further reading

Goleman, D. (2006) *Social Intelligence*. New York: Arrow.
Noddings, N. (2003) *Happiness and Education*. Cambridge: Cambridge University Press.
Rogoff, B. (2003) *The Cultural Nature of Human Development*. New York: Oxford University Press.

CHAPTER 5

What Does Neuroscience Tell Us About Cross-Curricular Learning?

One response to the practice outlined in the case studies is to suggest that cross-curricular teaching and learning is a result of changing political and social fashion. Recent developments in neuroscience imply, however, that integrated, meaningful and emotionally engaging approaches should become a new norm if education is to build capacity to address the accelerating rates of change outlined in Chapter 1.

As we begin to detail what interests, worries and motivates twenty-first-century children, improved technologies have helped us become more confident about the ways in which they think and learn. Chief amongst the new insights from science is the contribution of neuroscience. Applying neuroscientific insights to education raises fears of chemical interference in learning and behaviour reminiscent of Orwell's *1984* (see, for example, *Guardian*, 2006; Theroux, 2006). Some teachers suspect that in the hands of neuroscientists, ordinary human differences become pathologized. These and similar worries underline the importance of establishing dialogue and a shared vocabulary between educationalists and neuroscientists. Happily in both Europe and the USA, such dialogue has begun (for example, see Bransford et al., 1999; Howard-Jones, 2010; Howard-Jones and Pickering, 2005; Huppert et al., 2005; Perkins, 2009).

Dialogue has already shown that each side of the education–neuroscience debate sees a different truth. Neuroscientists and experimental psychologists rightly look for a 'scientific' truth represented by the evidence of numbers, trials and controlled experiments repeatable in the laboratory. Teachers tend to hold to an 'experiential' truth based on qualitative interpretation of their everyday experience in the classroom. Teachers may, for example, observe beneficial learning changes in children which appear to stem from the adoption of so-called 'brain-based' approaches to learning but which are dismissed as scientifically baseless by the neuroscientists (Howard-Jones, 2010).

Until recently, neuroscientists have most commonly been involved in thinking about children with various learning difficulties whilst teachers have been more interested in the implications of neuroscience for learning in all children. Conversations between scientists and educators are rich and fruitful, but teachers and other educators need to be aware of the detail and limitations of relevant neuroscientific research before they engage in the debate or apply findings. Neuroscientists are at pains to remind us that we are only at the beginning of understanding what happens in the brain and how it relates to action in the world. On the other hand, teachers have worked, researched and written about children's learning for millennia and perhaps need to feel confident of the validity of their own observations and experience. The most effective and transferable professional skills of the teacher perhaps more closely resemble an art than a science (Perkins, 2009).

The neuroscientific view on learning

Much current scientific thinking suggests that specifically human ways of learning conferred survival advantages on our species. It is unlikely we would have survived as a species if we were not self-conscious, able to develop complex language systems, make lasting relationships, understand and make signs or symbols, synthesize input via the senses, remember and create. We have seen how our species has achieved through social means (Chapter 4), sharing and building upon human abilities. Neuroscientists argue that the plasticity and complexity of our brains and our prodigious capacity to learn has made the success of the human race possible. Teachers need to make full use of the advantages evolution and society have conferred on us when they make choices relating to the style, means and context of the learning they offer their children.

Education in the twenty-first century will increasingly be influenced by the findings made possible by brain scanning and imaging techniques which were impossible only a generation ago. Through brain scanning, neuroscience offers independent corroboration of what teachers already 'know' about emotional and sensory engagement in learning, but it has also revealed a great deal of new knowledge about our learning. Teachers should know something about how information on the workings of brain is gathered and seek to be fully informed about the insights neurology brings (Blakemore and Frith, 2006; Goswami and Bryant, 2007).

Brain scans

Brain-imaging technologies such as functional Magnetic Resonance Imaging (fMRI), Positron Emission Tomography (PET) and Near Infra-Red Spectroscopy

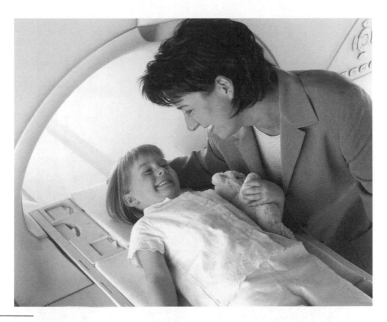

Illustration 5.1   *Child entering an fMRI scanner. Courtesy of Siemens*

(NIRS) have added new dimensions to our understanding of the ways in which we think and learn. Before extending the discussion to some significant implications for education, it needs to be remembered that fMRI scanners, the machines most often used to measure brain activity in children, are noisy, cumbersome, scary and very expensive. PET scans are not frequently used because they use a radioactive dye to indicate diseased or damaged areas of the brain. These costly scanners are confined to universities, hospitals and neurology departments and, until very recently, their main use has been to research or diagnose abnormalities. Medical beginnings may have resulted in the pathological tendency in neuroscientific–education research to concentrate on disability. Dyslexia, attention deficit hyperactivity disorder (ADHD), dyscalculia and autism and their treatment, rather than learning in general, have preoccupied neuro-researchers. It is still impossible to measure activity in children's brains while they are engaged in everyday learning activities. Neurological research into learning is therefore still very much in its infancy.

Neuroscientists have, however, been able to observe some significant aspects of normal brain activity and development in children. These observations have begun to influence our understanding of thinking, learning, the emotions, the influence of environment and the concept of self. Through findings in these areas, neuroscientific research is poised to make observations which could influence the curriculum our children follow. This is why teachers should be centrally involved in the debate. Since one of our assumptions is that learning is a consequence of thinking, we begin by considering the neuroscience of thought.

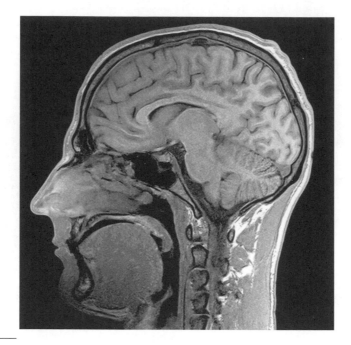

Illustration 5.2   *An fMRI scan of the head, showing skull, brain and other soft tissue. Courtesy of Siemens*

Thinking

Thinking is not a simple activity. Our brains and bodies work as an integrated organism with individual parts taking on a variety of functions depending upon which other parts are working with them. Connections within the 100,000,000,000 neurons (or brain cells) which make up the normal brain, control everything that happens in and through our body. We are not conscious of the activation of clusters of neural connections responsible for survival and most physical operations. Such neural activity cannot be called thinking. Even complex and conscious movement, such as playing a piano sonata or diving a car may for some become almost as automatic as breathing. When consciousness (or sometimes semi-consciousness) is involved in our mental or physical processes, we mark the qualitative difference with the word 'thinking'. The thinking elements of our brain – aspects of memory, planning, monitoring, learning, language, feelings, emotions, spirituality and self-consciousness itself – we call our mind. These faculties depend on even more complex linkages between brain networks, the rest of the body and our environment.

Close your eyes and place the tip of the index finger of your right hand on the base of the underside of the index finger of your left hand. Gently stroke your right index finger up to the tip of your left index finger. Even with your eyes closed, you can probably sense exactly where on your finger the sensation is. Each located sensation you register involves the connection of separate pairs and groups of neurons governing the feeling in that finger. When we think of the implications of this simple exercise, we are involving thousands of other connections: between aspects of memory and feeling, between neurons governing sight and sound, and between the networks which establish the present understanding of self and this book. Almost half the brain is involved in this activity (Blakemore and Frith, 2006).

Unlike living skin or bone cells, neurons generally do not replace themselves when they die, and they die when they are not used (see Giedd et al., 1999). Neuroscientists argue that exercising or simply using these neural connections is vital to the survival of individual neurons and our continued learning. Each working cell in our brain carries a minute part of the inherited or learned self. Most neurons are able to connect with others through some 1000 tiny root-like filaments called *dendrites*. Neurons 'connect' via the transmission of a tiny electrical impulse along an *axon* towards receptors on the dendrites of another cell. This pulse results in the emission of chemical neurotransmitters which move across the miniscule gap between an axon and a dendrite and are either accepted or rejected by the receiving dendrite. The meeting point between an axon and a dendrite is called a *synapse*. Neurons fail to connect when an electrical or chemical inhibitor is released at the synapse. In making consciousness itself and allowing the conscious act of thinking, these microscopically small synapses become the very stuff of intelligent behaviour (Keverne, 2005; LeDoux, 1999, 2002). Each concept we develop – pain, mother, comfort, tree, god – consists of networks of thousands of such connections, distributed across the brain. Individual linkages and wider networks which prove useful, become physically conjoined as a *myelin* sheath grows to protect and speed up the connection. Frequent use thus establishes networks of cells which fire almost simultaneously when required. Each human brain is wired up uniquely and, as Susan Greenfield observes, 'reflects, in its physical form and function, personal experiences with supreme fidelity' (Greenfield, 2003: 148).

An old brain trick illustrates the way these connections work in our mind.

Point to a piece of white paper and ask your audience what colour it is. Point then to a whiteboard or white teacup and ask again what colour it is. Repeat the question for two or three other white things in the room. Then simply ask, 'What does a cow drink?'

The immediate response to this quick-fire question is usually the (wrong) answer ... 'milk', after which people usually correct themselves and say, ' no, water'.

(Continued)

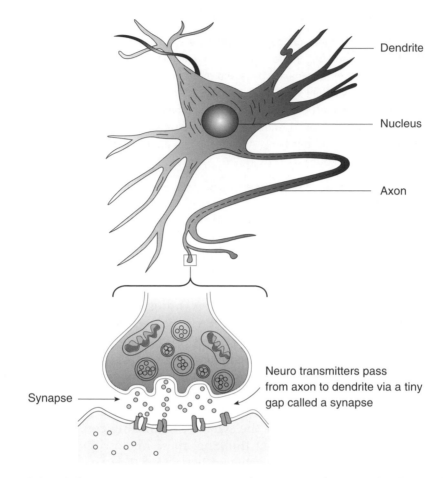

Dendrite

Nucleus

Axon

Neuro transmitters pass
from axon to dendrite via a tiny
gap called a synapse

Synapse

Figure 5.1a   A diagrammatic representation of a neurone, showing: dendrite, cell, body, axon and nucleus

(Continued)

What has happened in our brain?

When the concept 'white' is visually brought to mind, all previously experienced mental associations with white – summer clouds, milk, snow, drawing paper, the colour of a childhood bedroom or a hated school blouse – will also be brought into or near consciousness. So will the respective associations of each of those concepts. The areas of the brain involved with the concepts milk, paint, blouse and snow, 'glow' and are ready for action if needed. When the aurally introduced stimulus 'cow' is added, our brain circuitry races to fire up all the concepts related to cow. Since the concept milk is already primed by association with white, our reflex answer will be that a cow drinks milk, though we 'know' that only calves drink it. (See Figure 5.2.)

Structure of a Typical Neuron

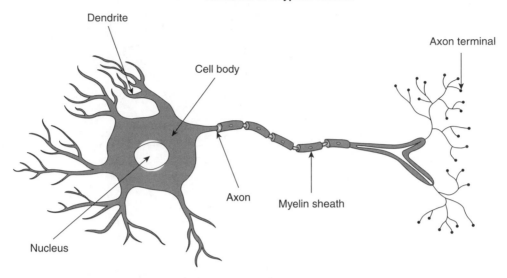

Figure 5.1b A myelin sheath develops to insulate the connection between an axon from one neurone and a dendrite from the next

The linkages between certain clusters of neurons via their axons and dendrites and across the synapses in the brain are the beginning of thinking. But thinking is not a purely cerebral activity, neither is it simple. A highly intricate system of two-way links between various parts of the brain and body is activated when we think. The advanced and developmentally recent frontal lobes or neo-cortex in the human brain have connections which link with much more primitive areas of the brain controlling the metabolism, senses, muscles, stomach, the immune system, emotions and memory. Neuroscientists now have evidence that these unconscious, largely automatic, but primitive systems, which we share evolutionarily with many other vertebrates, are involved in the conscious act of thinking. Thus, scientists are increasingly clear that what affects the body impacts upon thinking and that thinking deeply influences what happens within the body (Damasio, 2003; Goleman, 1997; Goswami and Bryant, 2007; LeDoux, 2002).

Since thinking appears to have given us evolutionary advantage, and is closely linked with senses, memory and emotions, neuroscience might prompt teachers to consider their use of the:

- sense of personal security
- multi sensory
- emotionally significant
- memory-using and enhancing faculties
- intellectually challenging.

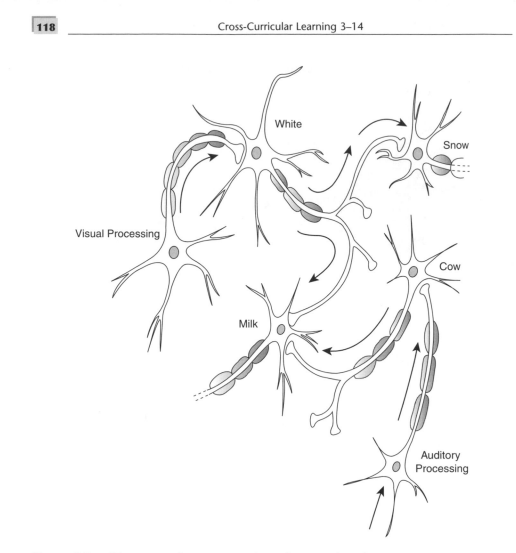

Figure 5.2   Diagrammatic representation of connections between neurons on processing sensory inputs relating to the concept 'white'

Such foci exploit the unique thinking ability of the human. Exercising the distinctive mix of mind/body skills in each individual is likely to enhance the sense of achievement in every child.

The maturing brain

More than a quarter of a century ago, scientists noted periods of especially rapid cell production in the growing brains of very young children. Confirming observations from developmental psychology, neuroscientists established that at 0–3 years, the neurons in the brain multiply at unusually rapid speeds. The volume of the brain does not increase significantly after about three years of age (Thompson et al., 2000) but scans show that the *matter* of the brain does undergo very significant reorganization as the density of the brain increases through childhood and early adulthood (see Illustration 5.3).

Between the ages of 8 and 14, there seems to be a second major 'growth spurt' of neurons with copious connection-making dendrites. Neuroscientist Jay Giedd and colleagues (1999) demonstrated that despite this extra capacity, the volume of the brain does not increase. Unused connections are rapidly 'pruned away' if unused. This finding suggests that the second period of neural growth may be as vital to optimum mental development as that of the early years. Giedd himself has commented:

> If a teen is doing music or sports or academics, those are the cells and connections that will be hardwired. If they're lying on the couch or playing video games or [watching] MTV, those are the cells and connections that are going to survive. (Frontline, 2002, website)

If the 'use it or lose it' principle applies to the immediately pre-adolescent brain, as other neuroscientists have suggested (Baird and Fugelsang, 2004 website; Keverne, 2007), then it is surely incumbent upon schools and teachers to ensure the experience of children is particularly rich, positive and stimulating in the years of puberty. This is especially true for those connections within the young person's brain most susceptible to environmental influence.

Over the period of our education, as more connections within our brain become 'hard wired', a physical change in brain density occurs. As we gain increasing control over physical and mental faculties, the fatty myelin sheath which develops over frequently used connections causes an observable change in colour from grey to white.

This colour change denotes maturity. But not every part of our brain becomes mature at the same time. Research (Gogtay et al., 2004; Thompson et al., 2000) has shown that the pre-frontal areas of the brain are not *fully* matured or 'wired up' until we reach our early twenties (see Illustration 5.3). Physical and sensory areas of the brain mature first, but the much more complex abstract-thinking, decision-making, impulse-controlling networks are among the last to mature. A research example (Luna and Sweeney, 2004) may illustrate this.

Adults and 14-year-olds were asked to perform a similar experiment which tested their ability to control a 'natural' impulse to look at a light. Whilst they were exerting this control, their brains were being scanned using fMRI. It was found that whilst many 14-year-olds showed the same degree of success in avoiding looking at the light, adults and teenagers used different parts of their brains to assert that control. Adults used a range of areas distributed throughout the brain whereas those used by young teenagers were very localized and easily susceptible to emotional 'hijack'.

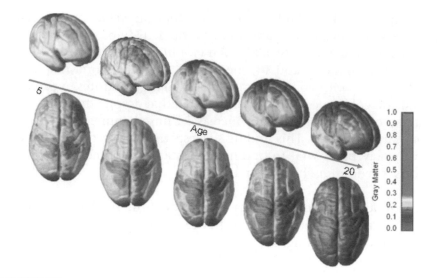

Illustration 5.3   *Thompson and Giedd's illustration of the maturing brain*
0–21 years. Increasing white matter (myelin-sheathed neural connections within the brain) is
shown by the darkening colours as the brain matures. Courtesy of Paul Thompson

Maturation involves the reorganization of the brain into more complex net-works consisting of numbers of checks and balances. Significantly, these include the ability to envision, or ask, 'what if?' or 'what are the risks?' and to mentally model alternative outcomes. These abilities generally show them-selves in the late teens and early twenties and the extensively dispersed neural networks which make such weighing up possible are now known to be amongst the last to mature. Again, these findings may have implications for education. Neuroscientists tell us the mature brain is one where connections and inhibitors are widely distributed and collaborative, and less susceptible to impulse or purely emotional responses. To help 8–14-year-olds' brains reor-ganize and refine in this direction, perhaps social collaboration and distribut-ing intelligence between various members of a group should be more frequently modelled in educational settings. This social activity in learning would be an external metaphor for what is invisibly happening within the developing brain. Future neuroscientists may well be interested in researching the impact of curricular and class organization attempts at such 'help'.

If the thinking, predicting, reflecting parts of our brain come slowly to maturity and if through education we can make an impact upon which parts of the brain mature more quickly, then this would tend to affect the curricula we plan. Findings from neuroscience might be used to suggest that the school experience of children aged 8–14 should:

- be social
- continue to be physical

- exploit all the senses fully
- not expect too great a degree of abstraction
- be fully aware of the strong impact of emotions.

It is worth noting, however, that currently in England many children between 7 and 14 years old are heavily tested. They have national tests at 11 and 14, and school-based tests at 7, 8, 9, 10, 12, 13 and 15. For significant periods when the brain is growing at its fastest and its higher functions are maturing, children are under the stress of cramming and tests. Large periods of time which should be devoted to new learning, are lost in what has been called the 'never ending cycle of demoralising, childhood-destroying examinations' (Dawkins, 2003: 70), which summarizes educational experience for many.

Excess stress may cause difficulties for younger children too, establishing negative attitudes to learning and the self as a learner. The neuroscientific research above may suggest that there are optimal periods for introducing material into the school curriculum. Both listening to and playing music, for example, has been shown to have a strong impact on the developing brain of young children. Several studies, for example, have shown close relationships between musical activity and high scores and improvements, particularly in maths (Jensen, 2000). If we know that the progress of brain maturation makes musical, linguistic and physical activities more readily learned in the early years, should we delay the teaching of subjects more likely to be abstract? If we find that good health, positive emotions and feelings of security disproportionately affect the

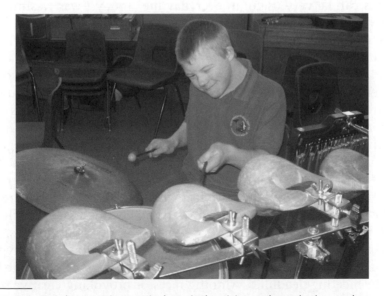

Illustration 5.4 *Involvement in practical musical activity, such as rhythm and tune, is primarily fun, but also helps develop skills of coordination, confidence, and an understanding of pattern and structure. Photo: Cherry Tewfik*

thinking of the young, should we angle the curriculum more towards activities which promote these things? Focused discussions between neuroscientists and educators are clearly overdue and should consider the following suggestions:

- Introduce physical, practical, sensory, emotional and language learning early.
- Maintain physical, practical, sensory, emotional and language learning throughout years 3–14.
- Do not expect abstract thought too early.
- Do not expect judicial behaviour too early.

Thinking can be good or bad, efficient or inefficient, complex or simple. One condition which apparently *prevents* some otherwise useful thinking connections being made is when we feel under some kind of physical or emotional threat.

Stress

Stress is a vital survival mechanism. We could not learn some things without a considerable degree of stress. The stress of being run over by a car has taught me to be very careful when crossing roads! To support us in stressful situations, the parts of the brain which control our secretions of hormones such as adrenalin become active. Our 'fight or flight' reflexes cut in, we think less consciously and react in a more reflexive way (Jensen, 1995; Smith and Call, 2000). This can be very useful in everyday life. Today I was washing up and was, not very sensibly, piling up the wet crockery too high on the draining board. When a cup slipped off the pile and headed for the floor, before I had time to fully register what was happening, my right knee had jerked up to block its fall. The cup then rebounded (unharmed) from knee to cupboard and my left hand was ready to catch it. I could never have achieved this feat of juggling if I had been asked to do it. This balletic response was a simple reflex action triggered at the lowest levels of my nervous system. It did not involve thinking or learning in the terms already discussed, though I have learned that I can trust my reflexes to get me out of trouble ... sometimes.

A degree of stress may be vital for learning. We should, however, make a distinction between stress which we feel when we lose control or are in danger, and *challenge*, which pushes us towards achieving a goal which may be currently just beyond reach. A *lack* of response to stress hormones, particularly the catechoramines, has been implicated in attention deficit hyperactivity disorder (Arnsten and Li, 2005). Many of us are very aware of the benefits of stress in meeting deadlines, winning races or provoking creative solutions to problems. But too much stress over too long a period, or stress which threatens our psychological or physical being, may be damaging. The hormone cortisol produced through stress, has been shown to provoke cell death in the

Illustration 5.5   *An upset and angry pupil. Note the position of her shoulders, the configuration of mouth, eyes and cheekbones and the closed body language. This information was provided by Clinical Tools, Inc., and is copyrighted by Clinical Tools*

hippocampus area of the brain (Lee et al., 2002: 89) and high levels of stress appear to impact negatively on blood pressure and glucose and cholesterol levels in the blood. (Djuric et al., 2008, website)

There is a close relationship between our immune system, nervous system and state of mind. Neuroscientist Francisco Varela goes as far as calling the immune system our 'second brain' (in Goleman, 1997: 50) in that it responds to emotions and external influences in a parallel way to our 'neurological' brain. The feeling of stress, for example, seems to affect the connections between neurons within the brain by restricting blood supply (Kawachi et al., 1994). It also causes the secretion of hormones that weaken the immune system, which of course affects our physical well-being. Physical disease in its turn directly affects the behaviour of the limbic system of the brain which, to complete the vicious circle, makes us feel bad (Goleman, 1997: 58).

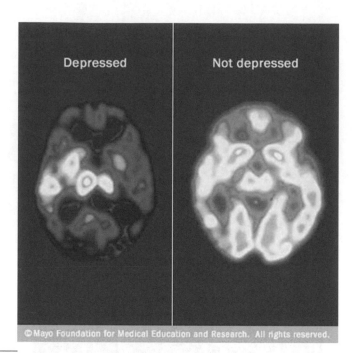

Illustration 5.6   *PET scans of a brain before (left) and after (right) treatment for depression. Notice increased blood supply (shown by paler areas) to the recovered brain*

Our brain has evolved a tendency to restrict blood supply to parts of the brain inessential to basic physical or psychological survival when under stress. The feeling of being 'unable to think straight' in times of stress can be very inconvenient – think of particularly nerve-racking examinations, angry teachers, unreasonable deadlines or stage fright when you were a child. Stress can restrict activity in the evolutionarily 'younger' parts of the brain – those involved in appraising situations, making fine judgements, analysing conse-quences, remembering, applying experience and planning.

The pair of PET scan images in Illustration 5.6 above show a depressed patient's brain compared with their brain after treatment. The lighter parts denote areas with a greater supply of blood essential to thinking. The frontal parts of the brain where thinking is most clearly registered appear relatively dark and therefore poorly supplied with blood. In the image on the right, taken after three months of treatment for depression, a much more general supply of blood is shown; this is especially evident in the frontal areas associ-ated with high-level thinking.

Recent neuro-scientific study therefore may suggest that:

- the stress of *unthreatening* challenge may be seen as helpful in some learning
- too much stress may actually reduce brain functioning
- our brains are likely to be less rational under stress

- if a child is feeling worried, embarrassed, sick or scared, they are less likely to be able to think or learn (Greenhalgh, 1994)
- a curriculum which is designed to produce challenge without stress is likely to maximize learning.

Emotions and feelings

The external manifestation of feelings – the smile, the frown or the grimace – we call emotion. These superficial features impact upon our minds and provoke further changes in our bodies. Psychologist Paul Ekman and neuroscientist Richard Davidson, working at the boundary between neuroscience and psychology, found that even pulling the face of happiness had a positive impact upon inner feelings (Ekman, 2004; Goleman, 1997). 'Whistling a happy tune' when we feel worried or upset really *does* seem to make a positive difference to our minds and bodies.

Both our externally shown emotions and our more secret inner feelings appear to be centrally involved in learning (Damasio and Immordino-Yang, 2007). The neurological connections through which body and mind are linked are well illustrated by examining what we call 'feelings'. A feeling is the word we give to our sensing of that exquisite network connecting memory, nervous and immune systems, muscular, visceral and intellectual systems as we respond to a particular event. Feelings, including intuition, serve to help us weigh up the pros and cons of a situation, decide on a course of action and plan our future actions (Claxton, 2003; Damasio, 1994, 2000, 2003; Goleman, 1996; LeDoux, 1999; Salovey and Sluyter, 1997) We are beginning to understand more about the complexity of these interrelated systems. British neuroscientist, Hugo Critchley, has shown how EEG, PET and fMRI scans can now be used to measure the impact of events on the living brain so that we are able to say with some confidence, for example, that *negative* non-speech intonations, and sounds like groans, sighs, squeals, shouts and cries, provoke increased activity in the parts of the brain which process threat, just as pictures and words associated with danger do. Numerous other imaging studies have confirmed the link between what is emotionally significant, current attention and long-term memory (Critchley, 2003), and it appears we can also learn to control electrical frequencies within our brain through neuro-feedback (Gruzelier, 2003).

Neuroscientist Damasio argues that a sense of joy or happiness is the optimum condition of the human organism. He examines biological evidence which supports seventeenth-century philosopher Spinoza's view that the brain/body is constantly seeking ways of promoting its physical and emotional survival. The goal of the human mind, he says, is to 'provide a better than neutral life state ... well-ness and well-being' (Damasio, 2003: 35). Translating this into a school context, we could take this to mean that children are likely

Illustration 5.7   *A happy face. Note the crinkles around the eyes, raised forehead, cheeks and eyebrows and the broad smile. This information was provided by Clinical Tools, Inc., and is copyrighted by Clinical Tools*

to be attempting to find aspects of their classroom life which generate those secure, relaxed, fully engaged and exciting feelings we interpret as happiness. Such feelings, whether provided by a stimulating curriculum or peer popularity gained in other ways, will affect body, mind and immune system positively – a condition we generally want to prolong. It is obvious that there is no guarantee that feelings of happiness are always generated by culturally or morally 'good' things. It does seem likely, however, that teachers and all those who work in schools would share the desire to provide in their classes:

- a comfortable and warm place where basic physical needs are supplied
- a place where positive experience for each individual is more likely than negative experience
- a curricular concentration on promoting the conditions of well-being
- a close knowledge of the lives of the children beyond the classroom.

Growing numbers of policy makers are convinced that 'emotional literacy' programmes, where pupils are helped to 'recognise, understand, handle and appropriately express emotions' (Sharp, 2001: 1; Young Foundation, 2010)

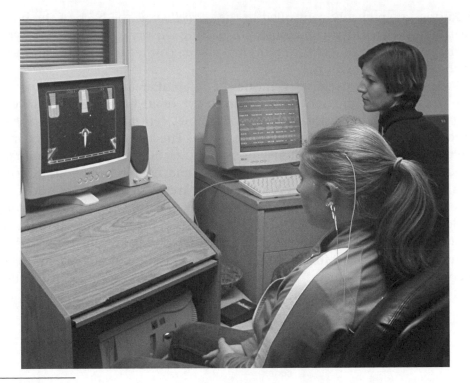

Illustration 5.8   *This student, linked to a computer which painlessly reveals electrical activity in parts of her brain, is learning, through neuro-feedback, to control aspects of her own thinking*

have a direct impact not only upon well-being, but on learning and achievement also. Research supporting a curriculum based around 'well-being' has only recently gained general prominence (Antidote, 2003; Frederickson, 2009; Hanko, 1999; Huppert, et al., 2005; Morris, 2005; Warnock, 1996; Weare and Gray, 2003).

Memory

Three different kinds of memory affect learning. The *working* memory involves present-time operations such as adding numbers in the head, remembering what you just said and following directions. These aspects of memory are controlled in various parts of the pre-frontal cortex and are very susceptible to even mild stress. The *declarative* memory (storage of facts, figures, faces and names, all experiences and conscious memories) is largely controlled by the limbic system including the *hippocampus*. We also have what is sometimes known as 'muscle memory', the memory of *procedures*, actions, habits or skills that are learned simply by repetition. These procedural memories are probably controlled in the *cerebellum* at the back of the brain. Learning is the result of consciously connecting sensory inputs, all three types of memory, language and the emotional charge connected with most aspects of the declarative memory.

We seem to store negative memories in different areas of the brain to positive ones. Equally, different organs within the brain have predominance in negative and positive situations. For example, centrally involved in even mildly threatening situations is the *amygdala*. The amygdala and other areas are activated in fearful situations and seem to facilitate rapid but minimally processed responses which evoke alertness and escape behaviour (Garrett et al., 2002; LeDoux, 2002). Even when we 'know' situations are not really threatening, such as those measured during a boxing scene in a DVD or a violent video, studies have shown that the areas of the brain linked to threat, escape and those which store long-term memory of (real) traumatic events are significantly engaged (Murray, 2007). The concentration of such events in the memory has been argued to affect the degree of aggression, desensitization and generalized fear experienced by individuals.

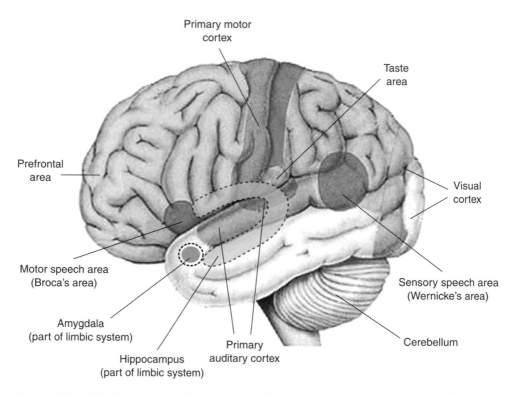

Figure 5.3   The brain marked with some of the major sensory, memory and thinking areas referred to in the text. The amygdala and hippocampus are deep within the brain

Positive emotional stimuli tend to arouse quite different and equally complex areas of the brain. Brain areas associated with relaxed, content, secure, 'approach' behaviour are generally distinct from those which provoke withdrawal behaviour typical of feelings of fear, pain and disgust. Even in young babies, the reflex response to their mother's approach activates the areas of the brain which in adulthood process positive emotion. Positive feelings appear to involve larger and more dispersed areas of the brain usually concentrated on the *left* side rather than the right. In emotionally significant situations, the engagement of these areas facilitates more detailed, measured responses and enables analysis, correction or reinforcement.

Neuroscientific research into memory would suggest that schools and teachers:

- provide many situations likely to provide positive memories
- avoid realistic negative scenarios
- cultivate 'approach' atmospheres and relationships in the classroom
- avoid situations where withdrawal is the natural response.

School learning, memory and brain science

Teachers and other adults are understandably interested in how thinking and learning are affirmed, provoked and reorganized. The links between learning and memory are vital and, again, neuroscience has helped us understand them. Learning happens when brain and body combine to make experience part of the conscious memory to be recalled to solve future problems. We have seen how the brain does not mature in a linear fashion, and this is true of the memory in particular. As the connections between senses and amygdala and hippocampus become hard-wired, we can memorize more easily. Between the ages of 3 and 14, memory is more reliable if our already matured senses are involved. Repetition also significantly helps us to memorize (Alexander, 2010; Blakemore and Frith, 2006). Through establishing repeated neural connections, we create permanent or semi-permanent changes in the brain. But context-free memory exercises are not the best way to generate mind change (Gardner, 2004).

Teachers generally aim at what might be called 'quality learning'. Quality learning is the kind of learning which benefits individual and society and is transferable to many situations. Quality learning may also include the ability to inhibit inappropriate behaviours and thoughts, focus attention and monitor our own actions – each of these abilities, Gogtay and colleagues' (2004) research reminds us, are subject to gradual maturation. Perkins (2009) also draws attention to fMRI studies which show that new knowledge on a particular subject, say the cause of thunder, tends to overlay pre-existing, or 'native' knowledge, rather than replace it, which is why 'backsliding' is so common.

Memory is also enhanced by frequently talking about the things we think are important. National or state curricula have helped us by establishing what *politicians* think is most important to remember, but each institution may arrive at other aspects of 'worthwhile' knowledge (see Chapter 8). By establishing and revisiting conversations, by metacognition, making links between present and past class activity and by connecting school learning with the rest of life, teachers can help build useful memory banks in each child's mind. Key, usually subject-based, vocabulary is important here also and forms part of the proposed lesson plans discussed in Chapter 11.

Adults construct much of the physical and emotional environment within which the child learns. Teachers plan progressive sensory and intellectual experience to support the child in building new concepts and reassessing earlier misconceptions. It is therefore of great importance that teachers and other adults involved in education keep abreast of research on the workings and development of the brain.

Many schools are currently using 'mind mapping', 'brain gym', visual, auditory and kinaesthetic (VAK) divisions or 'brain-based learning' methods.

Illustration 5.9 *Children engaged with an interactive museum exhibit. Photo: Dorothee Thyssen*

This interest in ideas traceable to neuroscience suggests that neurological perspectives have already made significant inroads into education. In the view of most laboratory neuroscientists, however, these 'brain-based' ideas are poorly understood, founded on faulty science and likely to be ineffective in the longer term. Such well-intentioned initiatives have been dismissed by neuroscientists and other academics as 'psycho-babble' (Howard-Jones and Pickering, 2005: 7) and consequently insights of potential worth may be undermined. A teacher's understanding of neuroscientific research is unlikely ever to be as detailed and deep as a neuroscientist's and, in any case, experience, agendas and audiences are very dissimilar. The popularity of brain-based approaches with teachers, however, says much about the contemporary need for 'quick fixes' and external verification from science to justify what might in the past have been called good and intuitive teaching. Neuroscientists already tell us with confidence that the developing brain seeks patterns, holds doggedly on to naive concepts, and learns socially and in multi-sensory ways (Goskami, 2007). An important challenge for twenty-first-century education is to ensure dialogue between educationalists and neuroscientists for the benefit of children. Schools in the meantime should:

- agree on what 'quality' learning and 'worthwhile' knowledge should be
- continue to use multi-sensory approaches shown to be effective in helping children learn and remember
- talk a lot about important principles, bits of knowledge and skills which have already been introduced
- assess the effectiveness of new brain-based approaches by small-scale research projects within school.

Multiple intelligences

Gardner's popular theory of multiple intelligences (Gardner, 1993, 1999b) is neuroscientifically founded. Its widening of the concept of intelligence provides academic support for teachers' genuine attempts to be more inclusive and positive. Gardner suggests a neuroscientific basis for his various 'intelligences'. An intelligence, he proposes, is 'a neural mechanism or computational system … genetically programmed to be activated or triggered by certain kinds of internally or externally presented information' (Gardner, 1993: 63).

Gardner suggests that the following are each discrete ways of making sense of the world, highly valued in at least one culture and capable of isolation through brain damage (see Gardner, 1999b):

- linguistic
- logical mathematical

- spatial
- bodily kinaesthetic
- musical
- naturalist
- intra-personal
- interpersonal
- existential.

Each of us has a mix of all intelligences but every individual has a unique profile of strengths and weaknesses. A related cluster of brain areas distributed across all areas of the brain is involved in processing each mode of mental processing. For example, the way we understand the world *spatially* uses observably different combinations of brain areas than those used to understand it *linguistically*. The same brain area, however, may fulfil a number of different functions and be shared by several different 'intelligences'.

Whilst it seems that in normal situations our brains work as a complex whole, each of Gardner's intelligences is argued to be capable of relatively independent existence. Usually, we use several intelligences to process what is going on around us, but nonetheless we may display positive dispositions towards one or more. So one of us may be more prone to understanding practically through the use of our body and gross and fine motor movements (Gardner's

Illustration 5.10   *These fully involved children are using musical intelligence to compose music based around the skin patterns of African animals*

bodily kinaesthetic intelligence), whilst another may prefer to understand through reflection and quiet analysis (using his *intra-personal* intelligence).

Since this neurologically based theory is seen as 'uncontroversial (in scientific terms), unthreatening and simple' (Howard-Jones and Pickering, 2005: 13), it is argued to be 'easily accepted and owned' by education. Whilst it might be owned, it may still not be very deeply understood. My observations in schools which purport to put this theory into practice would suggest that many fail to grasp some of its founding principles (Barnes, 2005a). Multiple intelligence theory was proposed to help teachers and other adults understand that children may learn and show their intelligence in various and contrasting ways. The dangers of encouraging children to pigeonhole themselves by deciding between nine categories of being 'smart' have become apparent. Such classifications run counter to Gardner's intentions. An understanding of the different ways a child could show intelligence was meant to suggest to teachers different ways of mobilizing the brain so that important content could be learned. Gardner is clear that he does not support the creation of a 'new set of losers' and accepts the strong possibility that the profile of intelligences may change with the situation, maturity or experience (Gardner, 1999a: 98).

Interest in Gardner's multiple intelligence theory might suggest the following changes in school:

- Avoid labelling children as having one intelligence or another – this will limit their development.

- Provide as many entry points to learning as possible – this will maximize the chances of engagement.

- Be more inclusive in the use of the term intelligence – look for *how* each child is intelligent, not *if*.

- Value equally all ways of being intelligent.

- Choose a curriculum which provides many powerful and multifaceted experiences to interpret in a wide variety of ways.

School environments

The nature–nurture debate has raged for centuries, but neuroscience is helping us see the two sides of the argument in more dynamic balance. Robertson and many others have argued that environment has as big an effect on intelligence and our neural circuitry as our genetic inheritance, and that our minds are susceptible to 'sculpture' by our environments. He quotes a number of studies which demonstrate a marked improvement in children's mental processing achieved simply by changing the home environment of children (Robertson, 1999, 2002).

Illustration 5.11   *Working in less familiar environments beyond the classroom can quickly involve children in memorable learning experiences. Canterbury HEARTS project*

Neuroscientists have been able to demonstrate that our brains, particularly the complex pre-frontal cortex (PFC), are especially shapeable by experience (see Goswami, 2007; Greenfield, 2003; Marks and Shah, 2005). The PFC is involved in cognitive, social and emotional processes such as the regulation of attention, planning, self-control, flexibility and self-awareness, and seems very sensitive to environment. Studies of children with neurological damage due to accidents have already shown that family and physical environment are key factors in the degree and rate of recovery from such injury (Yates et al., 1997), but the environment consists of much more than family. Neuroscientists have noted that the PFC is also involved in the working memory, mental imagery, audio and visual associations, mental representation of the body in space and the integration of memory with present circumstances. Each of these faculties are shaped and organized according to environmental considerations, including unique experience, class, peer group and geographical location.

The plasticity of the brain may be illustrated by a study on the brain areas concerned with topographical memory of London taxi drivers (Maguire et al., 2000). Taxi drivers' memory for streets, landmarks, routes and shortcuts is unsurprisingly increased by repetition and practice. This progressive experience results in observable growth in the relevant brain areas, chiefly the hippocampus, which was observed to become more complex, dense and enlarged over time. Similarly, experienced musicians have an auditory cortex some 25 per cent larger than control groups of non-musicians (Pantev et al., 1998).

Illustration 5.12   *Recording fine detail and personal impressions in a unique and authentic environment*

Brain scientists guess that other areas of the brain, particularly those involved in our feelings and emotions, are similarly responsive to the environment (Davidson et al., 2000; Marks and Shah, 2005).

Some educationalists have taken the concept of the plasticity of the brain to imply that it ought to be possible to teach other aspects of thinking and being. Gruzelier (2003) has shown how students can learn (through neuro-feedback via a monitor screen, see Illustration 5.8) to control the *theta* brainwaves associated by neuroscientists and experimental psychologists with creativity, improved memory, anxiety reduction, self-confidence and a sense of well-being. We have already seen how simple practice makes a great deal of difference to performance, but more complex neurological outcomes can result from particular approaches to learning. Given extra music lessons, for example, children made unexpected and considerable developments in mathematics, emotional literacy and language (Overy, 1998). Other studies have shown the value of music in managing emotion (Justlin and Sloboda, 2009). Such findings coupled with the neurological insights outlined in this chapter would suggest that schools may need to see intellect and attitude as:

- teachable and able to be changed through experience
- subject to non-maturational influence in particular supportive, stimulating environments
- responsive to learning situations throughout life.

Summary

The implications for education of modern neuroscientific study are only lately being discussed by educationalists (Alexander, 2010; Howard-Jones, 2010; Howard-Jones and Pickering, 2005). The techniques of brain scanning are still in their infancy and we should therefore be tentative about conclusions from neuroscience and wary of unthinkingly adopting 'neuromyths'. However, when neuroresearchers publish findings which match the experienced observations of teachers, it seems inevitable that teachers will take this scientific evidence as corroboration and support for their own professional judgements. When rapidly developing imaging technology makes it possible

Illustration 5.13   *Using emotions, senses, intellect and body in a holistic learning experience*

to see brain connections being made in response to particular stimuli, and when we are able to observe the neural effects of well-being in non-laboratory contexts, then the implications for schools and curricula would be huge. Schools must be prepared for this likelihood. The meeting points between neurology and education are still being forged, but this area is one of the most significant and potentially paradigm-changing developments of the present.

Neuroscientific research supports many of the principles of cross-curricular learning. A curricular approach which maximizes the use of the widest range of mental and physical faculties is likely to be more effective than one which only uses some. The faculties which evolved to ensure human survival and flourishing are those which continue to ensure the most productive learning. The common ground between cross-curricular learning and our current understanding of neuroscience of learning is in the following areas:

- the crucial role of the senses
- the unique human skill of making finely judged discriminations
- the centrality of emotional engagement
- the long-lasting effects of positive experience
- the positive impact of challenge
- the negative impact of threat
- the positive effect of stimulating and supportive environments
- the importance of rich, authentic and multilayered experiences
- the existence of multiple modes of interpretation.

Key questions for discussion

- Does neuroscience tell us anything new?
- Why do we need evidence from neuroscience?
- What is the difference between stress and challenge?
- What can teachers tell neuroscientists?

Further reading

Damasio, A. (2003) *Looking for Spinoza: Joy, Sorrow and the Feeling Brain*. Orlando, FL: Harcourt.
Gardner, H. (1999) *Intelligence Reframed: Multiple Intelligence for the 21st Century*. New York: Basic Books.
Huppert, F., Baylis, N. and Keverne, B. (2005) *The Science of Well-being*. Oxford: Oxford University Press.
LeDoux, J. (2002) *The Synaptic Self*. New York: Viking.

CHAPTER 6

Psychology and Cross-Curricular Learning

• Children often remark that learning seems easier when it makes sense to them. Educational psychologists are interested in how children create and sustain sense of experience. They observe children's behaviour and focus on what they *say*, think and do. Amongst many other questions, educational psychologists ask how the curriculum and teachers can improve the learning experience of children. They attempt to make use of experimental findings and test theoretical positions regarding learning and intelligence. Many findings emanating from psychology support the introduction of more cross-curricular practice in schools and this chapter will outline some of them.

Over the last few decades, psychologists have disputed old concepts of intelligence and suggested new ones. To take a few examples: Gardner (1993) and Sternberg (1997b) challenged narrow 'language and logic' definitions of intelligence by introducing wider more inclusive understandings of what intelligent behaviour could look like. Robertson (1999), on the boundary of psychology and neuroscience, helped establish the concept of the 'plastic' brain, an organism highly responsive to its environment. Psychologists like Jensen (1995) and Shayer and Adey (2002) introduced the concept of *learnable intelligence* which has become a common belief amongst teachers. Similarly, Perkins' (1995) idea of *distributed intelligence* which sees other people's minds, tools and technologies as playing a significant part in individual problem solving and 'intelligent' behaviour, is widely understood and accepted. Bandura (1994) showed how *self-efficacy*, usually arising from a positive social context, generates the sense that we are able to learn and are empowered to use that learning. John-Steiner (2006) used observations of *creative collaboration* amongst key shapers of the twentieth century, to argue that collaborative groups in educational settings can build more intelligent solutions. Picking up Gardner's ideas, Goleman suggested that *emotional intelligence* (1996) and *social intelligence* (2006) may be more important than Intelligence Quotients. Meanwhile, Barbara Rogoff (2003) and Ken Robinson (2009) challenged Western assumptions that intelligent behaviour was best nurtured in what she saw as the 'production line' techniques of current Western education where children are taught an economically driven curriculum in large groups of the same age.

Methods of instruction have been particularly subject to the ebbs and flows of fashion over the last 80 years. Teaching heavily focused on whole-class tuition, drilling facts, fixed knowledge, rote learning, texts, formulas, and 'the basics' of reading, writing and arithmetic, appropriate to a nineteenth-century industrial, manufacturing society, was not primarily intended to develop understanding. Such pedagogies are seen now by psychologists as engendering only short-term learning (see Gardner, 1999a: 82; Shepard, 1992: 319). Some have offered 'deeper', more transferable, longer-lasting models of learning. Marton and Entwistle pioneered work in this field in Europe (see Chapter 7 for more details of their work). They argue persuasively for active learning concentrating on understanding – transforming 'surface' knowledge by relating ideas to each other, looking for patterns and principles and extracting meaning. They suggest the most effective methods to generate 'deep learning' are within groups and in solving problems which are, or have been made, significant to pupils. The concept of 'teaching for understanding' (Blythe, 1997: Stone-Wiske, 1998) has become common amongst teachers and researchers who want to help students learn *how* to learn (Claxton, 2003; Entwistle, 2000; Rhen, 1995). It is the central argument of this book that relevant and meaningful cross-curricular contexts provide some of the most powerful motivators for such learning.

Cognitive psychologists suggest that we can and should learn *how* to learn. Some writers have popularized specific aids to thinking. Ideas like 'Mind Mapping'®(Buzan, 2002), the identification of Visual, Auditory and Kinaesthetic (VAK) learning styles, (Dunn et al., 1984), 'Six Thinking Hats'®(De Bono, 1999) and the 'new 4 Rs' of resilience, resourcefulness, reflection and reciprocity (Claxton, 2003) have, like 'brain-based learning' been embraced by teachers because they appear to help children and adults order and deepen their thoughts. Perkins called these tools designed to assist thinking, 'Mindware' (New Horizon, 1991, website). Neuroscientists, however, frequently cast doubt on simply expressed models of learning (Geake, 2009; Howard-Jones, 2010).

There are many possible answers to the question 'How do children learn?' locked away in erudite journals and rarely visited websites. Many approaches overlap significantly, however, in highlighting the importance of personal and transformative experience, passion, understanding and cooperation. Teachers wishing to make education exciting and motivating for all children may appreciate the suggestions brought together from current psychological research, under the following headings:

- Children thinking
- The 'thinking classroom'
- Children playing
- Children and their feelings

- Children and 'flow'
- Children and language.

Children thinking

Harvard Professor of Education David Perkins famously stated that 'learning is a consequence of thinking' (1992: 34). He continues to argue that rich, stimulating and multi-layered environments, real-world investigations and active participation in discovery and challenging questioning, all promote thinking in both cross-curricular and single discipline contexts (Perkins, 1992). But experience and stimulation alone are not enough to make thinking deep and learning transferable. Most cognitive psychologists argue that there are a range of other influences on the way children think: self-confidence, the ability to be metacognitive, the social and physical environment, the accidents of heredity, the example of peers, and perceived relevance may all play their part. The social aspects of thinking and learning have already been discussed but thought is also influenced by more hidden forces within the individual mind.

Humans' ability to examine and talk about their own thought processes must have provided enormous advantages in the primeval world – psychologists remind us that it is still vital now. Metacognition, or thinking about our thinking, is essential to 'deep learning' (see Chapter 7) (see Entwistle, 2000; Fisher, 2008). By calling to mind the *way* in which we think, we rehearse, externalize and buttress that thinking. Even at the age of five and probably younger, children can become aware that they think and think differently from others (Fisher, 1999) and this can lead towards them examining their own thought processes. Being asked to consider our own mental process appears to result in measurably positive benefits for young learners in mathematics, science and design technology. Grades dramatically improved in national and school tests in a number of London schools in which teachers encouraged children to think, explain and hypothesize about subject-based activities in which they were involved (Shayer and Adey, 2002). Shayer and Adey's research also suggested that the change of teaching and learning style provoked marked improvements in attitude, autonomy and motivation.

Thinking needs preparation time and teachers themselves need to be very aware of what works best. In 1994, Adey and Shayer provided five simple pointers to generating better thinking:

1 Prepare the child's mind with experience of concrete and practical examples and relevant vocabulary.

(Continued)

(Continued)

2 Arrange some kind of 'cognitive conflict', an apparent contradiction of common sense, a genuine challenge or a problem.
3 Work with others to construct an answer to the problem through speculation and collaboration.
4 Think about your methods of finding an answer to the problem.
5 Transfer the newly formed theory to a new situation. (Adey and Shayer, 1994)

When children explain their thinking, whether in a cross-curricular context like children's philosophy or in a single subject session, we quickly become aware that not everyone thinks in the same way. A simple musical listening exercise (shared by Fisher), will help demonstrate this:

Music and moving image

Find a section of video where a single slowly changing scene is depicted for about three or four minutes. Several sequences from the documentary film *Powaqqatsi* (1988) directed by Godfrey Reggio are highly suitable, but this will work with the opening sequences from many modern films. Play the same video clip through three times, but each time play it against a different musical soundtrack (perhaps one rock music, one reflective and quiet church music, and one silence). Ask children independently to write down or discuss with a neighbour what they saw in the video clip or what it made them think. A discussion after each clip will reveal that dozens of different connections have been made between the sounds of the music and the details of the image you have chosen. This will remind children of two important messages: that they are (a) all thinkers and (b) all different thinkers.

The suggestion that there may be many different ways of thinking has been developed by psychologist Robert Sternberg (1997b). Sternberg, a past president of the US Psychological Association, postulates some 13 distinctly different 'thinking styles' (or styles of 'mental self-government') and uses the metaphor of contrasting styles of political government to illustrate them. Within Sternberg's theory, some of us are *monarchic* thinkers who prefer single goals to think about and work towards. Others may be *judicial* thinkers who weigh up the alternatives before deciding on a goal. *Oligarchic* thinkers are motivated by several, sometimes competing, goals of equal importance. Other possible thinking styles are listed in Figure 6.1.

Understanding one's own preferred thinking style and the bias it brings to judgements and choices is clearly essential for all teachers. Without this

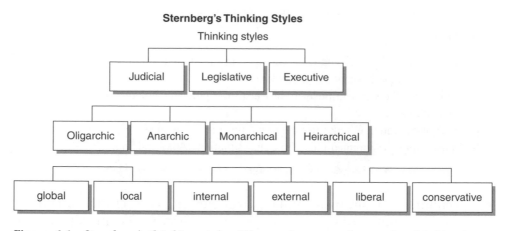

Figure 6.1 Sternberg's thinking styles. We may have a preference for thinking in one style in each group shown in the diagram. We don't all think in the same way, yet often assume others think like us

understanding, teachers might expect children to think in exactly the same way as they do, or at least aim to think like them. Sternberg argues that it is vital for teachers to expect children to think in many different ways and that none of them are intrinsically wrong – if they work. Different thinking styles may be effectively pooled in group discussions and collective activities to produce much more satisfying and rounded outcomes than would be possible through one style alone.

Sternberg has also made major contributions to our understanding of intelligence itself. His *triarchic theory* of human intelligence suggests that alongside requiring a good memory, intelligence consists of analytical, creative and practical ways of thinking which differ in each of us (Sternberg, 1997b, 2003). He describes research which shows that pupils taught by teachers who share their intelligence strength are much more likely to succeed, but those with a teacher with a different intelligence strength are more likely to fail. A child with a strongly analytical approach, for example, who finds themself taught by a highly (but exclusively) 'creative' teacher will more often receive bad grades and a negative attitude to learning itself. The obvious advice is for teachers to be aware of their own preferred style but also to plan for many different thinking styles and to aim to use a variety of entry points so as to maximize the number of pupils that can be reached.

Whilst psychologists continue to use IQ tests to measure the quality of children's thinking, many now believe that both thinking and intelligent behaviour are much more complex than simple tests and snap judgements suggest. Research on children's thinking has quite literally changed many teachers' minds as they seek to discover *where* the intelligence strength lies in each individual, rather than *if* it is there. The key suggestions that psychologists bring to teachers are that:

Illustration 6.1 Making sense of a view through the window – teacher and pupils thinking and learning together as equals

- we all think differently
- there are a wide range of thinking styles/preferences
- each child shows intelligence in different ways
- teachers can help children think better.

The thinking classroom

The design, arrangement and resources of the classroom itself can promote thinking. The concept of situated learning was first developed by Lave and Wenger (1991) in a business context, but the *setting* of learning may be of even greater significance for children. Displays, stimulus resources, learning aids, furniture, window view, corridor space, ICT and access to outside may each be used to help generate thinking. A classroom has social and personal dimensions too. Expensive and excellent physical characteristics are worthless unless the social, personal and spiritual classroom is equally well-resourced and cared for. Teaching experience shows that thinking is generated by an atmosphere where questioning is part of the classroom culture. Piaget and hundreds of psychologists since him remind us that learning growth happens when children are not frightened to make mistakes, where relationships are warm and supportive, and where instructions and goals are clear.

Illustration 6.2 *A group discussing a proposed drama. Each brings a different perspective to the discussion*

Psychologists argued that environment profoundly impacted on our thinking and learning well before such thoughts were confirmed by neurology. Beliefs about the relationship between environmental and inherited factors affecting learning have always coloured policy and practice in schools. The common view today is that environmental and inherited factors are so intertwined that it is difficult, and possibly pointless, to untangle them Psychologist Robert Fisher, for example, identifies three dimensions of the child's intelligence (1999): two of them, *developed intelligence* and *self-developed intelligence*, are clearly affected by environmental conditions. Fisher's third concept, born-*with* intelligence, sounds a biological absolute, but we know that environmental influences such as smoking, alcohol, poverty or violence each begin their impact upon the developing brain, shortly after conception (Gardner, 1999a).

The social, emotional and physical environment we live in is in many ways exclusive to us. Psychologist of language Steven Pinker suggests a roughly 50/50 split in environmental and genetic influences on our learning (Pinker, 2002). Fifty per cent of what we *are* (character, abilities, intelligence, even habits) is the result, he argues, of our genetic inheritance. The other 40–50 per cent is the result *not* of our generalized, home, family, school or cultural background (or nurture), but what Pinker calls our *unique environment*. The unique environment is what exclusively surrounds us as individuals; exactly what happened to us, where, with whom, what we heard, smelt, touched, saw, felt

Illustration 6.3   *Meaningful engagement found in a museum. How was each child's 'unique environment' manipulated by the teacher? Photo: Dorothee Thyssen*

and thought in the billions of separate incidents which make up our unique lives. Thus, identical twins, physically clones of each other, are likely to be nearer to 50 per cent alike in character and intelligence than the 100 per cent we might expect, because each of them inhabited a different unique environment from shortly after conception. Pinker's concept of the unique environment could have major implications for schools and teachers. Teachers, as influential adults, consciously and unconsciously control much of the physical and emotional environments that surround the child. Whilst the unique environment experienced by the child could never be directly under a teacher's control, teachers are still likely to influence its general character. Teachers can strive to build the kind of environment most likely to generate meaningful, positive, affirmative and constructive connections within the mind.

Many cognitive psychologists of the past 20 years have also agreed on the importance of meaning making in education (Bruner, 1996; Csikszentmihalyi, 1997; David, 2001; Eaude, 2008; Gardner, 1999a; Marton and Booth, 1997). Such writers argue that personal meaning may only be found if an appropriate and personalized language of learning is discovered. The personal often starts with questions of identity. Who am I? Who/what matters to me? What matters to us? How do I like doing things? When a teacher successfully introduces such personally meaningful questions, the experience of children is transformed as passion enters the curriculum.

The provision of multiple aids to understanding does not obviate direct teaching of facts and skills. The human child, and adult for that matter, seems to learn best through interpersonal and intra-personal relationships. Most psychologists involved in education argue for balance between structure and freedom, the didactic and the discovery approach (for example, Alexander, 2010; Hallam and Ireson, in Mortimore, 1999). Space in a classroom must be provided for instruction too. Many teachers have therefore taken to choosing furniture for its flexibility. They redesign their classroom term by term, or even weekly, to offer a changing palette of opportunities depending upon the term's theme and the most appropriate teaching and learning styles.

The challenge of working with a conceptual artist

Creative Partnerships UK (a pre-coalition initiative encouraging long-term links between schools and creative practitioners in the community) set up a project about the deliberate marooning of a conceptual artist on a mid-English Channel fort for a month. Local high school children with a wide range of barriers to learning were provided with well-resourced spaces for construction, music and drama activities. Using these spaces, they worked in mixed age groups to provide comfort, entertainment and food for the mind of the marooned artist. These were delivered to him on the dangerous and isolated fort. In the following term, the same groups of 11–14-year-olds worked in art rooms, comfortable common rooms and ICT suites to produce high-quality brochures and visual presentations on the project. Children reported very positively about their experience. The provision of multiple entry points changed the teacher's view as well. As a result of engagement in the project, their teacher said, 'I think at the start it was subject knowledge I was passionate about ... but now I think I'm more passionate about the children's learning and learning something new from each other' (Cremin et al., 2009).

Educational and cognitive psychologists suggest that learning which takes place in a relevant context is learning that sticks and is transferable (for example, Perkins, 1992, 2009; Shepherd, 1991). 'Situated learning' in school starts within a classroom made relevant for the activities the children will follow, but quickly moves to the even richer settings beyond the classroom. In such contexts, meaningful learning is easier to construct. Each context is real world, complex and stimulating. Each needs cross-curricular approaches to provide fuller understanding.

The work of cognitive psychologists suggests that classrooms should be arranged, resourced and 'ethos-ed' to generate intrinsic motivation and help the child become aware of their own thought processes. The concept of the unique environment suggests that we construct classrooms and curricula in which the chances of positive experience are greater than the chances of negative ones. In summary, recent research suggests that teachers need to:

Illustration 6.4   *Positive relationships between teacher, child and resources generate thinking and deeper learning. Photo: Dorothee Thyssen*

- make classrooms visually exciting and change the stimuli often
- resource classrooms so that children find it easy to construct mental images of new concepts
- arrange furniture and resources so that stimulus displays, artefacts, other people, tools, machines and technologies are all used to generate, sustain and deepen thinking
- use space flexibly to allow for teachers to move between being instructors, facilitators, observers and coaches
- capture learning in the classroom environment through celebratory and informative displays, exhibitions, gallery walks and collections
- widen the definition of the classroom to include views, corridor, school building, grounds and locality
- ensure that they spend as much time constructing a positive atmosphere as providing a stimulating room.

Children playing

After a gap of 30 years, greater emphasis has once again been placed upon play. Psychologists and psychology researchers since Jean Piaget have seen exploration, intuition and imagination as key sources of all, and especially early, learning (Claxton, 1998; David, 1999, 2001; DfES/QCA, 1999; Goouch, 2010). Guy Claxton argues that to generate more creative attitudes in children, teachers should make less distinction between work and play. Just is unstructured play with sound is an essential foundation for musical development at any age (Swanwick, 1994, 1999), similar playfulness with words, numbers, shapes, colours, objects, time, place and the physical capabilities of our bodies, provides the ground for learning in other disciplines. Research on the 'Forest Schools' of Denmark, Wales and some counties of England has added weight to the suggestion that simply having the opportunity to play in safe, stimulating environments adds significantly to social skills, self-esteem and positive attitude to learning (Laevers, 1994a; Maynard, 2007). Playing with language, the voice, body sounds, patterns, objects and social situations are part of the controlled risk taking and invention which characterizes childhood (David, 1999, 2001).

The humour, abandon and risk of playfulness have serious purposes for learning. James and Pollard (2008) point to the importance of informal learning in the world of the child. Children may play with power relations and the meaning of things, and this activity supports them in establishing social and conceptual boundaries. Laughter often accompanies play and helps children overcome inner anxieties, but its positive effects are frequently observable in the external world of children too. David has also discussed the importance of the irreverent, challenging and subversive behaviour of young children as they discover personal meaning, creativity and the possibilities of their personality. In play, children learn and practise the rules of their culture or sub-culture. The curricular implications of such observations are many and often cut across traditional subject boundaries, and the Curriculum Guidance for the Foundation Stage (CGFS) (DfES/QCA, 1999) recognizes this. There are times when simply to observe and record young children at play is all a good teacher needs to do to: 'Teachers need without intruding into their "tribal culture" or hijacking children's play, to capitalise on children's highly motivated and playful use of language [roles, objects and places] and learn to celebrate it and use it as a tool for learning' (David, 1999: 28).

At other times, the teacher's role may be to make learning take on the character of play. Opportunities to play with movement in dance, with sound to compose new music, with words to write an original poem or with the concept of roles, symbols or boundaries in history or geography abound in the National Curriculum. Equally, opportunities to play with the links between subjects are overtly encouraged by government advice (DCSF/QCDA, 2010; DfES/QCA, 1999; Ofsted, 2002; QCA, 2005, website). Permission to play with ideas on a cross-curricular level is already given, for example, in the case of drawing:

Illustration 6.5 *Play in the sand, making an imagined world real by involving all the senses*

Drawing, in a variety of media, is associated with play and playfulness in much early years teaching. Children often tell stories through their drawings, talking about what is happening as they draw. In secondary schools the potential of drawing for releasing and articulating ideas, while an integral part of art and design and design and technology (D&T), was also evident in other subjects such as religious education and geography. In one geography lesson, for example, Year 8 pupils produced annotated drawings of the potential effects of particular planning decisions on a local landscape. (Ofsted, 2003, website, para. 21)

Such advice is built upon recognition that children may enter an understanding of a particular subject from many contrasting starting points but it also points to the importance of play. Even at the Year 8 level, children are recorded as playing with ideas about the future through drawing. The recent work of psychologists has simply reminded us of the importance of a fundamental human activity.

Playing across the curriculum

Using an example from the classroom, teach children to take a tiny aspect of their world and weave it into a haiku poem (5 + 7 + 5 syllables). Suggest that the ideal haiku might have two lines of description and one (usually final) line which flips the reader onto a higher plane of thought level. One 12-year-old looking at a single candle in a cathedral wrote, for example:

> A lone white candle
> Hopeful against dark vastness
> Folly or symbol?

After this teaching, take children into the school playground and ask them to identify a tiny object, plant or corner that for a few minutes can be theirs. (They might choose a dandelion clock, a spider's web, a discarded crisp packet – see Illustration 6.6.) Allow them time to reflect and then write and correct their own haikus. On return to class, ask them to gather into groups of five or six and decide on one which might be a good candidate for putting to music. When children have chosen, give them time and resources to construct a piece of music to either accompany or even replace the haiku. It should have the same 'feel' as the poem. They may use the words imaginatively, recite, chant, sing or mumble the words as part of the music, or abandon words entirely and let the sounds speak for themselves.

Illustration 6.6   *Here a teacher joins in the haiku writing exercise with the children*

Research on the significance of play from Piaget, through Bowlby to Claxton or David, suggests that teachers should:

- consider plentiful opportunities for children of all ages to play with ideas, materials and senses

- shift the balance of their teaching towards the playful aspects of their subject
- not fear failure and encourage adventurousness
- observe children's play to get ideas for teaching
- play with the application of the skills in one subject to the understanding of another.

Children and their feelings

Psychological insights point to the importance of what we *feel* to be true about ourselves and our likes and dislikes. Goleman has brought together a considerable weight of research by neuroscientists and psychologists such as Bandura (1994), Damasio (1994), Ekman (2004), Gardner (1993), LeDoux (1999), Salovey and Sluyter (1997), and Saron and Davidson (1997) to support his notions of emotional and social intelligence (Goleman, 1996, 1999, 2006).

The identification of personal engagement in and ownership of the curriculum has been a favourite theme of UK educational writers too. They maintain that positive views of the self as a learner, a belief that mistakes are part of learning and a feeling of personal emotional security are fundamental to transferable learning. The focus on learning rather than teaching has arisen partly in recognition of the stubborn and sizeable 'tail of underachievement', disaffection and feelings of social exclusion which still remain after decades of government education initiatives intended to address them (Abbs, 2003; Arthur and Cremin, 2010; Black and Wiliam, 1998; Gipps and MacGilchrist, 1999; Halpin, 2003; Pollard, 2008; Seltzer and Bentley, 1999). The *Good Childhood* report (Layard and Dunn, 2009) showed how the sense of well-being has been compromised for many young people in our post-industrial societies. Whilst the USA and UK have become increasingly rich, there seems no appreciable increase in recorded happiness indicators (Layard, 2005; UNICEF, 2007). One UK government-sponsored report noted that depression and chronic anxiety are the biggest causes of misery and incapacity in Britain amongst 16–60-year-olds (Layard, 2006).

Schools, their staff and their children are all affected by the alarming statistics on depression. Encouraging debate on children's and teachers' feelings about themselves must be central in this new social context, and psychology has important contributions to make. Educational psychologists offer some practical answers chiefly through cognitive behavioural therapies, but they also offer teachers corroboration of their intuitive and experiential professional knowledge of children's learning. Good teachers quickly develop a knowledge and understanding of what works to promote children's learning but, if they are unsupported, often lack confidence to fully and adventurously apply it.

Illustration 6.7 *Look for the smiles and other facial signs of involvement in life and learning in classrooms*

The debate regarding children's and teachers' feelings about themselves and their learning, hinges on values. How highly do we value individual happiness? What is the importance of individuality? Where do we place children in our hierarchy of value? What is the value of a school, a community, a society? Educational psychologists are not above such questions, indeed they are subject to the same pressures and worries as the rest of the population, but they often offer some corroboration for the intuitive and experiential knowledge that teachers and others who work closely with children develop.

The sense of inclusion or exclusion deeply involves feelings. If a child or family feels excluded in school, it is unlikely they will enter into any meaningful learning contract with school. At its fundamental level, inclusion concerns each individual's emotional response to the people in institutions with which they come into contact. The internationally acclaimed research of Ainscow, Booth and Dyson (2006) has contributed centrally to the debate on inclusion in our schools. Their work, initially written against the background of the institutional failures exposed in the Macpherson Report on the murder of Stephen Lawrence (Stephen Lawrence Inquiry, 1999, website), suggests that a forensic examination of the social and structural character of our schools is essential before many adults and children begin to feel included.

At a personal level, finding an emotionally significant entry point to any subject is a powerful route to deep learning. Writer Peter Abbs (2003) suggests that not only is education a cultural and cooperative occupation but that it also has to be seen by the learner as an *existential* activity to be effective. Psychologists from Freud and Jung to Frankl, Seligman and Davidson remind us that the search for meaning is a typical human attribute. Sadly, the age-old pupil question, 'Why do we have to do this?' continues to be seen as a threat rather than a plea for personal relevance.

We have already seen neurological corroboration of the assumption that we learn better when we are happy. Psychologists confirm this intuition too. Recently, schools of 'positive psychology' have been established by psychologists who have argued strongly for a renewed focus on aspects of psychology which seek to study enrichment of the human mind rather than just its repair. Physio-psychologist Barbara Fredrickson and colleagues (Fredrickson, 2009; Fredrickson and Branigan, 2005; Fredrickson and Tugade, 2004) suggest, for example, that remembered states of 'positive emotion' provide a bank of positive scenarios which support us in developing resilience in times of difficulty. In her 'Broaden and Build' theory of positive emotions (Fredrickson, 2004), she argues that states of positive emotion such as calm, interest, security, fascination, joy, elation and love provoke the ability of the mind to broaden its 'thought-action repertoire'. By this she means that when we feel good, we are more able to make new links, explore new ideas, places or materials and make new and deeper relationships. She also suggests, from a wide research base, that adults in states of positive emotion show a significantly enhanced ability to build new ideas, to be creative and to integrate past knowledge and present circumstances. In states of prevailing negative emotion, she notes that experimental subjects were less able to think of new ideas, build relationships or explore possibilities.

A positive mindset results in a strong sense of 'self-efficacy', the ability to persuade oneself that one is able to reach a particular goal or set of goals (Bandura, 1994; Baron and Byrne, 2004). Numerous psychological studies have suggested a strong link between positive engagement with others and an expressed sense of well-being. Even more have shown that negative emotional experiences have a detrimental effect upon health, relationships and longevity (for example, Fraser-Smith et al., 1995). Scientific study now provides evidence that constructive relationships, affirmative experiences and an optimistic mindset can positively affect learning, intellectual activity, physical functioning and enduring personal resources (for example, Fredrickson, 2004; Isen, 2002). Positivity should never, however, obstruct moral stands against injustice and unkindness – it must be developed within a values framework.

Teachers do not have the time to read these serious and often tentative scientific studies, and it is left to others to summarize and apply their conclusions to schools and teachers. Inevitably, the work of these scientists is oversimplified and conclusions are overgeneralized. Popular books and courses of guidance on 'accelerated learning' (for example, Smith and Call, 2000), whilst sometimes accused of being based only tenuously on psychological evidence, have successfully challenged and changed the character of teaching

Illustration 6.8   *A positive experience shows itself in the detail and concentration shown by this five-year-old redesigning his playground*

towards a more inclusive, engaging and effective curriculum. It is perhaps unhelpful to demean such developments, considering the alternative of doing nothing to make the curriculum more engaging.

Research in psychology on the importance of emotions in learning suggests that teachers:

- make inclusion a priority
- create a classroom life which seeks to generate the secure, relaxed, fully engaged or exciting feelings we call happiness
- promote positive relationships in the classroom and school as a priority
- seek emotionally relevant starting points – 'speak to the heart'.

Children and language

From our first moments, language forms a key part of our environment. The six-month-old baby is able to recognize the specific nuances of her mother's language, probably by its dominant tunes and musical tones. Until the child is two or three, they may learn the *exact* tones and tunes of any world language they are exposed to – as Patricia Khul says, they are true citizens of the world. After our infancy, however, it becomes increasingly difficult to speak a foreign language exactly as it is spoken (Khul, 2002). There are possibly windows of opportunity for language development, opened at different times during a child's development that make language acquisition a programmed affair. Understanding seems to develop before spoken language, fluent and grammatical speech; using the home tongue or tongues come next and the detail of 'foreign' languages may come after. If we are deprived of opportunities to develop language until the age of 12, the case of *Genie* suggests that it may be difficult to learn any language (Jones, 1995).

The language we use and the ways in which we use it are powerful means of constructing the emotional and social setting within which learning might occur. Many parents and teachers recognize truth in Chomsky's arguments that the growing mind is dependent upon a brain apparently already wired up for language learning. Chomsky also argues for the existence of a universal grammar. Regardless of theory, style and philosophy, language is clearly the chief means of most school learning. An understanding of what Pinker (1994) has called the 'language instinct' is considered by many teacher educators to be a prerequisite to good teaching. Our brains seem prepared for ever more complex, symbolic and abstract uses of language, but clearly these need exercising. The challenge for the teacher is to continually find ways of enhancing the talk of children. Language can be significantly improved by attention to the learning context, and a recent study by anthropologist Shirley Brice Heath illustrates this well:

Research in the classroom

Language is so much part of what we as humans are, it is hardly surprising to find researchers identifying a pivotal role for language in a project linking art with science. Shirley Brice Heath watched and recorded the interactions between early years children and an artist provided by 'Creative Partnerships' over a year. She observed that whilst using drawing to help them understand aspects of the natural world, children's language developed as strongly as their understanding of science and art. She points out that in concentrating on drawing detail, careful observation of skulls, eyes, the face and fruit, children were subconsciously naming the minutiae of what they were observing, and refining their language accordingly. Their language skills – fluency, use of vocabulary, expression – were all significantly enhanced simply by the act of focusing so strongly on single objects during the act of drawing or painting. Their use of complex language not only improved dramatically through working with a 'real' artist, but Brice Heath notes that the types of language they used in art was remarkably similar to the language needed for science because both disciplines 'testified to the power of curiosity, fascination and mobility of thought'. She noted also that in talking about their art and the art of adult artists, ordinary children aged just 4–6 used complex, multi-syllabic words, and expressed complex and sometimes profound and emotional thoughts (Brice Heath and Wolf, 2005).

Language is inherently creative. We create new sentences moment by moment, and with great ease, to provide commentary on the unique situations which we encounter. We cannot assume that this commentary goes on in all households, however, and one of the roles of the school could be described as establishing a minimum base of language experience in a population. Helping children play with language is seen by many as a vital component in developing their creativity. Creativity requires more than simple consciousness of the moment – it requires, as Damasio puts it, 'abundant fact and skill memory, abundant working memory, fine reasoning ability and language' (Damasio, 2000: 315). The more words children can play with, the bigger their world can become (Deutcher, 2006, 2010). Language progressively gives children the ability to translate feeling and thoughts into words, and words back into feelings and thoughts. It gives them the ability to classify and to express the imaginary, and to be still more creative.

There is a language of learning too. When teachers and children build a shared vocabulary regarding learning itself, learning is enhanced. The language of metacognition has been vital to children finding success with Guy Claxton's *building learning power* programme, for example (Claxton, 2006, website). In metacognitive contexts, the ability of humans to be conscious of themselves means that children learn quickly to identify and improve the fine detail of their own learning. By using evaluative conversations, reflections, talking about their learning strengths and difficulties, they become conscious of themselves as 'independent learners'. How did I learn that? What difficulties did I find? How could I do it better next time? How did I deal with that distraction? How did I memorize that? Do I need to practise? Whatever the shared language of learning, it can be reinforced by being made visible in wall displays and social with 'talk partners' or a sustained learning dialogue with adult learners. In various commercial or 'home-grown' ways, cognitive psychology suggests that specific language should be used by children to track their own development as learners, thus externalizing and extending their learning.

Role play, 'hot-seating', discussion, 'exploratory talk', problem solving and making sense of authentic situations are time-honoured ways of extending language and the deepened thinking which emanates from a broadened language world. The National Literacy Strategy (NLS) and other strategies of the past six years may, however, have had the effect of diminishing the use of classroom dialogue, through an unintended narrowing of the curriculum (Smith et al., 2004). Guidance from the DfES/QCA (2003) used research findings from linguists, anthropologists and psychologists to reaffirm the importance of genuine dialogue, drama, debate and discourse in improving the speaking and listening of children aged 3–14 (see Illustration 6.9).

Recent work on language suggests that teachers should be aware that:

- the language world of children should be extended daily (Khul, 2002)
- art, music and science can very effectively stimulate language development (Brice Heath and Wolf, 2005)

- children should have multiple and contrasting opportunities to play with and extend their language world (David, 1999; Deutcher, 2010)

- using words to explain feelings, problem-solving techniques, new understandings, differences and similarities is an important part of extending learning (Shayer and Adey, 2002)

- teachers should strive to use the language of thinking: *hypothesis, hypothesize, believe, predict, guess, think, suggest, understand, compare, contrast, metaphor, analogy, analyse,* and so on (see Costa, 1991)

- teachers should provide a clear sense of progression in the complexity of language within a real context (Perkins, 1992).

Children and flow

The environment is, of course, not simply physical. We have already seen how classroom atmosphere can become the all-pervasive influence on what and how much is learned. There is general consensus that the most productive of

Illustration 6.9 *Children role playing an argument. The class notes down the changes in language they use. Photo: Dorothee Thyssen*

learning atmospheres is one in which all participants are fully involved in learning. Ferre Laevers is well known in Europe for the *Leuven involvement scale* (Laevers, 1994b), which attempts to measure such engagement. Differences occur when psychologists, pedagogs and others argue about the way to construct such an atmosphere. One answer has come from Hungarian psychologist Mihalyi Csikszentmihalyi, who coined the term *flow* to describe that sense of deep engagement (see Illustration 6.10). We are said to be in a state of 'flow' when we experience: 'that almost automatic, effortless, yet highly focused state of consciousness, which is so enjoyable that we will seek it at considerable risk and expense to ourselves' (Csikszentmihalyi, 2004, website).

These moments of flow remain treasured parts of our memory and seem familiar to all audiences in all cultures. From asking thousands of people from a wide cross-section of cultures, socio-economic backgrounds and ages, what this state of total involvement feels like, Csikszentmihalyi constructed the following list. In these periods of deep and satisfying engagement:

- time seems altered
- skills match the challenge presented
- present worries fade
- self-consciousness diminishes
- confidence is strong
- the activity is engaged in for its own sake
- there is a sense of fusion between self and activity
- there is rapid feedback (usually from the self).

Illustration 6.10   *Lost in the music. This five-year-old shows signs of flow as she listens to her favourite music*

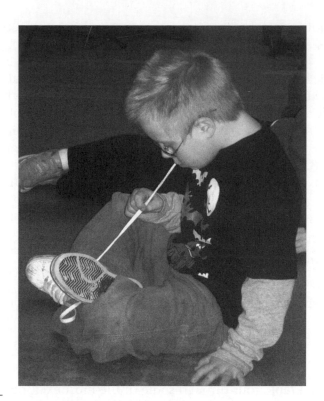

Illustration 6.11 *Concentration may show itself in many ways. Photo: Cherry Tewfik*

In further questioning, researchers discovered that apart from sex, the most common conditions to provoke the state of flow was during creative or physically challenging activity. Flow was not common when watching television or resting, neither was it recorded as being particularly prevalent in school, although frequently particular teachers were credited with stimulating it. These findings suggest that a curriculum which gives plentiful opportunity for physical and creative activity is one which would be most likely to generate flow amongst its pupils. This conclusion is of much more than academic interest, because Csikszentmihalyi goes on to argue that the condition of flow is the optimum condition for learning.

Many teachers will have experienced situations where children are in flow, for example when children are so involved in an activity in class that they do not want to go out to play (or come in *from* play!). Laevers describes such total involvement as follows:

The child is clearly absorbed in his/her activities. His/her eyes are more or less uninterruptedly focussed on the actions and on the material. Surrounding stimuli do not or barely reach him/her. Actions are readily performed and require mental effort. This effort is brought up in a natural way, not so much by will power. There is a certain tension about the action (an intrinsic not an emotional tension) ... the signals concentration, persistence, energy and complexity abound. (Laevers, 1994b: 39)

In the specific context of children and schools, Csikszentmihalyi has controversially recorded that the greatest concentration of flow activities are found in school club activities and practical sessions, in homes with plenty of books, in poorer communities, in children with *fewer* technological aids at home, in families where discussion is common and in families where group activities are common (Csikszentmihalyi, 2004, website).

Work on involvement or flow suggests, therefore, that teachers consider:

- providing more opportunities for creative activity in all subjects
- finding more time to involve children in physical/practical activities
- making more field trips and visits
- encouraging discussion both at home and in school
- encouraging the availability of a wide range of club activities.

Summary

We have made a rapid tour through some of the most exciting work in modern psychology. The conclusions are necessarily oversimplified and perhaps reductionist, but the work of these leaders of the field demands a thoughtful response from teachers. Much of the work discussed was not designed for direct application to the classroom, however many teachers will recognize the congruence between these findings and their own professional judgements. Gardner himself, in the introduction to the second edition of his book introducing the theory of multiple intelligences, writes:

> Whilst working on 'Frames of Mind' I viewed it principally as a contribution to my own discipline of developmental psychology and more broadly to the behavioural and cognitive sciences. I wanted to broaden conceptions of intelligence to include not only the results of paper-and-pencil tests but also knowledge of the human brain and sensitivity to the diversity of human cultures ... my eyes were not beamed toward the classroom ... In fact however the book has exerted considerable influence in educational quarters ... Psychology does not directly dictate education, it merely helps one to understand the conditions within which education takes place ... (Gardner, 1993: xii–xxvii)

Such thoughts remind us that what psychologists say is tentative, not focused on the realities of the classroom, and is always provisional (see White, 2002). Teachers must make daily decisions which affect children's lives and do not have the luxury of investigating ideas enjoyed by the experimental psychologist. Nonetheless, each research finding cited in this chapter has possible implications for schools and their curricula. Each has cross-curricular ramifications too. In summary, current psychological research suggests to teachers that:

- we should not blindly accept IQ, background, current ability, socio-economic status or apparent learning difficulty as a limit on children's aspirations or our aspirations for their learning
- we should see intelligence as learnable and the mind as malleable
- we should make the generation of thinking one of our prime concerns
- we should be concerned about the whole physical, social, spiritual and emotional environment for learning
- we should consider seriously whether a positive, affirmative and happy environment produces better teachers and learners
- we should reflect on and research the effects of multifaceted, contextualized and relevant learning settings
- we should carefully plan the learning experience of children to include a balance of instruction, coaching, facilitating and challenge
- we should seek to maximize on those learning experiences which promote flow or involvement
- we should take care to enrich understanding and perception by a particular concentration on new language acquisition.

Key questions for discussion

- How can we construct within our schools shared, social, intellectual and physical environments which optimize the chances of positive experiences for each individual?
- Do we need to change the curriculum to do this?
- If so, how must we change the curriculum to make the positive and secure learning experience more likely?
- Do we agree that we want children to be steered by a set of positive experiences in school?
- What sorts of positive experiences do we feel would be most valuable?

Further reading

Claxton, G. (2003) *Building Learning Power*. London: TLO.
Csikszentmihalyi, M. (2002) *Flow: The Classic Work on How to Achieve Happiness*. New York: Ebury Press.
Fisher, R. (1999) *Head Start: How to Develop Your Child's Min*. London: Souvenir Press.
Pollard, A. (2008) *Reflective Teaching: Evidence-informed Professional Practice* (3rd edition). London: Continuum.

CHAPTER 7

Cross-Curricular Pedagogies

'Start from where the children are.' This exhortation has been given to teacher trainees for generations. It can sound glib, simplistic, even idealistic, and yet as pedagogical advice it has profound implications for teaching philosophy, style and the curriculum itself. Paulo Freire, Brazilian activist, educator and thinker, clarifies the meaning of this big idea:

> The educator needs to know that his or her 'here' and 'now' are nearly always the educands' 'there' and 'then' … The educator must begin with the educands' 'here' and not with his or her own. At the very least, the educator must keep account of the existence of the educands' here and respect it. You never get *there* by starting from *there*, you get *there* by starting from *here*. This means ultimately that the educator must not be ignorant or underestimate or reject any of the 'knowledge of living experience' with which the educands come to school. (Freire, 1994: 47)

The daily lives of children should be central to curriculum decisions, but the 'here and now' of today's children is clearly not a homogenized whole. Children growing up in certain areas have to add the fear of gangs and gun crime to the 'traditional' fears of childhood. Happily, many still experience an ideal childhood of mindfulness, playful exploration, security and fulfillment, but significant numbers face the additional challenges of parental poverty, joblessness and alcohol, food or drug abuse. Such well-researched aspects of twenty-first-century life, plus the sometimes malign influence of the internet, mass media, celebrity and consumerism are obvious features of national and state life (see James, 2008, for example) and yet our nationally prescribed curricula almost ignore them. If, in Freire's words, we wish 'to change a wicked world, recreating it in terms of making it less perverse' (Freire, 1994: 55), issues from the daily and weekend life of children must feature in their weekly curriculum. The coalition government of 2010 reminded us of the flexibility within the existing national curricula, the possibilities for creative interpretation and the need to build more partnerships between the community and schools (*TES*, 2010, website). Such comments may suggest continued support for the well-justified, planned and understood integrated and creative curriculum, but the increased freedoms promised by government will be tempered by a prevailing 'back to basics' sympathy encouraged by the Department of Education's reading of Hirsch (1999).

Modern approaches to teaching in the UK and USA are a mix of liberal, constructivist ideologies and the economically driven language of competition, targets, objectives and accountability (see Arthur and Cremin, 2010). Beyond liberal Westernized education systems, however, and in the minds of many Western parents, the *delivery model* of teaching and learning is remarkably resilient. The delivery model suggests simply that schools are places where the teacher transmits packages of 'worthwhile' knowledge to children – worthwhile knowledge usually being defined as what the powerful have found useful. The view that in school children learn what teachers teach, seems to most lay people the obvious and proper way things should be. 'Traditional' pedagogical methods are however singularly inappropriate in a twenty-first-century society. The growth of the internet and other ICT, the general acceptance of scientific method, secularism, multiracialism, diverse communities, modern psychology and neuroscience, the politics of liberation, equality and children's rights have challenged and changed teaching. Aware of the growing gap between the educational experience of rich and poor children, many now argue for fundamental change rather than a retreat to 'tried and tested' methods (Ainscow et al., 2006; McCauley and Rose, 2010; Raffo et al., 2010; RSA, 2010 website).

Clarity of purpose, however, remains vital. Teachers' experience is central to the debate on the aims, values and function of education. As powerful agents of change and challenge, teachers work with, and think about, children's experience for much of their lives and build up an incomparable body of expertise and evidence. Teachers may be consulted with regard to public policy on education, but many feel their views are not adequately represented or consulted, perhaps because pedagogy is still not seen as an academic subject in the UK. The word *pedagogy* denotes what Pollard (2010) calls the 'art and craft' of teaching. Pedagogy is the fusion of theoretical knowledge, practical experience, environmental management and intuitive response demonstrated minute by minute in the practice of the 'good teacher'. Through daily interaction with large groups of children and their lives, the best teachers quickly become experts on:

- motivation
- social learning
- communication through good pedagogy
- creative solutions
- barriers to thinking and learning
- values.

Illustration 7.1   *The teacher physically coming down to the child's level will help equalize the relationship*

Motivating children

Motivating children is central to the work of the teacher. Children may derive motivation from a range of sources. They may be engaged by *belief* about the relevance of a subject so a teacher may need to appeal to, or attempt to change, beliefs in order to involve a particular child. They may be motivated by *fear* or a desire for *acceptance*, by *respect* for a teacher or *love* for a subject. Children may be motivated by the wish to *reach a goal*, to be *involved* in a specific activity or *to please someone* else. The expert teacher will orchestrate such diverse motivations in an attempt to involve all in the task ahead. In a culture where the child's voice is heard, the teacher may frequently follow the children's lead, opportunistically combining knowledge meaningful to them with life skills relevant to their community.

Social learning with the teacher

In the world of work beyond schools, most people work in teams and these teams tend to contain people with different skills and strengths. The 'economic' justification for group work and shared projects in schools is that they prepare children to contribute more fully to an economy where people work in teams. But perhaps

Illustration 7.2   *This student teacher in dancing with children demonstrates a playful aspect of social learning*

a more profound justification lies in the suggestion that working together, sharing experiences and solving problems in groups is beneficial to the physical and mental health of the child now. Self-awareness, empathy, motivation, managing feelings and social skills are obviously best developed in some kind of social setting. As current Department of Education and Department of Health (DoH) advice (DoE, 2010, website; DoH, 2005, website) make clear, such skills are not simply caught; they need to be taught within a whole-school framework.

Teaching social, emotional and behavioural (SEB) skills should not be a separate activity. Opportunities arise naturally from a curriculum designed around children's participation in meaningful, shared experiences and shared responses. Research quoted by the Department of Health/Department for Education and Skills (DoH/DfES, 2005) suggests that academic achievement, self-esteem, personal responsibility, mental health, tolerance of difference, workplace effectiveness, behaviour and sense of inclusion are all positively affected by a curriculum and ethos which takes SEB seriously.

Since the Labour government's *Excellence and Enjoyment* primary strategy (DfES, 2004c, website), schools have begun to abandon the perceived straitjacket of a rigid interpretation of the NLS and NNS. A more flexible approach, never specifically outlawed, is now evolving in many schools and this is encouraged by a new education administration. Teaching approaches which

Illustration 7.3   *Emotional and interpersonal aspects of learning dominate the day for both teacher and child*

use 'thinking partners', group investigations, problem solving, role play, links with other subjects and practical situations are now common. This change of style takes account of different school and cultural contexts, various styles of thinking and learning, multiple emotional needs and a variety of ways of showing intelligence. In best practice, the teacher becomes part of these groups and shares learning with the children.

> Recently, an experiment in alternative modes of teacher education, The HEARTS project (Barnes and Shirley, 2007; see Chapter 3, case study 7) took the idea of 'teacher as learner' still further. Third-year student teachers were given the opportunity to work in small groups of six Year 7/8 children on an open-ended project to 'capture the essence' of an unfamiliar place. They were instructed to avoid the words 'you' or 'I' and to give the role of deputy to any budding child-leader who arose in their group.
>
> Neither students nor the children knew the place. They only knew they had to prepare a presentation on the essence of the place for the whole school the following day. For this two-day session, there were no lesson plans, no clear objectives, no differentiation and no assessment criteria. The challenge strongly focused both students and children. The results of the two-day challenge were 15 powerful, inventive and highly creative presentations which were very well received by the school. But a key finding for researchers monitoring this approach was that students remarked that the social nature of the activities resulted in their feeling that they understood the children for the first time, though facing the same challenge together.

Illustration 7.4 *Classroom teachers rediscovering their own creativity on a staff development day*

Pedagogs may come to a variety of conclusions from examples like the case study above, but a number of issues are worth discussion:

- Are children genuinely working collaboratively when placed in groups?
- Are we as teachers genuinely planning and constructing opportunities to learn alongside children?
- Do our groups promote social, emotional and behavioural skills?
- Have we got the balance right between direct teaching and social learning?

Communication through good pedagogy

Formulaic, one-size-fits-all approaches to teaching are still very evident. To a degree, Initial Teacher Education (ITE) has fallen behind some of the more innovative and adventurous primary schools. The 'Standards' for Qualified Teacher Status (QTS) (TDA, 2008, website; TTA, 2003) have spawned a pragmatic approach to the preparation of teachers in which *training* has become the operative word. Initial Teacher Education courses and various series of teacher education publications encourage a 'training manual' approach to the art of teaching. Many books on how to achieve QTS are dominated by grids and instructions which advise on how to demonstrate the standards but give less help as to *how* to make curriculum choices that promote learning and thinking. There is a tendency to fall back on bland exhortations such as 'aim for effectiveness through efficiency' and the admission that successful teaching requires a considerable degree of confidence and practice (Hayes, 2003). Perhaps such confidence can only come after many years in the job, but since so many leave teaching in the first five years, maybe our ITE and in-service courses need to consider how their own students can themselves become deeper, more creative learners and enjoy the job satisfaction of more creative teaching and learning.

Teachers and teach*ing* have a vital role in promoting and shaping children's learning, but learning and teaching are not the same. The idea that armed with a basket labelled 'tips for teachers', teachers will effectively teach and children learn, denies the utter complexity of children's (and adults') minds. Ivan Illich reminded us in the early 1970s that most learning happens outside schools, casually and as a by-product of some other activity (Illich, 1971). The skilful and open-minded teacher recognizes that children come to school with a rich understanding of their world, which is already entrenched and largely sensible, but knows he or she can help the child develop and shape that knowledge. Understanding and respecting the child's world, his or her popular culture and 'knowledge of living experience' is very important for the student teacher, but the successful teacher needs more. Illich and that other arch progressive, Freire, also recognized the importance of discipline, the teaching of skills and subject knowledge. The good teacher should look for the deeper meaning of the content being taught, but not shy away from occasional decontextualization and simple direct teaching. The strongly motivated pupil, says Illich, 'may benefit greatly from the discipline now associated with the old fashioned schoolmaster' (Illich, 1971: 20). The disciplined approach to learning was as important as respect for the lives of the learners. Freire puts it clearly:

> Teachers who fail to take their teaching practice seriously, who therefore do not study, so that they teach poorly, or who teach something they know poorly, who do not fight to have the material conditions absolutely necessary for their teaching practice, deprive themselves of the wherewithal to cooperate in the formation of the indispensable intellectual discipline of the students. Thus, they disqualify themselves as teachers. (Freire, 1994: 69)

The teacher, in other words, should balance respect for the child's world with a craftsperson's skill at their subject, pedagogy.

Current advice on teaching effectively should take serious account of the child's world. Today their world is one in which children learn from their peer group, television and other media, but also still very much from adults. Gardner (1993: 34–8) has suggested three ways in which children learn from adults: direct or *unmediated* learning, where the child observes an adult

Illustration 7.5 *Roles are reversed as a child leads a 'blind' teacher in investigating an environment*

engaged in activity; *imitation*, where the child reproduces the actions of an adult who deliberately models them; and *outside the context* learning in which a skill is introduced and practised under adult supervision but in a situation unrelated to the need for the skill. He notes that most formal learning within 'modern technological societies' occurs in specialized institutions far removed from the context in which the knowledge will be applied. By implication, this would suggest that the de-contextualized learning which has become dominant in Western schools, leaves out major opportunities for unmediated and imitation learning.

Significantly, more children would reach their potential in school settings which valued the practical, creative, physical, spiritual and interpersonal as much as the symbolic and logical. Perhaps we should re-examine some old metaphors for teaching and learning, like David Feldman's 'The child as craftsman' (Feldman, 1976). In his analysis, Feldman suggested that teachers looking to an uncertain world future should start by seeing the child as a person who *wants* to be good at something, take a pride in his or her work and feel an increasing sense of mastery over an area or areas of experience. Feldman argues that:

- the sense of engagement and purpose involved in doing what one feels good at is not possible without developing the related subject knowledge
- mastery cannot be aspired to without a belief that knowledge and understanding within the field can be continually enhanced

- a child's capabilities can only truly be assessed once we have identified an activity which truly engages them
- what might personally engage child craftspeople will be found within 'the full range of activities that enrich and sustain social life … and diverse occupations' (Feldman, 1976: 144).

To work within this idealistic framework, teachers, Feldman suggested, combine four different teaching roles:

- To teach the core skills and knowledge of writing, reading, number, citizenship required by society for all, but to ensure they are taught in meaningful contexts.
- To teach bodies of knowledge in a range of other subject areas chosen by community or school and considered necessary for all children.
- To discover the 'propensities and proclivities' of each child and then to organize resources progressively to 'further the child's mastery'.
- To promote each child's engagement through introduction to and progressive guidance in the principles, key skills and attitudes of discrete areas of knowledge they have chosen.

As children develop between 3–14, they should have increasing opportunity to refine and deepen the subject areas which teacher and child have jointly identified as personally engaging. Working in a school community which 'fosters commitment, satisfaction and joy in accomplishment' (Feldman, 1976: 146) will require each child to go beyond the limits of their current understanding of their chosen craft. This, I would suggest, is especially likely when groups attempt to solve problems or examine a shared experience. Recent work by David Perkins has corroborated this analysis. Perkins (2006, 2009) suggests that children need experience of 'playing the whole game', undertaking holistic endeavours that make learning meaningful and engaging'. Playing *any* whole game involves receiving coaching, learning the rules, having opportunities to play 'junior versions' of the game, identifying with the experts, having chances to play and be affirmed publicly and, of course, finishing it. In the social settings which involve playing the whole game or being an apprentice craftsperson, children are likely to learn creatively. They will inevitably make unexpected links and connections between areas of knowledge, experience and relationships.

Such observers of teachers teaching suggest that we consider the following advice:

- Show respect for the child's background.
- Give attention to subject knowledge.
- Learn the arts of pedagogy.

- Identify the areas of strength in each child.
- Find what engages each child.
- Give plentiful opportunities for holistic, contextualized and meaningful learning.

Illustration 7.6   *Head teachers rediscovering the child in themselves*

Creativity (for teacher and child)

Creativity is one of a small group of features which distinguishes humans from other animal species. We know that birds, primates and dolphins may show a degree of creativity in their responses, but in terms of capacity, breadth and expression it is surely a quality which marks out our species. The ability to be creative currently makes us different from machines too. Arthur Koestler's (1964) definition of creativity which involves *bisociation* – the often unexpected coming together of two contrasting planes of thought – is central to understanding the purpose of cross-curricular learning. Creativity, according to Csikszentmihalyi, is 'a central source of meaning in our lives' (1997: 1). Its apparent rediscovery by governments, advertisers, economists, planners and many teachers may be a belated realization of the importance of maximizing those abilities which make humans distinctive. The language of *creative teaching, creative thinking, creative learning* and *teaching for creativity* in schools is a reflection of this preoccupation, but treating it as a temporary fashion would risk losing for many children all that is

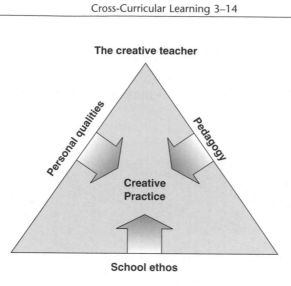

Figure 7.1 Creative practice depends on the interplay between a teacher's personal qualities of creativity (such as curiosity, humour, adventurousness, flexibility and enthusiasm), a creative pedagogy based upon multiple opportunities to make links and a child-centred supportive ethos established in the class and school

humanizing and sensitizing in the impulse to be creative. A number of government initiatives have creativity at their heart and in their title (Creativity, Culture and Education, 2010, website; HC, 2008; Ofsted, 2010; QCA, 2003, website) and provide further evidence that government advisers have accepted the advice of teachers, neurologists and psychologists that relevance is central to learning.

There are other important factors influencing creative learning too. The teacher's personal qualities, the ethos of the school and its particular pedagogical style all impact on the learning of the child. For learning to be creative, a particular set of characteristics needs to apply to each category.

The creative teacher (Figure 7.1) will be a personality who typically is playful, enthusiastic, flexible, committed and involved. His or her teaching style will commonly be personalized to the child, respectful, trusting, diverse and with a clear learning focus. The ethos in which the child is most likely to learn how to respond creatively is safe, secure and supportive of adventurous thinking (Cremin et al., 2009).

No kinds of learning can be 'conferred' on the child, but motivation to learn comes from many sources. Throughout time, good teachers have discovered myriad ways of creating relevance and engagement so that children will want to learn. Through force of character, story, anecdote, humour, display, drama, movement, music, games, debate, surprise, visits and visitors (but also by pressure, stress, threats and tests), teachers capture their audience. Ask a cross-section of teachers when their class seemed most engaged, most happy to work through playtime, and it is likely to have been during some kind of sensory creative or physical activity, perhaps a combination of all, such as a

Figure 7.2 The creative state of mind recognizes an inherent creativity in itself. Recognizing its own creativity may help it generate more connections, originality, questioning and autonomy

game, play, concert or dance. Research (for example, Brice Heath and Wolf, 2005; Harland et al., 2000) confirms the massive motivational and positive affective impact of the arts and artists in education, but the potential for motivation spreads far beyond the arts into every subject of the curriculum. Creative approaches to teaching and encouraging the whole range of creative activity can do far more than motivate, however; they can also engender the new connection making we earlier described as thinking (Cremin et al., 2009; Grainger et al., 2004).

Teaching is a creative act relying continually on chance meetings of ideas and materials, curiosity, flexibility and adventurous thinking. Although each teaching and learning situation is unique, there are a number of characteristics which seem common to most creative teachers. Creative teachers are simply those who adopt and apply a creative state of mind. This mindset on the part of the teacher seems particularly effective in promoting creativity in children. The core characteristics which appear to recur consistently in creative teachers and which result in creative practice are:

Illustration 7.7   *Collaborative creativity: a group of 14-year-olds planning their visual response to a haiku*

- curiosity and questioning
- connection making
- originality
- autonomy and ownership.

Thinking and barriers to thinking

Much of what we learn, whether creative or not, involves thought. Wherever we live and whatever we are doing, a stream of thoughts accompanies most actions. Through devoting focused attention to an aspect of our world, we bring together past and present thoughts and, if we do this with others, we also incorporate some of their thoughts as well. In thinking, groups of neurons also make connections. We know that these connections become insulated and 'hard-wired' if they are recalled or reused a number of times. We generally recycle such connections when they are relevant and meaningful to us. Thus, if we think, rethink and think *about* our thinking, we learn. If we agree that *learning* is one of the consequences of thinking, the obvious question the teacher must ask is, 'Am I promoting thinking in what I plan to do with these children?'

Children can be helped to think more productively and satisfyingly. A whole range of books on thinking for primary and secondary school children have become popular with teachers who recognize this important aspect of their role (see, for example, Fisher, 1999; Higgins et al., 2003). We know, however, that there are myriad barriers to children's thinking too. Good pedagogs are aware that they may be barriers themselves. Through reflection and evaluation, an effective teacher can consider the impact of his or her own differing thinking or learning styles, school or class ethos or interpersonal difficulties before blaming the child for not learning.

The good school will constantly ask itself the question, 'Have we erected barriers to children's thinking which are stopping them learning?' Is the 'hidden curriculum' that Illich referred to in the 1970s, stifling personal growth? One way of answering such questions is to use the comprehensive, whole-school approach recommended by the *Index for Inclusion* (Booth and Ainscow, 2002). The Index starts with questions for school self-evaluation, examining fundamental values and the way they influence school policies, practices and cultures. Going through such a procedure quickly reveals the hidden and often unarticulated barriers to inclusive practice in a school.

Children already know many of the barriers that hamper them. One Year 5 teacher in London recently took her children into an empty playground and gave them just such a theme to examine themselves. This is what she observed on her 'Barriers and boundaries' mini topic:

Barriers and boundaries

It did not take long for the children to realize that the list would consist of more than walls and fences – and they began to become engrossed as they came to realize that nearly everything can be a barrier or boundary – including flower beds, stinging nettles and other people. They began by asking 'Can I put down … ?' and when I asked them what they thought, and explained that there were no right and wrong answers so long as they could explain their reasons, they were unstoppable. We walked the rest of the school the next day, and if anything the children were even more motivated than the day before – there was no bad behaviour and their lists grew. One child working at level 1 in writing (and who had not produced more than a line or two of writing for me to date) produced a list of 30 items, often correctly spelt and all legible.

Illustration 7.8   *The open face of learning in an atmosphere of trust. Photo: Cherry Tewfik*

In class, we divided the lists into three columns: physical barriers and boundaries, signs (from the children's lists) and invisible barriers. We started the last column with language, which they had already identified, and the further suggestions (attitude, silence, culture, racism, hate, loss of senses, words) were very thought-provoking and although received mainly from children of high ability, were not exclusively so. Had there been time, there was a wealth of opportunities for the children to have more freedom to explore themes in Citizenship, PSHE, Literacy and Drama, Geography, RE, ICT, History and PE/Dance.

Given control of the agenda, children in the above example made multiple and unexpected connections. They were learning and, as the teacher noted, children were linking apparently unrelated areas (like spelling and concentration). Affording children this kind of respect, establishing dialogue between teachers and children, building on the 'social capital' already present in children's lives and their community, and making their 'lived experience' a focus of education are approaches powerfully argued by Freire. He was also one of the first modern pedagogs to stress the importance of learning to learn.

Teachers and all learners gain considerably by thinking about their own learning. Modern developments in psychology and neurology have helped us to learn more about the conditions in which we are likely to learn best, but few teacher education or in-service courses offer advice on *who* to learn from. Of course, the children we teach are rich sources of learning. Recent experiments where trainee teachers were instructed to pass the locus of control to children for an arts and the environment project (Barnes and Shirley, 2007) provoked significant and positive changes in students' respect for children as well as promoting major learning progress in the children involved.

As teachers, we should constantly and consistently examine our impact on the ethos of our institution and our classroom. The advice of key pedagogs suggests we consider:

- how we help children think
- where the barriers to learning are
- what are the unseen influences on the wider curriculum and atmosphere of the school
- the range of sources of learning we employ
- how to engage all children in satisfying learning.

Values: revisiting old absolutes

In a postmodern world, conscious of few anchor points, it is interesting to see an academic and educationally focused re-evaluation of 'old-fashioned' concepts such as 'hope' (Freire, 1994; Halpin, 2003; Wrigley, 2005), 'good' (Csikszentmihalyi, 2003; Gardner, 2004; Gardner et al., 2000), 'wisdom' (Craft et al., 2008; Sternberg, 2002), 'happiness' (Layard, 2005; Morris, 2005; Seligman, 2004) and 'love' (Bowlby, 1988; Darder, 2002; Goldstein, 1997; Goldstein and Lake, 2000). Pedagogs such as Comenius, Freire, Pestalozzi, Rudolf Steiner, Montessori, Dewey, Isaacs and Malaguzzi were unabashed at using terms like these. The progressive education philosophies of the past were anchored in clear understandings of such concepts, which were for them the ultimate purposes of education. These words, holding concepts that most of us feel we understand, remain personally powerful regardless of our religious or political beliefs. Perhaps they should be near the top of our consciousness as we think about the curricula our children follow. Old absolutes still form the basis of the 'here' and 'now' for most of us. Improving the emotional atmosphere of a school may involve using community discussions on hope, wisdom, love and good to help change many entrenched attitudes and practices.

We may need to examine our own institution critically and ask difficult questions. David Halpin, for example, feels that schools often fail to provide a learning environment which leads to a broad sense of security. He reminds us of proto-psychologist Sigmund Freud's use of the German word *sicherheit* (translated as 'security'). Freud regarded *sicherheit* as the chief gift of civilization and, by inference, the prerequisite for education:

> This word manages to squeeze into a single term, complex phenomena for which the English language needs at least three terms to convey – security being one, and certainty and safety being the other two. According to Freud, all three ingredients of 'sicherheit' are conditions of self-confidence and self-reliance, on which the ability to think and act creatively depend. The absence or near absence, of any of the three ingredients has much the same effect – the dissipation of self-assurance and the loss of trust in one's own ability, followed in quick succession by anxiety and growing incapacitation. (Halpin, 2003: 110–11)

For Halpin, no child should leave school feeling a loser. Equally, no teacher should end a school day feeling depressed. The cross-curriculum is well placed to turn the dream of a *liberating curriculum* into reality. Through it, children can be freed to be children. Teachers are in a persuasive position to work with communities towards achieving this utopia. They need only to agree on the meaning of the four exhortations at the end of Terry Wrigley's (2005) book, *Schools of Hope*:

- We need commitment to a better future.
- We have to be visionary.
- We must dare to dream.
- We will have to rethink education and not simply improve schools.

Summary

Even in today's largely secular, increasingly diverse and global culture, we cannot escape the fact that education is value laden and attitude rich. The values we display either consciously or in the equally powerful 'hidden curriculum' will not always match the official values of the school. Neither will the values of today be the same as those which sustained very different societies of the past. If we do not address values, then the learning experience of the

Illustration 7.9 *Fourteen-year-old pupils performing their own musical composition about a garden in the garden which generated it*

child has no coherent context and perhaps the majority will find little meaning in it. We should therefore not dodge questions such as:

- Who decides on what 'worthwhile knowledge' is?
- What is *good* behaviour?
- Who chooses the topic under discussion?
- How can we agree?

A suggested way forward is to focus on children's well-being and that of parents, teachers and others working with children (Young Foundation, 2010). This means discussing the questions above in the light of agreed concepts of well-being and designing a curriculum based around achievement, enjoyment, experience and personalized ways of making sense of the world. I would suggest that this is most possible through teachers and children working within a flexible, responsive and relevant curriculum.

Key questions for discussion

We should keep the debate open and free from extremes, and be aware of the provisional nature of any of our decisions on what worthwhile knowledge and good pedagogy is. In the light of previous chapters, key questions a school might ask before rethinking its curriculum might be as follows:

- Do we (adults in school) feel fulfilled and secure as people *ourselves*?
- Are we modelling lifelong learning?
- Is the teaching and learning in our classrooms promoting each child's well-being?
- Is the social, spiritual and physical environment we control helping to develop positive attitudes to learning and the self?
- What is the role of popular knowledge?
- Does each child have an opportunity to find and develop an area of expertise?
- Is the physical, emotional and intellectual environment we control keeping them safe?
- What content *should* we teach and learn? Who selects it and how do we decide how it is to be taught?
- What is the role of the teacher?
- Are schools able to change the world?
- Is our curriculum giving hope?
- Are we teaching wisdom?
- Is this school preparing all to make a positive contribution to future society?

Such questions are not very far from those posed by Plato, Comenius, Rousseau, Pestalozzi, Froebel, Dewey, Plowden or Alexander. As professionals, we are in a strong position to use the daily experience of today's successful primary teachers to help us judge which are the most appropriate attitudes, what is the most useful knowledge, the most helpful skills for children's lives *now*. Because we also serve society, we also need to seriously consider what kind of people we want to shape this increasingly fragile world in the coming years.

Further reading

Craft, A. (2005) *Creativity in Schools: Tensions and Dilemmas*. London: Routledge.

Freire, P. (1994) *The Pedagogy of Hope: Reliving the Pedagogy of the Oppressed*. New York: Continuum.

Richhart, R. (2002) *Intellectual Character: What It Is, Why It Matters and How to Get It*. New York: Jossey-Bass.

Wrigley, T. (2005) *Schools of Hope: A New Agenda for School Improvement*. Stoke-on-Trent: Trentham Books.

CHAPTER 8

What Principles Should We Apply?

We are all driven by our values. If we want to be effective teachers, we should be clear about why we want to teach and what we hope for children to learn in our classes. Teachers and children both need opportunities to develop their values and to have chances to discuss them. A thriving school is a place where debate about principles and big questions is alive and well. David Perkins once remarked: 'the quality of an organisation can be measured by the quality of its conversations' (Perkins, 2002). The conversations he was referring to were the ordinary daily chats in staffrooms, by the water cooler, in the playground and on the way to or from school. Overheard snatches of dialogue in successful schools are often sensitive, caring and concerning the deepest purposes of education. Such conversations feed and inspire novice teachers as they refine their values (see Gardner et al., 2000). They also sustain the seasoned teacher in times of pressure and doubt (see Barnes, 2011).

Schools need to subscribe to values as collegiate institutions. Without a clear and well-understood set of values, no organization can move very far forward. For some time, schools have published in their compulsory prospectuses 'mission statements', 'key aims' or 'overarching goals' outlining the values which underpin pupils' spiritual, moral, cultural and social development through curriculum and other activities (DfES, 2002, website). These statements can be the vital and often revisited core of everything schools do or little more than another bit of paperwork to be done before the next inspection. The US Department of Education's *No Child Left Behind* policy (USDE, 2002, website) and the UK's parallel *Every Child Matters* (HMG, 2004) have focused the attention of schools, local government, health authorities, social services and education policy on matters of principle. This is evident, for example, in the preamble to the abandoned proposals made by Sir Jim Rose for the primary curriculum for schools in England (DCSF/QCDA, 2010). The first section of this document is headed *Aims, values and purposes*, and seeks to establish clarity about underlying principles and to encourage schools to do the same. Similarly, Alexander (2010)

The sphere of shared values

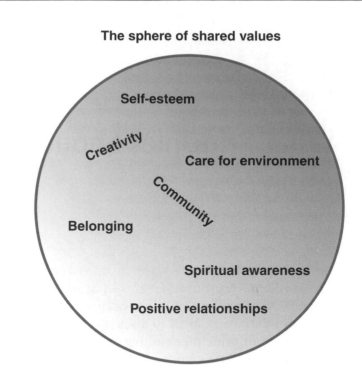

Figure 8.1   The sphere of shared values: discussing core values should be the school's first, most frequent and most important conversation

considers values early in his comprehensive survey of and proposals for the child's world and education.

Schools keep their values alive by talking about them (Jeffrey and Woods, 2003). The sphere of shared values, however, will be different in every school. Perhaps before they embark on any other discussion, a school community – teachers, children, leaders, support staff, parents and governors – should together decide on their individual and, eventually, collective answers to some of the following questions.

- What is education for?
- What is our attitude to children?
- How should adults behave towards children?
- What kind of children do we want our children to be?
- What kind of adults do we want our children to become?
- What kind of education do we want our children to have?
- What kind of education do *children* want to have?
- What are the most important issues for this community?

(Continued)

(Continued)

- What assumptions do we make about the wider context of which education is a part?
- What sustains, motivates and gives the adults in the school community optimism for the future?
- How can we build hope into children's lives through the curriculum?
- What things do we treasure most?

Taking the last two points first, it is arguably the teacher's prime professional responsibility to be optimistic (Booth, quoted in Dismore et al., 2008; Halpin, 2003). This optimism might stem from religious, political or philosophical beliefs, from a shared but non-religious spiritual understanding or from a deeply felt, personal attitude towards humanity, children and the environment. There will inevitably be a variety of answers, but even embarking on conversations which aim at shared understanding is valuable. A rational discussion on the meaning of education goes straight to the roots of our thinking. Education helps us all make sense of our lives and our world.

We mostly learn what is truly and personally relevant to us. In a postmodern, Western, educational context, Peter Abbs argues that without existential engagement there is no deep learning:

> education cannot take place against the intentions of the student or without his or her active participation … Learning may be released by the teacher but it can never be conferred – for it is not an object so much as a particular cast of mind, a creative and critical orientation towards experience. The student has to learn to be the protagonist of his or her own learning. (Abbs, 2003: 14–15)

The concept of education itself lies outside any single morality or world view. Education takes place in *any* and every cultural setting but only becomes really effective when it is meaningful. Meaning may be generated by fear, economic, cultural, political or religious obligation, duty, ambition, pleasure, self-fulfilment, self-actualization or a desire for the loss of self. In secular societies, the challenge is to find a commonly acceptable formula which can bring shared meaning to all. The outcome of such discussions, seriously held, should profoundly affect the content and organization of the curriculum.

There are a number of starting points for such discussions. The UK government provided a 'statement of values' by the National Forum for Values in Education and the Community (DfEE/QCA, 1999: 147–9) when the curriculum was revised after the Dearing Review. The Standards for Qualified Teacher Status (TTA, 2003) charges teachers to show 'positive values' and treat children with respect and consideration. Forty governments throughout the

Illustration 8.1   *A typical primary school classroom in action*

world lent support to the *Index for Inclusion* (Booth and Ainscow, 2002) which, through its sections on creating inclusive cultures, establishes a firm link between values and the curriculum. Japan's Soka schools, inspired by education philosopher Makiguchi, and the Ghandi-inspired schools of India, are inspiring attempts to link values, pedagogy and curriculum. More generally, the UNESCO-supported Association of Living Values (ALIVE website) is an example of an international organization offering support to schools wishing to think about their values.

Appropriately, half of the discussion questions above contain the word *children* and representing the child's voice in making curriculum decisions is now commonplace (see Burke and Grosvenor, 2003; Catling, 2005). Valuing the views of children alongside the experience and (hoped for) wisdom of adults ensures lively interchanges and broad-based support for and understanding of school policy. From an adult perspective, we might want education to promote creativity, make the world a better place, address the key issues of the day. Teenagers, however, may take a much more instrumental view of education, at best seeing it as the route to a better job and at worst totally irrelevant to their aspirations (Popenici, 2006). On the other hand, adults may feel that education should make our children more obedient, less challenging or more aware of 'high culture'. Either way, the curriculum will be the route through which we attempt to agree upon and achieve our aims.

Illustration 8.2   *Peace Art: school children in Uganda have worked with schools in British Columbia to turn their war toys into a whitened peace sculpture. Anthropological Museum, British Columbia, Canada*

One suspects the school curriculum would look very different if the world of 3–14-year-olds were truly taken seriously and represented.

As an example, let us take several commonly cited but general aims of education, gleaned from school websites:

1   To promote a feeling of well-being for all children.
2   To ensure that the beliefs and values of the Christian/Jewish/Muslim/ Sikh/Hindu/Buddhist faith underlie all we do.
3   To support the development of self-esteem and personal responsibility.
4   To promote lifelong learning.
5   To develop high standards across the school, striving to reach and go beyond national standards in all subjects and key stages.

These aims clearly imply a specific ethos which, in turn, should require particular approaches to the curriculum. Perhaps a progressive, creative and child-centred curriculum is suggested by the first aim. If we want to ensure that a particular religious belief system 'underlies all we do', our playground expectations, lunchtime rituals and our science, geography and English curricula will be affected as much as the RE curriculum. If we are aiming to support the development of self-esteem, this should show itself in the behaviour policy, but also has implications for the ways in which adults relate to each other as well as how they teach. The fourth aim focuses on positive attitudes to learning, whilst the last aim reflects the realities of a pluralist society.

Illustration 8.3   *Walking the talk: children from the Scottish Children's Parliament leading adults on their 'health and happiness' march. Courtesy of Scottish Children's Parliament*

None of these aims is likely to have come from children, though all can be readily understood and acted upon by them. They will most likely have been decided upon in good faith, by adults who feel they know what is best for children. It is surprising, however, that few school aims directly mention the environment, sustainability, relationships, new technologies or the global dimension.

Detailed aims such as the following examples may have more precise implications for their schools' curricula:

- To appreciate all forms of human achievement: scientific, literary, mathematical, artistic, physical, humanitarian and spiritual. (Wingrave C of E Primary School, Buckinghamshire, prospectus accessed 21 July 2005)

- To enable children to become innovative and creative learners who achieve the highest possible academic, artistic and technical standards throughout all areas of the curriculum. (Priory School, Slough, accessed 21 July 2005)

- Our school community is multi-cultural and we promote equality of opportunity, valuing all members of the school equally, regardless of race, class, gender and culture and we encourage religious tolerance through understanding. (Castlebar School, Ealing, prospectus accessed 20 October 2005)

- To be aware of the world in which they live and to realize they have both obligations to society as well as rights within it. We therefore see social interaction as an important factor in their education. (Marlborough Primary School, Wiltshire, prospectus accessed 21 July 2005)

- We aim to produce understanding citizens of the twenty-first century who recognize the need to participate in a caring and responsible way for the sustainability of our world. (St Mary's C of E (Aided) Primary School, Staffordshire, prospectus accessed 21 July 2005)

- The provision of philosophical and moral discipline and training through the visual arts and to maintain a state of intellectual and artistic development across all ages ... a belief in the importance of each individual's integrity, and the importance of the expression of that individuality. (Room 13 Scotland, 2005, website accessed July 2010)

Whilst words like *their, creative, obligations, produce, discipline* and *human achievement* may not have come directly from children, there is a sense that the realities of the children's world may have influenced these aims. There is perhaps a greater emphasis on enhancing and explaining the lives of children here and now, not simply preparing children for a future (adult-envisaged) world.

What, then, are the beliefs and values which might underpin the establishment of a curriculum which promotes cross-curricular links and activities? Some suggested principles may be linked under the five main categories:

1 Learning
2 Knowledge
3 Teaching
4 Children
5 The world.

The principles listed under these headings are not meant to be comprehensive, but are the expression of a personal ideology based upon 35 years in teaching. As such, they are fully open to criticism, major alteration, rejection and many additions. Use the suggested principles to prompt discussion about the principles *you* would argue for in your school. Each principle is intended to provoke a discussion resulting in whole-school agreement and implementation. Each can also be used to examine one's personal beliefs and attitudes towards education.

Beliefs about learning

As already discussed in Chapters 4, 5, 6 and 7, current work in social science, neurology, pedagogy and psychology has added much to our understanding of learning. However, the word 'beliefs' in the sub-heading is not accidental. Ultimately, as professionals in education, we have to decide what we believe to be right and true about learning. Hopefully, these beliefs will not be

Illustration 8.4 *Deep learning comes from deep thinking – these Year 2 children show signs of both*

uncritical or closed but based upon experience, our own research, reflection, conversation, knowledge of research and the theoretical perspectives of others, and always open to discussion. Some current beliefs might be summarized for discussion in the following list.

- There are many different ways of thinking and understanding ... each child has their own way of being bright.
- Generative topics and challenging experiences provide motivation to question, problem-solve and find answers.
- Learning is a consequence of thinking.
- Emotional, practical and personal engagement are essential to learning – group work, particularly in promoting conversation and other means of communication, is an effective way to promote learning.
- Modern technologies are powerful ways of promoting, sustaining and deepening learning.
- The resources that support intelligent behaviour do not lie only within the mind and brain, but are distributed throughout the environment and social system in which we operate.
- Learning happens in quiet, reflective and solitary moments too.

(Continued)

(Continued)

- Deep transferable learning is best facilitated by a general sense of 'positive emotion'.
- Applying the skills and knowledge of the subject disciplines is an effective way of making sense of experience.
- Children can learn how to learn through an introduction to metacognition and aids to thinking – intelligence is partly learnable.
- Enjoyment is an important part of the development of positive attitudes towards learning, self and community.

Such beliefs about teaching and learning can be linked into four categories: beliefs about *individual* learners; beliefs about working in *groups* or communities; beliefs about the importance of *environment*; and beliefs about subjects or *the disciplines*. These four aspects of pedagogy might be seen as the professional framework of beliefs which can be used to guarantee the liberation of the individual spirit.

Such beliefs do not become principles until they start to dictate action. So after discussing individual beliefs and attitudes, it is necessary to decide if they can be turned into a fixed statement about teaching, upon which all stakeholders can agree. Thus, a belief that each child may have their own way of being intelligent might be turned into the principle: 'We will act on the understanding that all children have different ways of showing intelligence'. Beliefs about the importance of enjoyment in learning may be expressed in the principle: 'We will seek daily opportunities to promote enjoyment of

Illustration 8.5   *Each individual expressing their own response to freedom. Courtesy of Scottish Children's Parliament*

learning'. In their briefest form, the agreed beliefs about education above might be expressed as the following principles.

We will:

- help each child discover his or her strengths and interests
- use relevant, powerful and challenging experiences to motivate learning
- attempt to promote high-level thinking in all learning situations
- ensure learning is practical and physical
- seek out emotional/personal links between desired learning and learner
- make frequent use of genuine group work
- find opportunities for solitary and reflective activity
- use modern technologies to support and encourage learning
- endeavour to create a sense of security and well-being in all
- help children learn to learn
- promote enjoyment of the learning process
- ensure all children have opportunities to achieve.

Illustration 8.6   *Drawing focuses the eyes and also the mind so that both visual and linguistic skills improve. (Brice Heath and Wolf, 2005; Creative Partnerships Kent, 2005)*

Understandings about knowledge

For most teachers, the only opportunity to think at length about their knowledge comes during their Initial Teacher Education. ITE, however, is so dominated by 'school experience' and assessments against standards that too little time is devoted to understanding knowledge. Knowledge is different from information. A library or the internet is full of information but this inert mass of data cannot become knowledge unless it is somehow internalized, organized and made relevant to the individual. Knowledge is not absolute but a matter of choice and degree; we never have 'the knowledge', rather we move towards what our culture says it is. It helps, however, if a teacher feels they are more knowledgeable, in at least one area, than most people (Cremin et al., 2009). The following list of statements about knowledge is arbitrary and personal, but can form the basis of a discussion on 'What is knowledge?'

- Knowledge outside the classroom is cross-curricular and organic in nature. It is not confined to single-subject disciplines.
- Knowledge is not absolute, but a matter of degree.
- Knowledge may be constructed through education.
- What constitutes worthwhile knowledge should be agreed upon by those involved in it.
- Progressive understanding of subject disciplines is essential to effective learning.
- All subject disciplines are equally valuable in understanding the world and no group of subjects should have special status.

If we found that we agreed with these statements of belief, then making them imperatives would turn them into whole-school principles which might underlie planning and teaching behaviour. The list might therefore start as follows.

We will:

- look at the world in cross-curricular ways
- get to know the school locality very well
- be open to change
- involve all in deciding what we should know
- use subject disciplines as useful ways of 'chunking' knowledge
- treat all subject disciplines as of equal value.

Attitudes to teaching

'Everyone remembers a teacher', said the Teacher Training Agency (TTA) advert. Many of the celebrities in the annual National Teaching Awards remember enthusiastic, encouraging, inspiring, caring, fascinated individuals

Illustration 8.7   *Teacher and pupil working together to display ceramic tile prototypes generated from looking very closely at a medieval building*

who clearly enjoyed teaching. Much research confirms the powerful impact specific teachers had on the development of individual interests and careers (see, for example, Csikszentmihalyi, 1997: 174–6). Perhaps understandably, little research has been carried out in the sensitive area of the damage teachers and schools have done to the confidence and self-image of pupils. Anecdotal evidence and emerging empirical research (see, for example, Riley, 2006) suggest that many teachers are fully aware that at times they feel driven to humiliate and emotionally harm children.

As in all areas of life, teaching is influenced by attitude. Our attitude towards teaching defines what and how we teach and our attitude to ourselves frames what kind of people we are. Research has suggested that simply ascribing words such as creative, original, expert or caring to individual teachers often makes a very significant difference to their feeling of worth and their confidence as teachers (Barnes and Shirley, 2005; Cremin et al., 2009). The need to feel we are 'making a contribution' is as important for the teacher as it is for the child. School leaders need to be fully aware not just that their staff is the crucial resource, but that each individual's personal sense of well-being is essential to the proper functioning of the school (Barnes, 2001).

A greater focus upon teacher well-being would transform staff development programmes. Currently, most staff development time is taken up by addressing externally driven initiatives, revising administrative requirements, preparing for or following up inspections, or making school self-evaluations or pupil assessments. Necessary though these may be, staff development time exclusively

Illustration 8.8 *Teachers planning creative activity for themselves in a staff meeting*

devoted to these things does little to develop staff as people. In contrast, the implementation of a planned and focused progression of personally engaging learning activities for staff is likely to transform both atmosphere and achievement in a school by positively changing adult attitudes. If five days per year were assigned to building up the intellectual, cultural, spiritual, physical and social lives of each staff member, current poor rates of teacher retention and recruitment are likely to improve.

Among the attitudes school leaders, teachers and others involved with children could consider developing are the following.

- The confidence to encourage 'safe risk taking', playing with ideas, using the imagination; a belief in the importance of making the time and opportunity to reflect on successful and not so successful lessons.
- The determination to avoid restrictive formulas with regard to teaching and earning.
- An enthusiasm for developing creative teaching behaviours.
- The expectation that teachers will plan genuine opportunities for creative thinking and action.
- An expectation that teachers will seek opportunities to develop their own creativity and interests as part of their staff development.
- A belief in the importance of formative assessment in adding to challenge and taking children forward.
- An awareness that their own subject knowledge can and should be constantly improved.
- An understanding that working together with staff with other areas of expertise enriches teaching and the experience of children.

Illustration 8.9   *A teacher dances a sea shanty with a group of children, enjoying their world with them*

Changing such attitudes into workable principles may mean using more child-friendly language to express them. It also makes very clear what the individual teacher is 'signing up to' by being part of the team.

In this school, teachers will:

- expect children to have fun
- plan activities aimed to interest children
- work with children to make the school a better place socially
- work with children to improve life in the community and local environment
- help children risk new ideas/uncertain answers
- give children time to think and dream
- make space for unique answers
- strive to be creative themselves
- help children achieve their plans and dreams
- try to include all children
- constantly be adding to their own knowledge
- work with each other to make lessons more engaging.

Attitudes towards children

If teachers' positive attitudes to themselves are an important part of strong cross-curricular planning, then positive, even idealistic, attitudes towards children are also necessary. Idealism does not have to deny the everyday realities of working in real, overcrowded, under-resourced classes and communities, it simply attempts to look beyond and above present realities to a positive and possible future. As well as being optimistic, maybe it is also the teacher's job to nurture the kind of idealism which many of them expressed during their job interviews. This idealism may be essential to maintaining the positive frame of mind which so often characterizes good teachers. Such optimism can be summarized in the following attitudes:

- a belief in providing frequent and multiple opportunities for children to discover what interests them as individuals – to develop passions
- a belief in the importance of education as meaning making in a social setting
- an understanding that the child's world is different from the adult's and that this needs to be taken into account when planning activities, curricula and environments.

Put clearly as guiding principles for a whole school, these attitudes might read as follows.

We will:

- provide the basic knowledge and skills children need to make a positive contribution to their world now and in the future
- help children see themselves as budding experts in a chosen area of knowledge
- help children see themselves as creative beings with original thoughts
- help children find personal meaning in school activities
- help children understand love and caring as central attributes of being human
- understand that the world of our children is different from that of adults
- support children in feeling good about themselves
- look from the child's eye view and value it.

An informed adult view of the world of the twenty-first century

The emphasis on children in the preceding paragraphs is an attempt to help redress the adult-centred balance of primary education. It would be wrong to assume, however, that adult views, beliefs and knowledge should be ignored or sidelined. We have seen too (Chapter 1) that, through the internet and television, today's children are much more in touch with global issues than in the past. Thompson and Giedd's research (Thompson et al., 2000; see also Chapter 5) into the maturing brain has reminded us that adult minds are in some ways very different to those of children. Adults may more easily see consequences, look into the future and plan strategies. At our best, we adults

Illustration 8.10   *Neuroscience confirms the human tendency to seek, use and create patterns from the earliest ages*

can offer the wisdom of experience, a wider perspective, and a more balanced and broad-based approach to knowledge and experience. However, there are as many adult viewpoints as there are adults – reality TV and the news remind us of this daily. Teachers, working with classes of children from families whose views range from permissive and liberal to fundamentalist and conservative, are charged with representing and understanding them all.

It is also expected of teachers that they prepare today's children for life in the world of the future. We currently believe that international and cultural conflict, pollution, water supply issues, unequal distribution of resources, AIDS, climate change, overpopulation and unfettered technological and scientific advance will colour the twenty-first century. Issues like these already impact upon our children's lives. It is probably essential that today's teachers have a view on these issues and address them at some level within the ITE curriculum and the curriculum children follow when in school.

As a starting point for discussion, the Royal Society of Arts (RSA, 2005, website) has usefully published its list of the 15 'global challenges' for the twenty-first century. These could form a basis for discussion. Each item requires a principled response; beneath the adult language, each raises an issue upon which children in our classes will already have a view. Each question can, at a practical level, be understood by a three-year-old, whilst each can be philosophically considered by a 14-year-old. Perhaps these or the United Nation's millennium goals (UN, 2000, website) could prompt discussion leading towards whole-school agreement on the big ideas behind school conversations, curriculum and culture.

The RSA's '15 global challenges' arose from their 'Future Gazing' Report in 2005 (RSA, 2005, website). What are the implications for education, the curriculum and our attitudes to children?

1 How can sustainable development be achieved for all?
2 How can everyone have sufficient water without conflict?
3 How can population growth and resources be brought into balance?
4 How can genuine democracy emerge from authoritarian regimes?
5 How can policy making be more sensitive to global long-term perspectives?
6 How can the global convergence of information and communications technologies work for everyone?
7 How can ethical market economies be encouraged to help reduce the gap between rich and poor?
8 How can the threat of new and re-emerging diseases and immune micro-organisms be reduced?
9 How can the capacity to make decisions be improved as the nature of work and institutions changes?
10 How can shared values and new security strategies reduce ethnic conflicts, terrorism and the use of weapons of mass destruction?
11 How can the changing status of women help improve the human condition?
12 How can transnational organized crime networks be stopped from becoming more powerful and sophisticated global enterprises?
13 How can growing energy demands be met safely and efficiently?
14 How can scientific and technological breakthroughs be accelerated to improve the human condition?
15 How can ethical considerations be more routinely incorporated into global decisions?

Summary: what have principles got to do with cross-curricular learning?

Every age has its major challenges. The big difference in this millennium is that the challenges cannot be kept local. Our global economy, instant communications and global pollution have meant that whatever happens in one place quickly affects every other. If they want it, ordinary adults, and particularly teachers, are now in a position to exert some influence over the interrelated future of this world. To do so effectively, teachers and children need to be very clear about (a) what they value most and (b) what parts of our society, environment and the wider world they feel we can effectively influence. The answers to these questions and those like the

UN's or the RSA's global challenges could and should underpin all our education decisions.

This book suggests that a cross-curricular approach is the approach most suitable to addressing core values in the learning context of children's own lived experience. I have selected and examined four key areas where the formulation of shared values in a school is a pressing need: learning, knowledge, teaching and children.

Each of these areas is subject to a number of often contrasting beliefs and attitudes. A school's first priority is to work towards turning its combined beliefs and attitudes into a set of agreed principles, which will inform all decisions about staffing, resources, curriculum, time management and classroom organization. Such principles will also guide school self-evaluation and parents' and children's views on the achievements and qualities of the school. A school's statement of principles, or its fundamental aims, should be the result of an in-depth and frequently revisited conversation between all stakeholders. In many ways, this conversation is the most important policy decision that the school can make. The discussion on school principles should:

- involve parents, governors, children, volunteers and other adults working in the school, as well as teachers and the head teacher
- be regularly discussed and often revised
- be used to make internal evaluations of the success of the school
- be expected to be used by both stakeholders and external bodies to judge the quality of the school.

Teachers are amongst the key individuals who can help our populations face the unprecedented challenges of the twenty-first century. They must therefore have a clear understanding of global issues and a principled view on how to help tackle them. Teachers must start by becoming growing, learning, positive and interesting people themselves.

Key questions for discussion

- What do we stand for as school teachers and a school?
- What do we believe is important in framing our teaching?
- What has all this to do with the UN's millennium goals?

Further reading

Gardner, H., Csikszentmihalyi, M. and Damon, W. (2000) *Good Work: When Excellence and Ethics Meet.* New York: Basic Books.

Halpin, D. (2003) *Hope and Education.* London: Routledge.

Robinson, K. and Aronica, L. (2010) *The Element: How Finding Your Passion Changes Everything.* London: Allen Lane.

CHAPTER 9

What Themes are Suitable for Cross-Curricular Learning?

> The brain learns best and retains most when the organism is actively involved in exploring physical sites and materials and asking questions to which it actually craves the answers. Merely passive experiences tend to attenuate and have little lasting impact. (Gardner, 1999a: 83)

Any subject can be suitable for cross-curricular learning. Themes as disparate as a well-read story, a visit from the community police officer, a child's visit to relatives in Tyneside or Tobago, the death of a beloved hamster, the discovery of a spider's web in the playground or a birthday trip to the adventure playground, can all generate deep learning. Any topic presented with enthusiasm and careful planning can be approached using the skills and knowledge of almost any discipline or help children forge links between different areas of knowledge. I have argued that personal significance and limited subject focus are important features of successful projects, but so too is the learner's own sense that they are learning.

External features such as postural, facial and attentional characteristics are probably the most accessible indicator that a child might be learning. Laevers (1994b) argues that signs of *involvement* are the first we should look for. His and other's work has suggested that signs of genuine involvement in learning might include:

- facial expressions of enjoyment, concentration and motivation
- a bodily posture of positive tension
- relaxed relationships with peers and other co-workers
- a performance which matches or exceeds the known capabilities of the child
- a reluctance to be distracted.

In addition, and in the light of the emphasis I have placed on principles (Chapter 8), we should also consider whether the kind of learning happening could be described as:

- worthwhile
- meaningful
- good
- right

or

- helping develop 'big' concepts like beauty, truth, justice, etc.

Research into deep learning suggests that those who strive or who are helped to make *meaningful* connections between themselves and new knowledge, retain and are able to transfer their understanding more effectively. This approach to learning was implicit in Plowden (DES, 1967) and was picked up by researchers contributing to the Alexander Review (2010) (see Chapter 2). A combined interest in fostering knowledge for its own sake, establishing a broad and balanced education and enhancing thinking skills are common features of schools attempting to create a curriculum accessible to all (Ofsted, 2009a,b).

Meaningful projects

In the 1970s and 1980s in our patronizing way, many teachers chose topics which we 'knew' children would be interested in. Topics like 'pirates' or 'buried treasure' were popular with teachers. We argued that all children liked pirates, lots of their films and books were about them and we'd all read and enjoyed *Treasure Island* as children and seen the TV serializations too. Whilst there were stunning examples of very motivating, memorable and successful 'topics', I believe we were mistaken in many of our choices. Certainly in my classes, children quickly saw through the pirate maths and pirate RE, pirate poems and pirate geography. They tired easily of measuring planks to walk upon and 57 doubloons plus 25 doubloons was still just 'sums'. Whilst the complex 'Topic Webs' we constructed were often impressive and should have won prizes for ingenuity, they shoe-horned subjects into spurious themes and the deepest thinking was the teacher's. Indeed, provoking *thought* in children was possibly the last thing on the teacher's mind and any sense of relevance came more by luck than judgement. Children were indeed more engaged than in the days of simple 'chalk and talk' but perhaps we omitted to ask whether such work leads to significantly raised standards. When teachers today say that current cross-curricular approaches are 'going back' to the topics of the 1970s and 1980s, I worry, because there was a great deal wrong with them. How then do we arrive at relevant and contemporary themes and projects which avoid these pitfalls?

I would suggest at the outset that the following guidelines could apply:

1 Consult the children about the theme and key questions.
2 Plan a shared and powerful experience related to the theme.
3 Choose only subjects which clearly add understanding to the experience.
4 Plan the subject skills, knowledge and progression required in each of those subjects.
5 Aim at a state of *flow* in children.
6 Finish with a performance of understanding.

Use the whole-school community as a resource. Chapter 3 demonstrated how some schools have used community links to develop speedy and more deeply rooted learning in children. Working with adults who are not teachers can help some children develop a greater sense of the everyday relevance in their school activity. But a teacher's growing professional and personal understanding of the daily lives of children will increasingly generate relevant and meaningful themes. The aim is to elicit the kind of responses expressed by children in terms like these:

> *It's just like I have discovered a new world of music that I never knew existed.* (Alisha, Key Stage 3 pupil talking about a sound composition project)

> *We were sitting there actually **enjoying** learning.* (Year 7 pupil talking about a history project enlivened by an artist)

> *I'm going to spend my birthday money on getting the equipment to set things up at home.* (Year 8 pupil talking about a pinhole camera project)

Consulting the children

> My dream school would be a school which would let me explore the world and tell me human knowledge ... At the start of every year the children will choose the topics they are most interested in. There are no compulsory time-tables.) Five professors will help the children in each place. Gautier, Key Stage 2 (quoted in Burke and Grosvenor, 2003: 62)

Recent thinking on citizenship in schools draws contemporary attention to the importance of pupil participation (e.g. Alexander, 2001; Potter, 2002; Ruddock and MacIntyre, 2007; Wrigley, 2005). The UN Charter for the Rights of the Child (UNCRC) Article 12, makes it clear that children should be consulted on *all* decisions affecting their lives (UNICEF, 1989, website). The establishment in the UK of the Children and Young Persons Unit (CYPU), Children's Commissioners in England, Northern Ireland, Scotland and Wales (e.g. Children's Commissioner, 2010, website) and other policy implications of *Every Child Matters* (DfES, 2004a, website), means that the idea of the children's voice being heard can now become mainstream. A preliminary research document to the Children Act of 2004 makes the following points in its summary:

- 'Taking account of what children say is what makes their involvement meaningful ...'
- 'Acting on children and young people's views brings positive outcomes in ... increasing young people's sense of citizenship and social inclusion and enhancing their personal development' (Kirby et al., 2003).

So what kinds of theme do children choose? Students are often surprised at the social awareness children display when school councils ask for projects on:

- conservation of the rainforest
- protecting our local environment
- the earthquakes in Pakistan or Haiti
- fair trade
- poverty
- cleaning up our town
- our links with ... [a school in the developing world].

Commercial companies have taken up this moral and politically aware theme amongst our young people. The International Primary Curriculum (IPC, 2006, website), for example, offers popular units like:

- the oil industry
- rulers and governments
- current affairs and the media
- sustainability
- being fit for life
- artists' impressions of the world.

Recent national and local authority developments which will inevitably influence children's curricular choices include:

- the adoption in many schools of 'Circle Time' (Moseley, 1996), aimed at developing empathy, relationship skills and personal values

- the growing local authority and school management interest in emotional literacy (Goleman, 1996; Morris, 2006, website)
- school councils where elected representatives have a meaningful role in school decision making (School Councils, 2005, website)
- pupil representatives on some governing bodies (in secondary schools at least)
- children's commissioners and children's parliaments.

Some schools have always included children centrally in their decision making with regard to the curriculum. In Steiner schools for almost 90 years, parents of each class have regularly met as a body to discuss the curriculum their children follow and general concerns about their children's physical, spiritual, moral and intellectual development. Whilst the curriculum follows a prescribed and adult-led route, the realization of the themes is strongly tailored to the holistic needs of the growing child and the personality of the class. Thus, for example, they study *volcanoes* and *revolutions* at the same time as their bodies and relationships are in the upheavals of puberty.

However, children also continue to love the traditional – a recent survey revealed that colourful and exciting topics of the past are still popular, such as:

- Egyptians
- castles
- Greek legends
- space
- light
- bubbles
- our pets
- Kenya.

When I asked the head of a case study school (Barnes, 2005d) what their curriculum themes would be for 2006, she answered that staff did not know because they had not asked the children yet. Some schools decide upon themes well in advance to ensure curriculum balance or guarantee consideration of issues relevant to school context, policies, aims or philosophy. Others use published schemes or state education policies as starting points. Each of these sources of ideas for projects has its strengths. It is also legitimate for adults to make decisions about what it is important to learn because schools are seen as society's way of inducting the child into itself. However, children can be helped to feel centrally involved in the choice of theme and that the choice is meaningful to them. In a culture which increasingly raises children's awareness of their rights, the school which denies children's participation at the curriculum level is in danger of adding to the atmosphere of disaffection we outlined in Chapter 1.

Planning a shared experience

We all love trips, and we can learn so much from going out and seeing things. Numeracy hour and literacy hour can be boring. LET US OUT! Kimberley, 11 (Burke and Grosvenor, 2003: 75)

Current trends towards individualized learning may run the risk of divorcing us from our physical, social and sensory selves. The now abandoned Digital curriculum introduced by the BBC in January 2006 was targeted on establishing an interactive dialogue *directly* with learners while leaving scope for parents, carers and teachers to mediate the resources. (This digital curriculum proposed catering for up to 50 per cent of National Curriculum coverage throughout the United Kingdom, not only potentially leapfrogging contact with the teacher but also lesson-time interaction with the rest of the class.) A modern manifestation of these same issues is likely – some of our newest schools and 'academies' already boast of their independent workstations instead of classrooms. It is possible, even common, to access the whole curriculum without personally experiencing the real world or getting hands dirty. Having the technology to ensure an education based in cyberspace is possible, but it may not be good.

Personal, social and physical experiences are great teachers. The strength of active, real-world and interpersonal learning is that it will inevitably be interpreted in many different ways and mean something different to each individual. Such variation in response can be harnessed to promote creative outcomes to problems or dilemmas arising from themed study. Active, communal and physical experiences may ultimately be preferred by children because their social, physical and sensory coordination develop first (see Chapter 5). Certainly, shared, dynamic and bodily activity more effectively use the exquisitely combined faculties of touch, smell, taste, feeling, movement and hearing that gave the human animal advantages over other animals. The evolutionary reward for these preferences is in the pleasure creative and physical activity gives us.

If we add our range of sensory accomplishments to the huge species advantages of language, self-conscious thought and culture, then arguments for learning together, in real life and relevant contexts, become difficult to refute.

Most objects and sounds that surround us generate personal memories and associations. These 'objects' (including categories of place and people) form part of the memory bank we unconsciously 'call up' whenever appropriate. If your class shares time at the circus, lakeside, theatre, car park or supermarket, each member will bring a different mind to the experience. Shared experiences can include:

- a public event (such as a carnival, charity fair, parade, Olympics, festival, political or state visit)
- any fieldwork within the school grounds or building
- fieldwork in the school locality or in some contrasting locality (such as on a school activity holiday)
- a visit (to a museum, supermarket, theatre or nature reserve)
- a special visitor (such as a grandparent, local nurse, poet, builder or gardener)
- a themed week (such as a 'Science week', 'Technology week' or 'Africa week') or day (e.g. 'Red Nose Day')
- a performance (such as a play, opera, dance, gymnastics, a musical or concert)
- a collection of objects (from a school collection, museum, school dig or visiting expert)
- a school event (such as sports day, open day, Victorian day or anniversary)
- a combined construction project (such as building an adventure playground, sculpture garden or 'robot wars' vehicle)
- a reflective activity (such as meditation, a quiet day, a church/temple or mosque visit)
- the writing of a class story, set of poems or book based upon aspects of the local environment or using detailed knowledge of a local place as the setting.

Some schools start their cross-curricular theme with a shared activity, whilst others choose to aim for such an event at the end of a term's interdisciplinary work. Any shared event will communicate *something* to participants. Your professional skill is shown in the ability to make something useful from the predictable diversity of response. The 'teacher as choreographer' makes a dance of individual responses to experience and helps craft the responses into a meaningful expression of community and cultural values.

The provision of strong, emotionally engaging experiences has become the stock-in-trade of initiatives like creative partnerships, cultural and community groups, and the various science and PSHE theatre projects touring the country. In a single Local Authority district, a sample of secondary and primary schools have recently based their curriculum around:

- a conceptual artist marooned for six months on a First World War mid-English Channel fort
- the creation of a pair of 'sound mirrors' with one in northern France and the other in Kent

- a cultural, song, games, dance and drama project based on links with a school in Sierra Leone
- the residency of an artist in school for two years
- the building of a new school entrance in an Infants school
- a new school play area in a junior school
- the creation of a community cinema within a community secondary school
- the musical *Jesus Christ Super Star* performed to sister high schools in the USA and eastern Europe as well as to its own community
- the production of a Shakespeare play
- the building of a geodesic dome in the school quadrangle
- the creation of a recording studio in a cupboard for trying things out
- live links, by letter, email and video with a school in Tanzania
- a massive community operatic and dramatic 'event' involving 20 primary and secondary schools, community clubs and organizations in a single district.

Children's voices best capture the impact of such powerful experiences:

The Sierra Leone project was one of the best parts of school in my life. My overall highlight of my time with Usufu was one game, one song and one dance ... when we performed the dance to the rest of the school they were all jealous of us and at the end of the dance the children clapped till their hands were red. Chris, Key Stage 2 pupil (Creative Partnerships Kent, 2005)

... the cupboard lets me learn in my own way, in my own time, by my own choices, its like you are given the helmet to put on yourself, or they put the helmet on *for* you. The helmet that's given to you is your own choice. You can leave it away or you can take it ... that's natural learning and the other is forced learning. (Josh, Key Stage 3 pupil)

Choosing only subjects which add understanding

The cross-curriculum models of the 1970s and 1980s often foundered on the contrived inclusion of *all* subjects on every Topic Web. In today's best cross-curricular practice, only two or three subjects are necessary to bring a balanced understanding to a theme. A serious danger of interdisciplinary work is that the boundaries between the subject disciplines become less distinct and progression within subjects is weakened.

Case study: Research into a cross-curricular project

A school in the USA chose the year 1492 (when 'Columbus sailed the ocean blue') as its theme for a term. Apart from the obvious history focus (What was it like then? What happened? Why? How do we know?), pupils studied from the perspective of science (What is true? How have living things changed over the last 500 years? How do plants adapt to change?), and using a geographical lens, children looked at diverse eco-systems which represented contrasting parts of the country in 1492 (they made a series of maps, discussed human–environment interactions and specifically the impact of humans since 1492). Using storybooks, the internet, non-fiction publications, practical experimentation, fieldwork, the application of mapping and diagrammatic skills, the different perspectives of scientist, historian and geographer were explored. The linking theme of a single year drew children into much wider debates and understandings of the ways in which historians develop interpretations, scientists develop explanations and geographers develop descriptions. The researcher (Roth, 2000) reflecting upon this project noted, however, that science learning within the theme was not as deep as social studies learning.

My own research (Barnes and Shirley, 2007) suggests that in delivering cross-curricular themes, teachers should:

- identify and focus on clear, appropriate, subject-based learning objectives
- continually monitor the depth of understanding by informal assessment during the activities
- avoid compromising subjects in efforts to 'fit them' to a theme
- be prepared to drop the theme for a period in order to teach subject-specific skills and knowledge
- give children early opportunities to *apply* newly learned skills and knowledge when returning to the theme
- strive to generate a genuine questioning stance in the children
- be prepared to intervene in any group activity in order to help raise standards and meet challenging objectives.

Planning the skills, subject knowledge and progression required

The National Curricula of England, Wales, Northern Ireland and the National Guidelines for Scotland are permissive and flexible documents. On careful reading, they are not as content-heavy as many complain they are, but allow considerable leeway in terms of delivery. QCA, NNS and NLS documents, whilst heavier in knowledge and skills content, are not statutory but provide useful guidance and frameworks to work within if needed. The great benefit of the various statutory curricula is their attention to progression and measures of achievement within each subject. The various attainment levels are clearly progressive in complexity and depth and provide very helpful guides as to age-appropriate achievement. If you are planning learning within a theme, the attainment targets and their levels are good places to start. There is a strong interrelationship in language and concept between the levels, whatever the subject.

Table 9.1 Generic National Curriculum levels 1–5

Attainment level	Generic concepts	Typical generic activities
Level 1	Literal	See, experience, respond, describe
Level 2	Organization	Arrange, compare, contrast, classify, put into own words
Level 3	Evaluation	Make choices, give reasons, ask questions, find and use, present
Level 4	Inference	Work out, explain, select, combine, make educated guesses
Level 5	Appreciation	Justify, generalize, look for qualities, modify, establish own conclusions

(The author is grateful to Jane Heyes and Brompton Westbrook Primary School for this analysis)

Working from subject-specific statements of attainment and the generic concepts above, the teacher can devise clear, measurable objectives for each lesson. Through constant interaction, concentrated feedback, open-ended (and occasionally closed) questioning, the teacher can ensure achievement is raised. With clear objectives, either directly stated to the children or elicited after the activities ('What do you think I wanted you to learn from this?'), the teacher can ensure that subject skills and knowledge are not lost in what Roth calls the 'bland broth' of interdisciplinary study (Wineburg and Grossman, 2000). Looking above and below the average level for the age using the generic concepts in Table 9.1, the teacher may plan for differentiated support and appropriate progression within each subject represented.

Aiming at a state of flow in children

The school I'd like … could slow down a little. Hugh, 6 (Burke and Grosvenor, 2003: 74)

Csikszentmihalyi's concept of flow brilliantly summarizes that sense of complete involvement we teachers often see when children are fully engaged in an activity over which they feel they have some control. The state of flow is described as the sensation we feel when ideas, thoughts and life itself seem to run freely. His research suggests that when we reflect on this feeling, the following features of flow are most frequently described:

- complete involvement in an activity for its own sake
- confidence that our skills match the challenge we have been set
- awareness that time seems different from ordinary experience
- less self-consciousness
- less fear of failure
- the fading of current worries
- feedback which comes immediately and mostly from the self
- the feeling of being most alive, and having most sense of meaning.

Intrinsic motivation, as we have seen in Chapter 6, is often observed in the school playground, in participation in the school play or concert, or in engagement in certain practical, sporting and creative sessions. It is in combining feelings associated with play, physical activity, challenge, opportunity for creative connection making and relaxed and friendly relationships with newly acquired knowledge and skills that flow is most likely to occur.

Case study: flow in action

In a school serving a deprived, 'raw, rough and unsociable' area of the bankrupted of city Berlin, a group of 250 young people were asked to join a project to learn and perform a ballet to Stravinsky's *Rite of Spring*. Sir Simon Rattle, a famous conductor, and choreographer Royston Maldoom led this social project, expressly designed to change minds and counter disaffection through involvement in a cross-arts project. These young people had never had contact with Western classical music, had never danced and many were battling severe social, emotional and health problems of their own, with some very reluctant to participate. The story of their transformation from low aspirations and negativity towards a more hopeful, positive, confident and sensitized life is told in the film *Rhythm Is It* (Sanchez and Gruber, 2005, website). At one point in the film, choreographer Maldoom says, 'Don't think you are just doing dancing. You can change your life in a dance class!' The film ends with extracts from the final rehearsal and performance in which one can observe flow in action in the faces and bodies of the children. The film portrays the combination of real, hard and painfully earned skill and a high challenge which two months before had seemed insurmountable and which clearly resulted in some transformed lives.

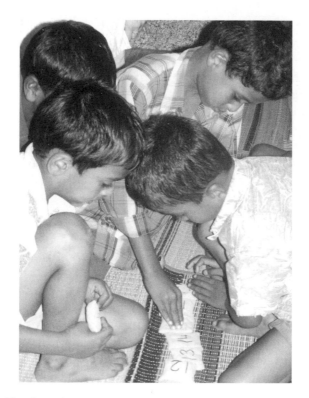

Illustration 9.1   *Flow in action*

The state of flow seems more likely in school children when they are involved with other people, when they have plenty of books at home and space they can call their own, and when they have fewer electronic entertainments. As we have already seen, Csikszentmihalyi also observes that it is most common when people are engaged in creative and active pursuits. These observations are powerful arguments for a curriculum which operates outside the limits of the normal classroom in the real and multi-disciplinary world outside.

Finishing with a performance of understanding

In terms of principles for the teacher to consider, the most effective means of monitoring and formatively appraising work done across several curricula is the *Performance of Understanding* (Perkins in Blyth, 1997). In this kind of assessment procedure, children create some kind of demonstration of the degree of their understanding. Assessment generally and specific attention to the performance of understanding will be the subject of Chapter 10.

Themes

It is clear that there are as many relevant and fascinating themes as there are objects, places, feelings, ideas and living things in the universe. There can be no definitive list. The essence of a theme which will generate learning is one which both teacher and children can feel enthusiastic about and can therefore sustain commitment to. For cross-curricular work to be successful in raising standards through motivating children, there is no alternative to thorough planning, ongoing assessment and continued attention to specific objectives within focus subjects. The short lists below are some themes which have recently and successfully been used in schools since the publication of the Primary Strategy, *Excellence and Enjoyment*. I have chosen to identify themes which perhaps suggest one major focus subject in order to emphasize the fact that key learning objectives within the subjects need to be restricted within each theme so that subject learning is not 'watered down'. A foundation stage or Key Stage 1 theme with a science focus like 'Why won't my seed grow?' (de Boo, 2004) will lay the foundations for science later on in school by helping children handle, tend and think about seeds and growth, but true to good early years practice, children will also sort and classify, count, draw, construct, make musical instruments and listen to and invent stories. The *Knowledge and Understanding of the World* or Key Stage 1 science objectives may be 'to identify the features of living things', 'to be able to relate the life process of a plant' or 'to identify similarities and differences in natural things'. The teacher will know the expected range of levels of understanding by looking at the level descriptions and thus be able both to differentiate and encourage children to higher levels of achievement. Each of the *non*-science activities will also have a levelled objective (e.g. 'sort objects and talk about sorting', 'initiate communication with others' or 'be aware of the needs of others'). Through these and other relevant objectives, teachers and Teaching Assistants will be helping children grow in the areas of creativity, communication, mathematics and personal, emotional and social development.

Some themes with a science focus

Systems

Models

Turn on the light

Patterns of change

Interactions

Colour

Bubbles

Why won't my seed grow?

Why is water important?

How many legs?

Some themes with a geography focus

Our street/our neighbours

Improving a derelict site/school playground

Weather

A building site

A basket of fruit from …

A day out in the town/country/seaside/India

A linked school in a distant locality

Finding our way/maps and mapping

A local river, lake, dam or coast/geographical processes

Getting there/transport systems

My footprint/sustainability and me

My home/systems that serve us

What's in the news and where is it?

Some themes with an RE focus

People

Journeys

Celebrations

Stories

Special places

Symbols and signs

Judaism, Sikhism, Buddhism, Islam, Christianity, Hinduism, Shamanism, Animism

What's in the news?

What is beauty?

What is truth?

What is good?

What is bad?

Some themes with a history focus

Change

My birthday

My family

A particular building

Grandma Brown's visit

Florence Nightingale and Mary Seacole

The Olympic Games

The Gunpowder Plot

In an artist's/engineer's/scientist's shoes

Our school

The 1851 Great Exhibition

A visit to the museum

A mystery object

Summary and key questions

Perhaps you might consider the following questions before coming to a firm decision on a theme:

1 **Consulting the children**
   - Does this theme fit with the school's wider aims?
   - How will I make it relevant and meaningful to the children?
   - How can I involve children in decisions?

2 **Planning a shared experience**
   - How can I involve and enhance community links though this project?
   - What are my overarching goals for this theme? In what big ways do I want the children to be different at the end of this topic?
   - What shared experiences can we plan?

3 **Choosing only subjects which add understanding**
   - What two or three (maximum four) curriculum subjects best throw light on this theme?
   - What are the curriculum needs this term/year/week?

4 **Planning the subject skills, knowledge and progression required**
   - What level of skills and knowledge in each subject do I need to help children demonstrate?
   - What experts from the community can I call on to help me?

5 **Aiming at a state of flow in children**
   - What can I do to generate a state of flow in the children during aspects of this theme?

- How can I make this project personally meaningful to the maximum number of children?

6 **Finishing with a performance of understanding**

- In what ways can the children demonstrate the depth of their learning?
- How can I help children show that their learning is transferable to other situations and settings?

Further reading

Kerry, T. (ed.) (2010) *Cross-Curricular Teaching in the Primary School*. London: Routledge.
Rowley, C. and Cooper, H. (2009) *Cross-Curricular Teaching and Learning*. London: Sage.
Wyse, D. and Rowson, P. (2008) *The Really Useful Creativity Book*. London: Routledge.

CHAPTER 10

How Can We Assess Cross-Curricular and Creative Learning?

Cross-curricular learning is often difficult to assess. In opportunistic, multi- or inter-disciplinary contexts, learning occurs on too many levels and in too many domains to be susceptible to summative assessment. This book has attempted to make the case that cross-curricular learning is a powerful way to generate creative thinking – creativity is also notoriously difficult to assess. *Formative* assessment, or assessment for learning, however, can and should form part of all creative and cross-curricular activity. Assessment that promotes further learning allows for several different kinds of assessor: self, peer group, audience, expert practitioner, interested observer or teacher. Constructive approaches to evaluation ideally empower the learner both to appreciate their progress and hunger after new and deeper understandings.

The most significant and lasting of assessments are those we make on ourselves. In periods of deep and positive engagement, concentration is sustained, even deepened, by the feedback we give ourselves. In children, self-assessment often comes in the form of 'self talk', the spoken commentary that commonly accompanies play (see Barnes, 2010b). Self-talk is generally internalized as we grow older but forms an ever-present critical appraisal as we act out our lives. This personal feedback is added to by the often wordless reactions of others close by, who by body language and the occasional comment tell us how we are doing. These often subtle and unconscious sources of feedback are vital components of the flow state described earlier (Chapter 6). Teachers observe this kind of self and peer assessment when school work takes on the nature of play and exploration – a desirable characteristic of cross-curricular learning.

What to assess

Teachers continually assess. We quickly sense the 'atmosphere' of a room full of pupils, we judge the verity of an explanation after a playground spat, we evaluate the amount of work going on even before we crouch beside a table of working children. As we listen to the questions, comments and chatter of children engaged in activity throughout the school day and beyond, we cannot help making value judgments, comparing and checking. Assessment has not always been made against progressive, planned, articulated and monitored learning objectives. In the past, rather than being linked with future learning, assessments were often more to do with capturing the quantity of correctness. From the earliest days of formal education, teachers kept detailed mark books and made annual reports: summative assessments of individual progress in reading, writing, tables, arithmetic, Latin, general knowledge. From surviving school assessment records, we can see, for example, that Isaac Newton, Albert Einstein, Winston Churchill and John Lennon were clearly destined for lives of failure!

More frequent, stringent, statutory, uniform and formalized assessment has become a noticeable feature of teaching since the 1980s. With the advent of SATs, voluntary SATs, booster classes in English and maths and published league tables of school results, English children are now amongst the most assessed in the world. These assessments have a number of functions. They provide regular updates on a child's progress to parents and carers. For governors, they give confidence that the school is fulfilling its legal responsibilities. Assessments also serve to inform of school progress (usually in the core subjects only) against other similar schools or its own previous record. For school principals, heads or subject coordinators, they may serve to monitor the success of a particular teacher in delivering a subject. An Ofsted inspector may use records of assessments to judge curriculum coverage and age-appropriate expectations and to ensure an adequate degree of accountability on the part of the teacher. Whilst assessments are expected in all foundation subjects and RE, the assessments most consulted during inspections are the core subjects of English, mathematics, science and increasingly ICT. None of the official functions of assessment matter very much to most children, and yet assessment intended to promote *further learning* can be a most productive and positive part of a teacher's interaction with the child.

The kind of curriculum promoted by this book aims at the personal growth and fulfilment of children. Illich (1971), and many since his day, remind us that personal growth is ultimately immeasurable. But if teachers are to feel confident that they are supporting children in their journey, some means of capturing progress may need to be developed. If creativity is to be promoted through our school system, then we have to evolve some ways of finding out if and to what degree it is happening in our classes. The following sections are intended to inform discussion on how assessment can be both integrated in the learning process and inform teachers of the effectiveness of their teaching. In cross-curricular work intended to take learning at all levels forward, we should therefore assess attitudes towards and progress in: self-understanding, understanding of others, collaboration, understanding of issues significant to the community and understanding of global issues as well as disciplinary understanding.

Formative assessment

Formative assessment is assessment intended to take the child forward on their learning journey. The concept of formative assessment or 'assessment for learning' has been current for many years. British schools paid lip-service to formative assessment throughout the 1990s, when the National Curriculum was being launched. However, the NACCCE report in 1999 (paras 200–11) noted its relatively minor importance in school procedures and argued for a more privileged place for formative assessment (Recommendation 5). In the same year as the NACCCE investigations were being conducted, researchers Black and Wiliam (1998) found that, at its best, formative assessment could achieve the following:

- raising children's attainment
- increasing their self-esteem
- giving them a greater stake in their learning
- enabling a greater prospect of 'lifelong learning'.

In an 18-month project on formative assessment, led by educationalist Shirley Clarke, teachers were introduced to now familiar terms such as 'learning intentions', 'success criteria' and 'pupil self-evaluation' (Clarke, 2001, website). Even after only a term of serious application, teachers felt able to credit the *assessment for learning* techniques she had introduced with the following benefits:

- Children liked knowing the learning intentions and success criteria.
- Most teachers saw benefit in sharing the learning intentions and success criteria.
- Seventy-five per cent of teachers said that children understood tasks better.
- Almost all teachers said that sharing learning intentions and success criteria had had a positive effect on their teaching.
- Just under half of lessons involved successful use of self-evaluation questions.
- Most teachers said children were no longer afraid to make mistakes and were more able to admit to difficulties.

Table 10.1   Asking the right assessment questions

Assessing	Examples of key assessment questions
Self-understanding	In what ways has this person added to their understanding of their own character, likes and dislikes, talents, weaknesses, strengths and influences? What are their attitudes to their own work and learning? What are the next steps they could take?
Understanding others	In what ways has this individual added to their understanding of the feelings and strengths of others? In what ways do they demonstrate understanding of the minds of others? What social skills do they need to develop or nurture?
Working with others	In what ways does this person work and play with others? How do they use their knowledge of others (a) to influence (b) to empathize (c) to collaborate? What do they need to learn, celebrate or control?
Creativity	In what ways and in which areas does this individual show originality, the ability to link ideas or to make valuable new contributions? In what ways have they been able to make connections between the skills/ knowledge of one subject and those of another? How can these things be cherished, fostered and developed?
Community issues	To what degree is this individual aware of the dominant values of their community? What do they understand of the important issues for their community? How are these things shown? Where do they need to go from here?
Global issues	To what degree is this person aware of the major issues facing our world? In what ways are they aware of their role in addressing these issues in their everyday lives?
Disciplinary understandings in two or three subject disciplines	At what level is this individual's understanding of the skills, knowledge, attitudes and values of each of the subjects combined in this cross-curricular study? How have they built on past understandings? How have they shown their new understandings? What are the next steps in each subject?

- Half of the teachers said that children of all abilities are able to access self-evaluation questions.

- Two-thirds of children had some perception of the true point of self-evaluation.

- Of the teachers who tried pupil self-evaluation, almost all said it had a positive effect on their teaching.

Findings like these are highly relevant to assessing cross-curricular activities in the classroom. The personally meaningful, less formal and open-ended nature of much cross-curricular learning, lends itself well to the idea of self-evaluation and the creation of a positive atmosphere which accepts mistakes as a vital part of learning. There are many ways of managing formative assessment: the informal feedback of the concerned teacher as he or she moves around the class offering help, posing questions and listening to observations; the formal marking of class work; or the informal testing of certain factual knowledge in order to identify barriers to learning. However, each of these can be something of a 'bolt-on' assessment, not truly integrated with the, hopefully, vital activity of the topic of study. The concept of the performance of understanding was devised by David Perkins, Tina Blythe and their associates at Project Zero (Project Zero, 2006, website), the educational research arm of Harvard's Graduate School of Education.

Performances of understanding

The idea of *presenting* understanding before a final performance will be examined in closer detail with the suggestion that such presentations are potentially a key growth point in any medium-term scheme of work (see Chapter 11). Children grow in understanding through their own presentations. They become aware of the gaps in their own understanding, they receive more easily the advice of their peers with whom they have shared the challenges and problems, and they grow in confidence.

The performance of understanding as a form of formative assessment was mentioned briefly in Chapter 7 when suitable themes for cross-curricular learning were discussed. This is a term coined by Professor David Perkins and expounded upon by Tina Blythe in her book, *The Teaching for Understanding Guide* (Blythe, 1997). Simply expressed, the performance of understanding is a curriculum opportunity for a child or a group of children to demonstrate the depth and degree of their learning by applying it in a new situation. This 'performance' is not literally a dramatic or musical performance (though it might be), but a chance publicly to show learning. It may be:

- a collection
- a construction
- a dance
- a debate
- a demonstration
- a diagram
- a poem
- a poster
- a reading
- a recital
- a song
- a talk

- a led discussion
- a map or plan
- a meal
- a mime
- a newspaper article
- a piece of music
- a play

- a walk or guided tour
- an annotated drawing
- an essay
- an exhibition
- an experiment
- an exposition.

or any combination of these and other ways of communicating understanding, but the essence of the performance of understanding is that the 'performer(s)' have not previously expressed their understanding of the topic in this way (Illustration 10.1).

A class in a performing arts school in Kent has been carrying out cross-curricular learning related to the earthquake in Haiti. The theme was planned to cover six weeks (see Table 10.2 below). Using skills and learning the relevant knowledge in geography, they were introduced through maps, videos, newspaper reports, diagrams and photographs to the landscape, weather and economic conditions in the area. They were also given a direct teaching session on what causes earthquakes. They studied the normal daily lives and religion of a community living there through both RE and geographical perspectives. Their PSHE lesson with newspapers told them a great deal about conditions there directly after the earthquake and about different ways of reporting such news. A friend of the school who was born in the Caribbean spoke to the class about his life there and

Illustration 10.1   *A performance of understanding. Children explaining their responses to a 'health and happiness' workshop in Scotland. Courtesy of Scottish Children's Parliament*

answered questions during another PSHE/Citizenship lesson. In another geography lesson, they considered in detail what conditions must be like in the community they studied and used an email link with a charity to get up-to-date information on the aid effort. They have learned about Caribbean cooking and culture from a local cultural group and some parents.

Since the school was based in a large area of open countryside with considerable grounds, rural science and gardening formed a significant part of the curriculum. The children decided to use their work and talents to grow food for sale to friends and parents in order to raise money for their identified project connected with the disaster. This was to extend aspects of the theme and the associated learning through the next term.

The final taught week of this very relevant and emotive theme consisted of children planning and mounting a charity collection for the victims of the natural disaster. The teacher was on hand as adviser, but had little idea of what aspects children would choose as the focus of their final week presentations to parents. The charity event eventually planned included four themed PowerPoint presentations on a village in Haiti from a group of four children, who used their own maps, photographs found on the internet and information from aid agencies. Caribbean food and drink were prepared, presented and served by an appropriately dressed group of six children. A further five decided to mount their own exhibition on the current state of affairs in the region using their own maps, material sent by an aid agency, collected newspaper cuttings and re-presented information from the internet. A group of six chose to perform a short play based upon a Jamaican tale about helping the hungry and homeless. Three other children created a detailed and accurate backdrop of palm trees and sea. Finally, a group of five children decided to write and duplicate a newspaper-style fact sheet for parents and guests to take home with them. This was extended in subsequent terms to bring news of the money-raising fruit and vegetable sales.

During the preparation week before the final day of performances, each group was asked a number of times to rehearse what they were going to do/say/show to the rest of the class, and the class was encouraged to offer advice or ask questions which resulted in improvements. This process of refinement significantly raised the stakes and markedly improved standards through peer assessment. On the last day, each activity refocused attention on the main theme (and in the process generated a great deal of money for the cause) but throughout the week, teachers were able to use the various demonstrations of subject understanding to help them assess the level of learning of each individual against National Curriculum levels.

These assessments were in no way summative; they were part of the day-to-day learning and were intended to have a positive effect on future learning. In the last week of the project, teachers were able to act less like

Table 10.2 The Haiti earthquake: a six-week plan leading to a fund-raising event

Week 1 theme	Week 2 theme	Week 3 theme	Week 4 theme	Week 5 theme	Week 6 theme
Introduction With video/ newspapers Children's comments and questions	Physical geography Maps Diagrams	What happened to the villages? What life is like now for the survivors	What religion tells us about natural disasters/helping our neighbour	Caribbean culture: food, clothing, music, dance	Fund-raising week for the victims of the earthquake
Demonstrating subject understanding	*Demonstrating subject understanding*	*Demonstrating subject understanding*	*Demonstrating subject understanding*	*Demonstrating subject understanding*	*Performance of understanding*
Geog. cit. Asking geographical/ citizenship questions	**Geog.** Constructing maps Understanding diagrams and photographs	**Geog.** Making intelligent guesses based upon geographical understanding. Suggesting possible improvements and solutions	**RE** Asking spiritual questions Understanding the spiritual dimension **Cit.** Our role in disaster relief The role of aid agencies	**D/T** Cooking, designing a menu **Music** Recognizing pattern, pitch and applying knowledge to own compositions	**Geog.** PowerPoint presentations on geog of Haiti **RE** Replay on caring for hungry and homeless. **Cit.** Haiti – in the news; the facts **D/T** Caribbean menu, planned and served.

instructors and more like coaches. In this role, they were able actively to point to possible improvements or ask formative questions during the mounting of exhibitions, painting of scenery or cooking of food. During and after the event, they were able to involve the children themselves in their own self-assessment.

Children's peer assessment questions

- What went well? Why do you think it went so well?
- What did you enjoy most? Why?
- Whose work do you think communicated best? Why?
- What did you like about [N's] presentation?
- What would you do to improve your presentation, if you had another chance?
- What still puzzles you about what [N] said/showed?
- Has the project as a whole left you with any questions?

Throughout this project, teachers had multiple opportunities to record the level of subject understanding displayed by individuals. Teachers noticed the questions children asked of other groups, their responses to the suggestions of others, individual application within their own group and the level of subject understanding shown in rehearsals and performance. On average, one teacher assessed six children a day, and on some days subject coordinators were invited to make subject specific assessments. The organizing teacher

Illustration 10.2   Peer assessment in action. Children passing focused and positive comments to other participating groups after a practical workshop. Courtesy of Scottish Children's Parliament

made a further 15 assessments during the final performances. The collected observations and records during this themed term honoured a host of individual achievements which coloured end-of-year reports. In the following term, children were in a strong position to build upon past learning and had new strategies with which to acquire new skills and further knowledge in other subject areas.

Presentations and peer assessment

In learning through the arts, a cycle of activities known as the *Processes of the Arts* (Robinson, 2001; Robinson and Aronica, 2010) provides a useful model. The cycle of activities may start at any point, but includes activities generic to the arts, such as exploring, forming, presenting, evaluating and performing. The concept of *presenting* is considered quite distinct from performing and I believe this distinction may usefully be applied across the curriculum, well beyond the arts. Presenting in Robinson's model consists of taking time out of a creative process to show colleagues what has been formed, learned, understood *so far*. There is no pretence that this is a performance; it is 'work in progress' and has an important peer assessment function. When a group or individual has the chance to demonstrate subject understanding in an overtly provisional setting, where everyone knows it is 'not finished yet', a real opportunity to 'raise the bar' presents itself (Illustration 10.2).

In cross-curricular settings like that outlined above (and in Chapter 3), groups within a class will commonly be engaged in related activities.

Illustration 10.3   *Student teachers presenting their understanding of place for their peers to comment upon*

Hopefully, the class ethos is one of mutual support, confidence and a relaxed attitude to mistakes; each group will understand the issues confronting the others. When each group presents their work in progress for comment, feedback from others who have trodden a similar path can easily become personally engaging, relevant and wholly formative in character. Children report that it is in these situations that they learn the most – their peers have become their teachers (Barnes and Shirley, 2007; Dismore et al., 2008). Perkins makes 'distributed cognition', that is, thinking shared across the group, the central theme of his views on learnable intelligence (Sternberg and Williams, 1998) (Illustration 10.4).

Table 10.3 A simple format for (individual or group) peer assessment

Assessment focus	Examples
Say two things you really liked about the presentation.	• I really liked the way you started that piece off with a very simple tune and then changed it in little ways each time we heard it. • I especially liked the way you told us how you thought about a castle servant's life.
Ask about two things which puzzle you.	• Why did you decide to paint on the frame as well? • What made you think of using water for power instead of air? • Did you think of using any other instruments? • Why did you finish in that way?
Offer one point of advice.	• Next time you present this, I think you should … • Have you thought of …? • Do you think you could …?

Self-assessment

Here are two haikus on the subject of barriers, which started with observations in the school playground. They were composed by eight-year-olds. How would you formatively assess them? What would you pick out as particularly good? What would you want to ask? Do you have any advice?

(Continued)

(Continued)

Joshua   Wedresday 20th
July 2005.

Soft Silky cobwebs
attached apon the great wall.
Silk - caperter's lodge

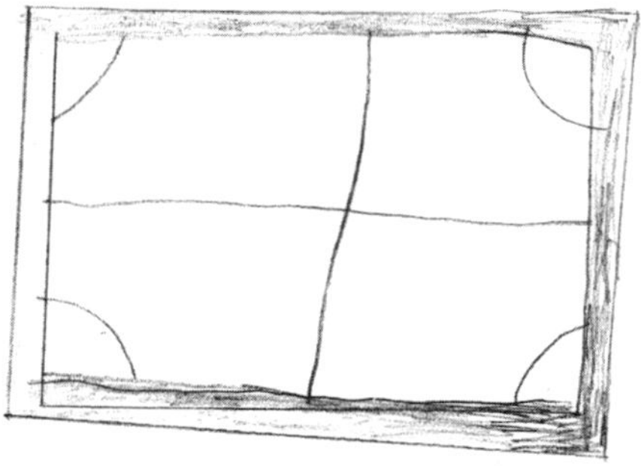

Figure 10.1   An eight-year-old responds to the tiny detail of his immediate environment

(Continued)

(Continued)

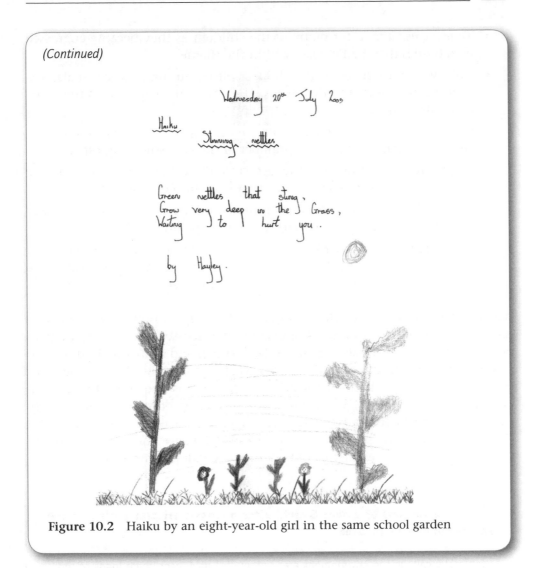

Figure 10.2   Haiku by an eight-year-old girl in the same school garden

The benefits of presentation do not end with peer appraisal. Presentation can be a non-threatening way of provoking self-criticism. In publicly presenting understanding so far, the presenters themselves are more likely to be made aware of the gaps in their own understanding. Presenting itself can become a form of learning, with feedback coming instantly from the individual self or the 'group self'. This links back to Csikszentmihayli's concept of flow, one of its universal characteristics being 'rapid feedback', which often follows naturally from a self wholly engaged in an activity. Indeed, as you look at the examples of cross-curricular activities in the previous section or Chapter 3, you might see that *all* the conditions of flow are likely to be present.

- *Time seemed altered* for many of the children as they became engrossed in activities they had chosen within the theme.

- Skills were introduced to the children either during cross-curricular sessions or in subject-specific lessons. These were then applied in the cross-curricular context.

- Playground, home or relationship *worries* apparently *diminished* during cross-curricular activities in a number of the case studies quoted.

- It appeared from observing the faces and interactions of children during case study observations that they were *less self-consciousness*.

- The *confidence* of children during presentations and performances was one of the features most remarked upon by parents and teachers.

- The intense engagement of children in the activities observed and described suggests that they were being enjoyed for *their own sake*. There was frequently a sense that individual children became *'lost' in an activity*.

Cross-curricular learning will, of course, only generate flow within the supportive and secure environments already fully discussed. It will only flourish when curriculum challenges are carefully planned and individualized so as to put specifically introduced skills and knowledge into action. Full engagement is only likely when a theme or activity has taken on some kind of existential significance for the child. Under these circumstances, cross-curricular activity itself may generate formative assessment of a highly personal and meaningful kind. Such reflexive self-assessment will also prepare the child's mind to receive supportive assessments and additional challenges from others.

Written reflections of a Year 6 child after a cross-curricular project in the school environmental area

I felt really calm in the environment area, although I have been there loads of times before I hadn't really paid so much attention to everything … My favourite activities were the object focus and when we laid [*sic*] down and looked up at the sky through the eyes of our object. I felt really quiet as I studied my chosen object, and we all know that doesn't happen very often! It felt kind of nice and relaxed and peaceful, but the time went really quickly and I could have spent longer out here … I feel that we are working so well together …

Assessing engagement

Looking for the outward signs of flow is a good way of assessing the degree of engagement, and therefore learning, in a child. Much of the significance can be missed if teachers fail to look at the faces and postures of their children at

Illustration 10.4 *The detail and care taken by this five-year-old as he planned additions to his playground is an indication of high levels of engagement. Describing his choices, he reveals the level of his understanding of design/technology principles and his views about improving the quality of his environment*

work (Barnes, 2005e). Student teachers should consider the facial and bodily expressions of involvement an integral part of their evaluations. All teachers should be aware of and responsive to the non-verbal signs children give us. Ferre Laevers has been influential in formulating a useable five-point scale to measure the physical signs of such involvement (the Leuven Involvement Scale (LIS)). According to this scale, a child's degree of participation can be classified as shown in Table 10.4.

Table 10.4 Measure of a child's degree of participation

Level 1	No activity, the child is mentally absent and there is stereotypic repetition of elementary movements.
Level 2	Actions with many interruptions.
Level 3	Actions more concerted, but concentration seems lacking and motivation and pleasure are lacking.
Level 4	Moments of intense mental activity shown by times of concentration beyond the routine.
Level 5	Total involvement expressed by full concentration, signs of enjoyment and absorption. Any disturbance or interruption is experienced as frustrating.

Source: adapted from Laevers (1994b)

Linking this work with the research of Ekman (2004) and others into facial expression, teachers and others working with children quickly come to recognize the range of facial expressions of engagement. Responding unconsciously to such facial and bodily nuances is probably part of our biological inheritance, but bringing that understanding into consciousness and attempting to generate particular expressions of engagement or enjoyment could significantly add to the effectiveness of teaching.

Summary

Whilst summative assessment may be helpful at the end of a key stage formative assessment, using it as part and parcel of daily learning activities makes it a more effective learning tool. Assessment should be a social and collaborative process involving children as well as adults, and should be linked to the wider aims and values of the school as well as subject learning. Assessments can be performed more usefully and accurately through giving children opportunities to apply new knowledge to real situations. The concept of 'performances of understanding' is a helpful model of meaningful assessment for both child and teacher.

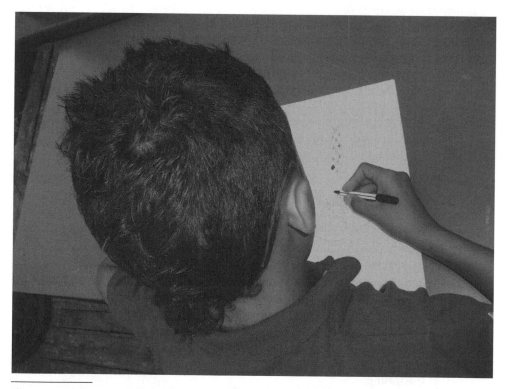

Illustration 10.5 *Look for the signs of enjoyment and absorption*

- How can we make assessment meaningful and a useful learning tool?
- How can we promote distributed cognition as part of the daily experience of children in school?
- What should be the balance of flow experiences and more mundane activities in class?
- Should subject skills and knowledge be assessed in a different way from their cross-curricular application?

Further reading

Clark, S. (2008) *Active Learning through Formative Assessment.* London: Hodder.
Glazzard, J., Chadwick, D., Webster, A. and Percival, J. (2010) *Assessment for Learning in the Early Years Foundation Stage.* London: Sage.
Laevers, F. (1994) *Defining and Assessing Quality in Early Childhood Education.* Leuven: Leuven University Press.

CHAPTER 11

How Should We Plan for Cross-Curricular Activity?

Planning before the paperwork

Planning is essential if teaching is to be transformed into learning. Planning cross-curricular activity requires paperwork, just as any other curriculum planning, but arguably its most important features come before anything is written. Thoughtful conversations should come first. We have seen (Chapter 4) how learning is a social activity and so teaching should be too. Conversations between all involved in teaching need time, structure and direction and should first be used to establish coherent and consistent values. The values conversation is probably the most important conversation to hold before formal planning starts. Chapter 8 suggested values discussions should be a regular and dynamic part of school life and include all involved. Ofsted (2009a, 2009b) has consistently noted that successful schools are clear about their values, but values conversations *should* arrive at different conclusions, different priorities and those priorities may change according to circumstances. Whilst no single set of values is applicable to all schools and communities, there may be significant overlaps. The values underpinning this book suggest that planning should be founded on beliefs in the importance of:

- inclusion and participation
- recognizing, allowing and nurturing creativity
- subject-based knowledge and skills
- a sense of progression in all learning
- meaningful and shared experiences
- strong and positive relations with the community and locality
- outdoor learning
- safe and stimulating spaces for learning.

Each item above has a planning implication; each needs talking about. Curriculum conversations should be thoughtful too, with thought given to how the application of values will affect individuals young and old connected with the school, and to ensuring the proper inclusion of all stakeholders. Finally, and still before the paperwork, thoughts about planning must address the balance between generating motivation and fulfilling the demands of national requirements. This chapter shows how National Curriculum expectations (with particular attention to the key skills) can become a meaningful, lively and even satisfying part of planning. It emphasizes the planning of powerful shared experiences which generate both motivation and creativity and supports its conclusions with reference to current research and practice.

Inclusion and participation

Cross-curricular approaches should provide the most inclusive and participatory of learning opportunities. Participation needs to be planned, however, and the principles of inclusion must be fully discussed, understood and agreed upon. Booth and Ainscow (2002) have provided a principled resource to support schools in developing this conversation, but cross-curricular pedagogies can provide a curriculum context to express and extend these pivotal values and aims.

Whether teaching and learning use hierarchical, multi-disciplinary, inter-disciplinary or opportunistic approaches, I have suggested that the prime motivators for learning should be shared, relevant, meaningful experiences. Shared experience is by definition inclusive; meaningful and relevant experience motivates participation, but such experiences need careful planning. If experiences are truly shared and genuinely meaningful, then they are likely to reach all children at the level appropriate for them from the outset.

In a broad and balanced curriculum where each subject has parity of prestige, there would be no need for a 'special needs' group, because children would be encouraged to work from their strengths. In the first case study in Chapter 3, school teachers supported one boy who had difficulties in working with numbers and other aspects of mathematics. They used his fascination with creepy crawlies found on the woodland walk to give him the job of classifying each collected creature by number of legs and length of body. He had little difficulty in handling numbers or dimensions in this practical and outdoor setting.

Teachers should plan for inclusion by using their knowledge of each child's strengths to predict the most appropriate entry point through which they may learn. The inclusion statements of the national curricula of each country of the UK make it abundantly clear that progressive learning of skills and knowledge in all subjects is the birthright of every child. 'Schools have a responsibility to provide a broad and balanced curriculum for all pupils'

(DfEE, 1999: 30), the general teaching requirements of the National Curriculum begins. This means that in the vast majority of cases, language, ethnicity, lifestyle, immigration status, intellectual or physical ability should make no difference to a child's opportunity to experience the whole curriculum.

For some, learning will be more easily provoked and extended by the use of modified equipment, extra staffing or specific practical aids, but an experience-led curriculum may be the best way of involving all children, regardless of barriers to their learning. Narrowing the curriculum to one dominated by the core subjects will inevitably narrow the potential of large percentages of children (see RSA, 2010, website). Thankfully, the concepts of literacy and numeracy are constantly widening – literacy can include non-verbal, visual, tactile and aural means of understanding the world. Numeracy has for many become an opportunity for meaningful and progressive play with numbers, measurements and shapes. The wordless, sensory and practical aspects of any subjects introduced to make sense of a cross-curricular experience are often noted as a transformative entry point to wider learning and social communication for those who find verbal expression difficult (see Roberts, 2006, for example).

Recognizing, allowing and nurturing creativity

The development of creativity has been implicit throughout the examples used in this book. Chapter 7 discussed in more detail definitions and implications of creative pedagogy, but planning for creativity is a contentious issue. Creativity often does not occur when planned. By definition, creativity is founded upon our ability to be imaginative and original and neither mental facility is easy to control. Yet I believe planning does affect creativity in three ways:

- teaching creatively
- teaching for creativity
- creative thinking and learning.

Teaching creatively

First, each teacher needs to understand that they are a creative being. Every individual's unique inheritance, history, social milieu, personal environment and neural connections ensure that at some level originality and imagination are possible in all. What varies is our ability to recognize our inherent creative strengths and our motivation to use them. When asked to identify creative teachers, the tendency is to look to the artistic or rather theatrical member of staff, whilst others may often deny any sense that they are creative. However, research (Cremin et al., 2009) has shown that working alongside non-teacher creative practitioners from any field – town planners, website designers, film

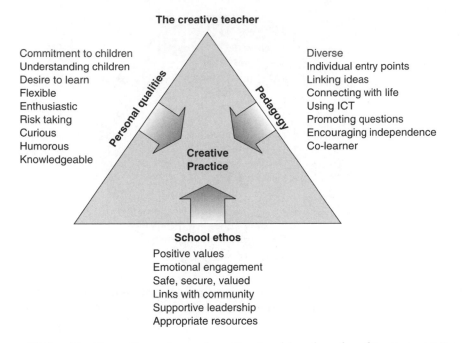

The creative teacher

Commitment to children
Understanding children
Desire to learn
Flexible
Enthusiastic
Risk taking
Curious
Humorous
Knowledgeable

Diverse
Individual entry points
Linking ideas
Connecting with life
Using ICT
Promoting questions
Encouraging independence
Co-learner

Personal qualities

Pedagogy

Creative
Practice

School ethos
Positive values
Emotional engagement
Safe, secure, valued
Links with community
Supportive leadership
Appropriate resources

Figure 11.1   The three dimensions of creative teaching, based on literature review (Cremin et al., 2009; copyright Cremin, Barnes and Scoffham, 2009)

makers, landscape gardeners, architects, research scientists, photographers, lighting designers, electronic engineers, as well as musicians, sculptors and artists – has awoken dormant creativity in teachers. Some teachers recognize their own creativity for the fist time when working alongside members of the community who have 'creative' roles. It is important that in every way possible, teachers are helped to discover that and where they are creative.

Conversation helps in developing creativity too. Two teachers discussing how to approach a particular topic or shared experience will inevitably bring different mindsets to bear on the same problem … such differences open the door to creative teaching. The synthesis of ideas, the recognition that other solutions exist, the unexpected viewpoint or different starting point can each generate new ideas for presentation/support or assessment.

Creative teaching, however, requires a blend of personal and institutional characteristics, most of which are either learnable or subject to managerial decisions. A thorough literature review suggested that a range of personal characteristics such as curiosity, flexibility, enthusiasm, humour and a thirst for knowledge are usually displayed in creative teaching. A particular set of pedagogical skills is also frequently evident – these include liking children and knowing the entry points for learning in each individual, using diverse approaches, a tendency to make links, adopting a questioning stance and encouraging questioning, independence and responsibility.

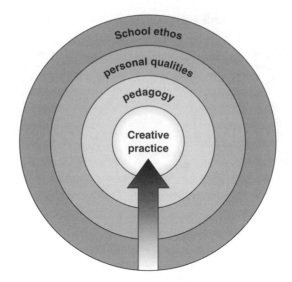

Figure 11.2   A revised model of the dimensions of creative teaching (Cremin et al., 2009; copyright Cremin, Barnes and Scoffham, 2009)

However, our research in eight primary and secondary classrooms showed that even if all these characteristics were in place, creative teaching was not sustainable unless there was an ethos of support and encouragement. Such an ethos cannot usually be generated by lone teachers, it generally depends upon a supportive management team and community. Rather than three equal dimensions of creative teaching, we suggest that there may be a hierarchy – the ethos permitting the pedagogy of creativity and that acceptance encouraging the use and development of the personal skills that make creative teaching such a wonderful, varied and stimulating resource for children and the community.

Teaching for creativity

If we agree that unlocking the innate creativity in every pupil is a suitable aim of education, then our planning and teaching should make this possible. Teaching for creativity means teaching so that confidence, link making, speculation, imagination, originality, questioning and safe risk taking are encouraged and part of the day-to-day experience of the child. Early years practice has for many years successfully developed a pedagogy that depends upon such characteristics in the context of play and exploration. The *Curriculum Guidance for the Foundation Stage* (CGFS; DfES/QCA, 1999) was seen as cross-curricular from the start. The language of this document avoids reference to separated subjects and speaks of 'areas of learning' to underline this. The promotion of a strong self-image and strong self-esteem are specifically mentioned as aims for the curriculum. The CGFS accepts that real, relevant and personally engaging experience interpreted through several areas of learning is most likely to promote both confidence and creativity.

Only lately have schools recognized that what stimulates creative learning in 3–5-year-olds also motivates older children and adults. Speculative and imaginative attitudes are commonplace at the cutting edge of research in every subject/discipline. If such creativity enlivens both ends of the learning continuum, perhaps it is time that the 5–14-year-olds in the middle experienced teaching styles that promote more unexpected, original thinking and connection making across the curriculum.

Creative thinking and learning

We cannot make children think and neither can we force them to learn, but as teachers we can create the conditions where both are more likely. Creativity in essence is unpredictable and does not always result from plans, but the atmosphere in a classroom can be planned and resourced. A creativity-friendly classroom will result from decisions that range from the arrangement of furniture and temperature to the timetable and treatment of individuals.

When two or three subject perspectives are used to interpret an experience, topic, problem or question, overlaps between them are inevitable. Creative advances in both the child's and the adult's world often happen at the boundaries between subjects and cultures. Well-planned cross-curricular approaches combined with a mix of playful attitudes and authentic challenges have a high chance of generating creative ideas and exchanges.

Subject-based knowledge and skills

One of the personal and pedagogical qualities in teachers deemed creative by their peers is that they have considerable subject knowledge (Cremin et al., 2009). There is no escape from the conclusion that a good teacher knows things, is enthusiastic to learn more things and is good at communicating both knowledge and enthusiasm. Subject knowledge is not an optional extra in cross-curricular teaching and learning – without a clear understanding of subject progression, neither appropriate challenge nor appropriate skill development are possible. In an early years or primary context, the need for subject expertise in cross-curricular learning once again asserts the importance of teachers talking to each other and planning together.

The HEARTS project (Chapter 3, case study 7) found that learning took place largely when the teachers used the motivation of the children as an opportunity to teach new skills or provide greater challenges. Where teachers only observed, or accepted contributions without applying subject rigour, little new subject learning occurred. There is of course a time for observation and simple acceptance – in the early years, children often learn most effectively when there is *less* adult intervention (Goouch, 2010). Children of all ages learn informally, away from classrooms and teachers most of their lives (Pollard, 2008), but as they get older the role of the teacher becomes ever more complex. Shirley (2007) sees this multiple role as like a dance – different with each child – where the teacher skillfully steps between leading, co-learning, instructing, training, quietly watching, encouraging and facilitating.

Subject knowledge is not the only knowledge essential to the teacher. The good pedagog knows his or her pupils well, knows children well, knows how to engage and calm them, how to lead them and how to let them lead. Part of knowing children well is knowing where and when they are most likely to learn, and the move towards learning beyond the classroom (Austin, 2007; DfES, 2006d, website) is in recognition that many children find outdoor learning more enjoyable and memorable. The Forest Schools (2010, website) which have developed all over England, Scotland, Wales, Northern Ireland and the Channel Islands offer stimulating, safe, flexible spaces and well-trained leaders for play-based learning out of doors and for all age groups. An increasing number of schools use these sites and practitioners as a major part of their curriculum. Many schools now repeat their visits to the woodland sites a number of times in a term or year to build community links and ensure a progression of learning in a wide range of subjects. Activities on site include: construction, way-finding, plant and animal identification/classification, traditional crafts, estimation, physical, personal and group challenges. The learning arising from such activities is inevitably cross-curricular since the overarching philosophy is founded on values of sustainability and child-led, exploratory and active learning. Schools report significant development in personal, social and emotional skills too and Forest Schools' principles of mutual respect and environmental responsibility support schools in their wider aims.

The use of outside, usually non-teacher, experts to boost subject knowledge and skills and to develop community links has been championed by all political parties. Between 2002 and 2010, together with Creative Partnerships, teachers benefited from all kinds of local joint ventures with experts from the locality of the school. This was not an abrogation of teacherly responsibilities or a compromise of their skills. Research (Brice Heath and Wolf, 2005; Roberts, 2006) has found that expert outsiders with the support of teachers can both persuade children to attempt greater challenges and achieve higher standards and improve the quality and range of teaching skills.

A sense of progression in all learning

Progression in learning results from the teacher providing suitable challenges for children. Csikszentmihalyi has shown that if we wish children to enter the productive and satisfying state which psychologists call flow, teachers need either to raise the challenge for children who are bored, or raise the level of skills for those who are anxious about learning.

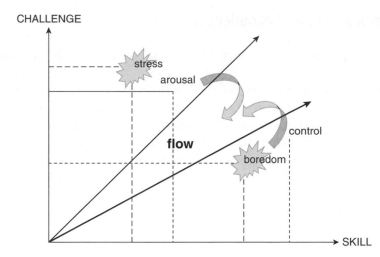

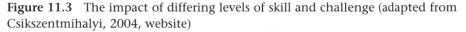

Figure 11.3 The impact of differing levels of skill and challenge (adapted from Csikszentmihalyi, 2004, website)

The national curricula of each UK country gives detailed attainment targets in the form of levelled descriptions for each curriculum subject. Subject specialist teachers can identify separated progressions of skills and knowledge from these lists and support colleagues in planning for progression. Progression is not simply a product of teaching, however – there needs to be progress in attitude and application on the part of the learner. The development to be planned starts with ensuring and measuring *involvement*, moves on to sustaining *engagement* and then, using individually crafted challenges, gives the child a sense of *progression* and finally results in a consciousness of real *achievement*. The progression from involvement to achievement is one that needs as much planning time and conversation as the details of knowledge and skills.

Children in a nursery class had seen a hedgehog in their garden. The teacher involved all in looking carefully as it moved towards the hedge, but she wanted them to have an opportunity to take something lasting from the experience. The teacher decided on leading the children to make a clay model of the hedgehog. Engagement was ensured by giving the children the experience of feeling the cold damp clay in their hands and shaping it into an ovoid, and it was deepened by the suggestion that they stuck multiple matchsticks into the clay to make the spines. Children moved from engagement to a sense of progression as they noticed their featureless ovoids looking more and more like hedgehogs. Finally, the children felt a real sense of achievement as they presented the carers with their finished models.

Meaningful and shared experiences

Planning for relevance does not just mean the teacher chooses a topic which he or she thinks is significant in the child's world. Neither is it always as simple as finding an appropriate entry point from everyday life. Teachers may be correct in their choices, but those choices must be made to *feel* meaningful within the minds of the learners before they enter into a learning contract with the teacher. Experienced teachers have become masters at this kind of negotiation. I gathered the following set of short examples during a single working week:

- A teacher in east Kent made *longshore drift* relevant to her Year 8 geography fieldwork class, by getting part of the class to dance the zigzag movement of the pebbles on the beach as she described their movement.

- A class teacher in Rotherham used his class's ringside seat at the demolition of the old school building as an excuse to bring old members of the community into the new school building to be interviewed.

- A Year 3 teacher made transparency and opacity relevant by asking groups of children to make trendy sunglasses for the class teddy bear.

- A teacher in Whitby significantly improved the creative writing of all her pupils by asking them to include their detailed observations of her precise movements as she wandered furtively between the ruins of an old monastery the day before.

The learning gained from such activity is a product not simply of good teaching, but of detailed attention to the emotional setting of learning. Relevance can be created by planning child-centred spaces for learning and ensuring a wholesome social and moral atmosphere. The emotional and intellectual content can also be planned for relevance by setting up meaningful links and structuring each learning experience with the child centrally in mind. In doing this, the teacher can make even the most unpromising pile of stones seem meaningful and generative.

Strong and positive relations with the community and locality

The coalition government of 2010 proposed far-reaching plans to make education more community based. Successful schools were encouraged to consider taking academy status, to develop a curriculum appropriate to the community and to find local sponsors to fund them. Both primary and secondary academies would operate outside local authority control and have considerable freedom to teach and arrange learning in ways felt to be appropriate communally. Such a policy shift will leave many schools in a position where they have to make decisions on curriculum that previously were made for them by local authority or government 'advice' via government circulars and the now disbanded Curriculum and Qualifications Development Agency (QCDA). It is hoped that this book and others like it will provide guidance on how to approach this newfound freedom.

Support in developing community links relevant to a creative and cross-curriculum already mentioned include the Engaging Places website, Creative Partnerships (now privatized under various local names, e.g. *Future Creative* in Kent, *A New Direction* in London, *Creative Futures* in Cumbia), English Heritage, Cadw and Historic Scotland, the National Trust, English Nature, Scottish Natural Heritage, Royal Society for the Protection of Birds and countless local museums, galleries, factories, theatres, concert halls and historic houses which combine nationally relevant education programmes with local contacts, sites and communities.

Teachers planning a relevant programme of experiences and interfaces for their children might start with a visit to their local library with a request for sites and organizations with an education officer. All education visits to English Heritage, Cadw, Northern Ireland Environment Agency or Historic Scotland are free so long as an educational booking is made. It is in the best interests of every organization with an education interest to make a visit to their site as positive as possible and so help with planning, structuring or following up a visit is often available.

Safe and stimulating spaces for learning

Planning for the most effective learning experience starts with the careful consideration of the spaces in which children learn. This, for example, has been a preoccupation of those who plan learning spaces for the children of Reggio Emilia in northern Italy. In pre-schools of Reggio, great attention and considerable resources are devoted to the fine detail of the children's environment. The fabrics, the design and materials of coat hooks, the colour of furniture, the lighting, the placing of services such as the school kitchen, or the views from windows are all carefully considered. There is a distinct child-centredness to all these decisions, immediately evident in the child-friendly levels of window sills, door handles and taps, as well as the powerful use of light, colour, fabrics and soft edges.

Jerome Bruner has worked with Reggio's pre-schools and has isolated three essentials for the pre-school child learning space. These principles for learning spaces could be profitably applied throughout education. For Bruner, a learning space must be:

- *mine, thine, and ours* (it 'needs to provide places for each individual who occupies it … but must be communal as well')

- *in and of the broader community* (it should be in the physical community and its activities should arise from the community)
- *a learning community* ('a place to learn together about the real world, and about possible worlds of imagination ... where the young discover the uses of mind, of imagination, of materials, and learn the power of doing these things together'). (Bruner, 2003: 137)

The exquisite learning outcomes of such attention to detail are well known and provide ample evidence of the ease of generating high levels of achievement in child-centred conditions (see Reggio Emilia, 2006, website).

Clearly, in Reggio, generous local funding and the economic profits of fame have worked together to construct exciting places and learning tools for the children. Reggio Emilia 'principles', however, are applicable in any setting. The first principle is to put the child at the heart of the decision-making process. The implications of this have recently been explored in an English context by Shirley Brice Heath in a community school in Hythe, Kent. Here Nursery, Reception, Year 1 and Year 2 children worked on a project to redesign and oversee the building of a new reception area for their school. The 3–7-year-olds worked with architects, an artist and interior designers to plan and follow through plans for a truly child-centred entrance and route way through their school (Brice Heath and Wolf, 2004). Through frequent planning and orientation meetings, questionnaires and a major exhibition of their

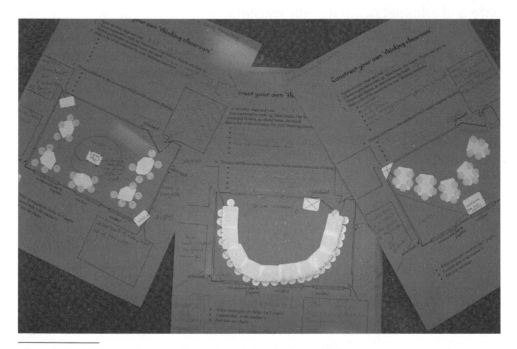

Illustration 11.1   *Student teachers' plans for a 'thinking classroom'*

plans and ideas, the children and architects arrived at a brief for the rebuilding and redesign of large areas of the school. The official brief to the architects and designers was to explore 'how good design can improve the quality of life in schools by listening to the voices of the consumers. It inspires pupils by putting them in the driving seat, giving them control and responsibility as clients' (Brice Heath and Wolf, 2004: 9). But the children's brief to the architects was in the form of a mighty exhibition. Designer Ben Kelly who worked with the children recounted:

> We posed questions to them and their response was this exhibition; that's how they overcame the practical problems of communication. They communicated in the way that young children do best, by chucking a load of stuff out from within themselves; drawings, paintings, models, collages, written stuff, tons and tons of it – all over the walls! Their brief/exhibition was incredible. It had such vigour, life and enthusiasm. It really was stimulating. It was the key that unlocked the process. (Brice Heath and Wolf, 2004: 14)

Children's decisions about space for learning and celebrating their learning were taken seriously by adults and the results were far in excess of expectations. Profound discussions about morality, security, culture, beauty, life and

Illustration 11.2 *Children proudly introduce their display in the entrance they designed with architects. Courtesy of Creative Partnerships Kent*

death were common in this context. Children decided, for example, that they did not want their reception area to be boring, 'just about sitting', they wanted to move people around and they wanted to showcase the art they were so proud of. They planned a display system and 'Barbie pink' carpeted route way around their displayed work which was in many ways to be the heart of the school. Interestingly, adults took on the playfulness of children in their design and the children took on some aspects of the seriousness of adults. The deep implications of these genuine and meaningful interactions between adults and children may be summarized in a single comment from Jack: 'We learned to make things. My favourite was the bucket lights [yellow ceiling lights made to look like sand castle buckets from the nearby beach] – they looked cool. When I walk into this reception area after it's built, I think I'll feel famous' (Brice Heath and Wolf, 2004: 19). Such a sense of specialness, accomplishment and meaning which results from involvement in creative acts, could be argued to be every child's birthright.

The Hythe project was cross-curricular in every way. Children were involved in this project for a whole year before the building was complete. They richly developed their language at both its most practical and most symbolic levels.

The Hythe pupils used and extended their art to make objects which truly became a valued part of their environment and developed a range of

Illustration 11.3 *Infants school entrance designed with 'big art' and buckets as light shades by the 5–7-year-old pupils. Courtesy of Creative Partnerships Kent*

design/technology skills and principles. Additionally, they learned that even at four years of age they could generate real change for the better in their community. It is not difficult, however, to translate this ambitious project into the more prosaic context of every primary classroom. What about the following questions which any class could fruitfully be involved in addressing?

- How could we rearrange the classroom furniture so that we can combine private space to work quietly on our own and opportunities to work together?
- How can we decorate the walls to make this classroom really reflect us as people?
- How can we improve the view from our classroom window?
- How can we address one of the millennium goals in this classroom this term?
- We have £200 to spend on some new furniture/equipment/resources for this room this year, so what shall we buy?
- How can we find out what local people *really* want in the redevelopment of part of the school grounds?

Such questions are authentic and open, and can be used genuinely to elicit the views and more importantly real-world actions and products of children's thought. Answers which generated action would involve children and adults together in a co-learning situation in which a range of skills and knowledge from design and technology, art, language, mathematics, science or geography might be taught and quickly and meaningfully applied. Genuine and thoughtful solutions would change the children's environment. They would be arrived at through compromise, empathy, problem solving, creative thinking and a host of other cross-curricular skills. But answers to such questions might also communicate important messages that ordinary folk *can* change things, and that we can agree on principled ways of improving our community.

Throughout the CGFS and the UK national curricula, we are reminded about linking subjects. 'Stepping stones', areas of learning, programmes of study and general teaching requirements are wide open to imaginative and school-specific interpretation. In its first pages, the English National Curriculum recites the now familiar mantra regarding education being a route to 'spiritual, moral, social, cultural, physical and mental development, and thus the well-being, of the individual'. It clearly states that the curriculum orders are intended to:

enable us to respond positively to the opportunities and challenges of the rapidly changing world in which we live and work. In particular, we need to be prepared to engage as individuals, parents, workers and citizens with economic, social and cultural change, including the continued globalization of the economy and society, with new work and leisure patterns and with the rapid expansion of communication technologies. (DfES/QCA, 1999: 10)

Most curricula are flexible enough to support the cross-curricular planning and creative thinking implicit in recent government-sponsored guidance. If words like those above are not mere rhetoric, they must result in a highly flexible, constantly revised curriculum, sensitively tuned to contemporary lives and communities. Even without revision, most national and local curricula allow for the kind of challenging curriculum experiments we saw represented in Chapter 3. Criticisms of curricula are common, but perhaps it is more productive to take a different *attitude* to existing guidance and link learning more precisely to the lived worlds of children themselves.

In many ways, the writers of the *Curriculum Guidance for the Foundation Stage* (DfES/QCA, 1999) blazed the trail towards broader, richer, more creative approaches to the curriculum. The QCA – in its response to *All Our Futures* (NACCCE, 1999), the Roberts review (2006) and the select committee report (HC, 2008) – the Department of Culture Media and Sport (DCMS) through sponsorship of research, Sport England, the Arts Council and Creative

Illustration 11.4   *Secondary School children making links between history, creative writing and movement*

Partnerships and the Healthy Schools campaign (DoH/DfES, 2005) have all spread a similar message about creativity. *Every Child Matters* and the resulting proposals relating to personalized learning and the re-conceptualizing of schools as multipurpose 'children's centres', heralds the development of a new mindset towards education. Government documents of both left and right seek broader definitions of learning, concentrating on lifelong, transferable, personally tailored, significant, confidence-building, global and community-specific features. It is up to teachers and others in schools to take control of this agenda for the betterment of their children.

There is evidence that schools are moving towards accepting a role where staff and pupil well-being have equal importance with curriculum content. This is in line with a government focus on measuring well-being across the population. This balance is particularly well served by cross-curricular and creative approaches to teaching and learning. The government White Paper on education, *Higher Standards, Better Schools for All* (HM Government, 2005, website), explicitly expresses the importance of the pliant, personalized and positive approach: 'Children and young people learn best with a curriculum which enthuses and engages. We are already seeing increasing curriculum flexibility and helping schools to make the most of this'.

To be effective and sustainable, a curriculum should link effortlessly to an established and school-based framework of shared values and assured relevance. A rationale which is clear to all stakeholders, which genuinely values all and aims to ensure personalized progression seems much more likely to raise standards.

When a teacher helps make a subject personally relevant to children, they do so by helping the child discover physical, personal and emotional links between the subject and their own lives. Working in this way, teachers attempt to make the existential connection which Peter Abbs (2003: 3) found so lacking in his geography teacher and which possibly millions still fail to find in their daily exposure to education. Many readers will instantly recollect the teachers who have really 'spoken' to them and have somehow imbued their subject with a sense of personal meaningfulness. The social, neurological, psychological and pedagogical research cited in this book leads me to believe that planning for such *emotional* identification engenders deep learning.

The Foundation Stage curriculum

The CGFS (Curriculum Guidance for the Foundation Stage) is very direct regarding how teachers and other adults must plan for real experiences from which children learn. Essentially, such learning experiences should feel like play. Planning for generative play is a key and wholly natural way for all children to learn. To make learning likely, however, adults need to consider structures to plan within. In teams, teachers of pre-school and reception class children should consider how to:

1 provide the physical and emotional security which allows for safe risk taking and encourages a positive view of mistakes
2 introduce the element of challenge into the planned play activity
3 support the play without intervening too much
4 extend the activity and the learning
5 ensure that spontaneous play is likely
6 add to the child's language world (see Illustration 11.5).

These generic thoughts aside, the most effective spaces and situations for challenging and generative play are often outside the classroom. The kindergartens of Germany, Switzerland and Scandinavia, the Forest Schools and the playgrounds of the Reggio Emilia pre-schools each use the semi-natural world of playground, woodland, fields, nature trails and parks nearest them as major resources. Rain or shine, within these outdoor environments, children may be asked to find their way, travel, imagine, collect, classify, build, record or express themselves within wider themes such as:

Ilustration 11.5   *Six-year-olds effectively linking art, language and science by working with an artist on careful looking and drawing. Courtesy of Creative Partnerships Kent*

- getting bigger
- going on a bear hunt
- life around us
- people who help us
- shelters
- journeys
- feeling happy; feeling sad
- finding the way home.

Within the classroom, the world of the imagination may take children much further away. Questions such as:

- What do angels look like?
- What do I look like when I'm peaceful?
- How do we think the internet works?
- How do television pictures get to us?
- What would the world look like if I was a bird/germ/giant/ant?

can extend the thinking, socialization and motor skills of every child.

Getting down to the paperwork

The thinking, talking, deciding and reflecting having been done, the paperwork aspects of planning should be more straightforward. Schools must have long-term plans to address particular issues identified in school self-reviews and/or inspections. They are likely to have medium-term plans covering a six-week school term and each teacher will have a series of daily lesson plans often called short-term plans.

Long-term planning

Long-term planning needs to take account of:

1 National/local curriculum subjects – designed to help children understand their world *now*.
2 Cross-curricular strands – designed to help children make a positive impact upon *the future*.
3 Own or others' research – intended to support teachers in combining personal and societal objectives.

National Curriculum subjects

Each country of the UK has differing groupings of subjects as indicated in Chapter 2. Chapter 3 showed how one school divided time between the subjects nationally required. The timing allocations between subjects are, however, not mandatory and core subjects may, with thorough planning, be incorporated into cross-curricular study. As schools become more independent of local authority and central government influence, no doubt many inventive curricula will couple the right for a broad and balanced curriculum with the continuing pressure to raise standards in literacy, numeracy and ICT. If we aim to take account of individual differences in learning and help each child become a self-regulated learner, then the cross-curricular skills identified in the 1999 curriculum remain a helpful guide.

Cross-curricular strands

Each UK country has different National Curriculum subjects and different cross-curricular strands, but regardless of regional priorities, the acquisition of certain skills running across all curriculum subjects are considered vital. These are:

- communication
- application of number
- information and communications technology (ICT)
- working with others
- improving own learning and performance
- problem-solving.

Communication

Reading, writing, speaking and listening would be encouraged in meaningful contexts across all school experience. Other powerful forms of communication through play, pictures and symbols, through music, numbers, dance and mime, and in facial expressions and body language would also be centrally represented. Schools could maximize alternative modes of communication by offering children a wide range of different methods to present their learning. Understanding in PE might be better communicated in movement or a game, geographical understanding might be clarified by a map, table, diagram, drawing or journey, history by an exhibition of artefacts or music by a composition.

Application of number

Number might well be one of the languages through which children understand a more general curriculum theme. In topics centred on design and technology, art and PE, we may practically apply concepts of weight, measurement, symmetry and balance. In a geography and history project, distance, graphs, statistics, scale and time are key to understanding the wider world. A theme illuminated by the perspectives of music, RE, MFL, English or science may need number to help children understand sonic, spiritual, linguistic and natural patterns around them.

Information and communications technology (ICT)

The challenge is not simply to use ICT, but to ensure it supports the progressive development of skills, knowledge and understanding in each subject. For example, a Year 1 class might use digital cameras to record significant aspects of their locality and then classify them into four categories: 'natural life', 'our historic environment', 'working in our village' and 'what's changing?' The degree and development of their local understanding could easily be recorded from the discussions, selections and poster presentations which accompanied this activity.

Working with others

School is the only place where most children regularly relate to a range of age mates, so group work on real-life, curriculum-based challenges can be a key opportunity to build new relationships and develop emotional literacy. Empathy, the capacity to relate, leadership or 'followership', and coping with disagreements and disappointments are all part of the experience of working on combined projects. Most great strides in human culture have not resulted from lone efforts but have arisen from the creative collaboration of groups (John-Steiner, 2006). Group investigations, games, murals, model-building, musical improvisations and compositions, and problem solving in teams will develop social skills and provoke more effective and creative solutions (see Illustration 11.5).

Improving own learning and performance

Reflection is not simply a pleasant and calming activity but has profound effects upon learning and performance. Five- and six-year-old children in a Cognitive Acceleration study (Shayer and Adey, 2002) were asked questions which provoked thinking at a level not usually associated with their age. In a practical science session on materials, teachers asked questions such as:

- What do you think we are going to have to think about?
- What could you do if you have problems?

- How do you know that?
- What might make this easier?

Other cross-curricular stands

Governments have variously attempted to boost the economy through education by promoting education for:

- financial capability
- enterprise.

Increasingly, governments have become concerned about the social, mental and physical well-being of their populations, resulting in cross-curricular strands such as:

- sustainable development
- PSHE/citizenship
- values education.

Similarly, 'Thinking Skills' are recognized as central to the properly educated mind. The thinking skills isolated by the English National Curriculum are:

- information processing
- reasoning
- enquiry
- creative thinking
- evaluation.

Research in teaching and learning

Increasingly, teachers are encouraged to formalize the analysis and data collection they do as a normal part of their work (Alexander, 2010). Formalized and written down for others, the routine observations, records and reflections of teachers becomes research. The development of teacher researchers is particularly relevant to curriculum planning (Wilson et al., 2010).Throughout this book, the research of professional researchers in neuroscience, psychology, sociology or the study of education has been cited in support of the suggestion that cross-curricular activities are appropriate, motivating and educationally beneficial to the vast majority of children. Summarized, the research already cited in this book suggests that teachers:

1 Create a positive, secure and comfortable atmosphere.

2 Ensure a range of practical, creative and analytical activities for each child.

3 Have clear goals, challenges and individualized targets pitched a little above current ability.

4 Use a manageable number of relevant subjects to throw light on the topic.

5 Build emotionally significant links to the life of each child, engaging all the senses and using tools and objects to support and promote thinking.

6 Involve developmentally appropriate progression in skills, knowledge and understanding.

7 Work within structures and a wider framework which includes concepts, subject skills, knowledge and attitudes.

8 Emphasize individual and cooperative thinking and learning throughout.

9 Provide supportive assessment procedures which build security and include time and tools for reflection.

10 Offer a wide range of opportunities to discover engagement, enjoyment and other positive emotions.

Education research also suggests that the best schools aim at personalized learning and effectively address emotional health and well-being for all. These schools develop philosophies which value and aim to develop resilience, problem solving, emotional intelligence, differences and cooperation between individuals and groups (DfES, 2003; Ofsted, 2009a and b). Planning in this context goes far wider than individual lessons or learning modules – it touches on every aspect of the experience of teachers and children in school.

Planning also involves the very language of pedagogy. Metacognitive questions like: How are we going to do this? What might happen if … ? I wonder what it would be like if … ? Are there any other ways this can be done? ensure improved performance by deepening thinking and apply to all subjects.

Medium-term planning

In applying the principles suggested elsewhere in this book and in the early part of this chapter, it is clear that planning cross-curricular modules of work from a few days to a term, will involve decisions on:

- limiting subjects
- planning powerful experiences
- maintaining a balance between open experience and structured learning.

Illustration 11.6 A team of two discuss their design and technology solution with a creative practitioner. Courtesy of Creative partnerships Kent

Limiting subjects

Whilst it is probably possible to bend every subject to fit a chosen theme, we have seen that this can be confusing and counterproductive. Limiting the subjects to two or three has been discussed in previous chapters, but in medium-term planning, specific detail of the programme of study and attainment targets for each subject should be included.

The simple appearance of a subject in a cross-curricular module is not enough. The deeper contribution of that subject and progression need to be evident in plans. A sense of progression and deeper meaning can often arise from the formulation of key questions within the subject.

Key questions

Key questions should address the issues within a subject perspective which preoccupy people at any intellectual level. Both the university professor and the young child are interested in the big questions of life: Who are we? Where are we going? What's the meaning of it all? Peter Abbs (2003) would suggest that any questions which touch upon the existential would be likely to draw the child into active participation in his or her learning, for example:

- What is my responsibility to the environment? (a geography key question)
- What are my dreams for the future? (a PSHE key question)
- Who is my neighbour? (an RE or PSHE key question)
- What does it mean to be alive? (a science key question)
- What is war like? (a history key question)
- How does learning about other cultures help me understand about myself? (an RE key question)
- What is beauty? (an art/music/PE/English/mathematics key question)
- What does fit for purpose mean? (a design/technology key question)
- How can I express emotion without words? (a music/art/PE key question)
- What is good/evil? (a history/RE/PSHE key question)

Subject progression

The easiest route towards ensuring subject progression is to ask each subject coordinator/specialist/team to look at the attainment targets and levels for their subject, found in the back of the national curriculum. From this list, specialists can build up a series of steps towards mastery of their subject under the headings *skills, knowledge* and *attitudes*.

Planning powerful experiences

Children (and probably most of us) learn most easily through actually being *physically* involved in exploring sites, materials and ideas. It is incumbent upon schools to create and control those experiences to stimulate involvement and learning. This can be done by planning not just for the physical and social environment the children work in, but the experiences they will learn through. Perkins (1992) calls such experiences 'generative experiences', and they can become the motor for a lively and meaningful curriculum. Planning generative experiences is better done by a team if possible. The progression of experiences a child has in his or her school career needs careful mapping throughout the key stage and beyond. Some experiences will be revisited, such as a second or third workshop with a theatre group or a trip to the local church, forest or mosque. As in Forest Schools, multiple visits will each have a different focus. A curriculum based around experiences will clearly need a whole-school approach and adults planning it might consider the following suggestions.

Planning learning

Not all learning comes from experience. Some learning is handed down from past generations, some is gathered from sources such as the internet, films

Illustration 11.7 *A First World War 'sound mirror', designed to detect the presence of approaching enemy aircraft, captures the attention of a pupil. Courtesy of Creative Partnerships Kent*

and books and some is passed on by peers, friends or family. Experience remains, however, a powerful means of kick-starting learning and motivating the deepening of that learning. If experiences are shared and if they are in some way meaningful to the participants, then frequently they will generate thinking and learning. Experiences can of course be big or small. They can be physical, social, creative, cerebral, emotional or practical, but to have personal and emotional meaning they need to capture and hold the attention.

Every lesson will include a number of small shared experiences, perhaps a well-read story, a science experiment or a new song, but big shared experiences need more planning. Major class experiences capable of sustaining interest and engagement over several weeks, should be planned for at least six occasions through every school year, one per six-week term. It is inevitable that a host of literacy skills will be developed as a result of every experience. Case study 3 (Chapter 3) showed a year's generative experiences for a Year 1/2 class. The vignette below records contrasting responses to generative experiences for a Year 8 class.

Illustration 11.8 *An impromptu classroom display after a reception class walk in the playground. Photo: Cherry Tewfik*

One Year 8 class in Birmingham was taken to the top of the Malvern Hills for an enriching and inspiring geography field course. Their teacher reported on her return that they were totally unmoved, uninterested and unfocused. When the next week the same group were taken to their own shopping street for well-prepared and detailed fieldwork on the shops and services there, the class reported that it had been their best day's work ever. When asked to explain, a female student said, 'We were really happy you had taken the trouble to find out lots of stuff about our place'.

Balancing experience, skills and knowledge

Experiences cannot become generative of new learning without interpreting them through the skills and subject knowledge of the disciplines. The disciplines provide a specialized vocabulary and structure to understanding and any engaging, sustainable and relevant curriculum should balance subject craft skills and knowledge, on one hand, and opportunities for personal responses, on the other. The six- or seven-week timetable suggested below (Figure 11.4) uses half the week for cross-curricular experience using two subjects and the other half for ongoing courses in the remaining national curriculum subjects. Through a year, a curriculum structure like this would allow for both coverage of each subject and opportunities to put subject learning into practice.

Such a timetable is flexible enough to allow for the essential visit, visitor or responses to specific issues arising from the visit. In the example above, science, geography and English are the focus subjects, but other curriculum subjects are still taught every week. In the following term, substantially more time may be given to mathematics, history and PE. In the subsequent term, art, design and technology and modern foreign languages may have the floor. A timetable like this is not very radical and fits easily within established approaches. More adventurous schools may wish to devote more time to the theme, but half a week each week for six weeks is sufficient to build successfully upon the generative experience for each child.

Monday	Core Literacy/ English	Core Numeracy/ Maths	RE (Core learning)	Geography (C-C theme)
Tuesday	Core History	Literacy/ English (C-C Theme)	Cross-curricular (C-C-theme, geog. and sci. focus)	Cross-curricular (C-C theme)
Wednesday	Core Numeracy/ Maths	Core Design and Technology	Core PE	Core Art
Thursday	Science (C-C theme)	Science (C-C theme)	Creative Literacy/ English (C-C theme)	Core Music
Friday	Core Literacy/ English/MFL	Ongoing Investigative Numeracy/ Maths	Cross-curricular (C-C theme, geog. and sci. focus)	Cross-curricular (C-C theme, geog. and Sci. focus)

Figure 11.4 A primary school curriculum for a six-week term where Geography and Science were focus subjects

Alternatively, a school may wish to plan a unit of work based on Blythe and Perkins's (Blythe, 1997) concept of 'performances of understanding' (PoU) but applied by the teacher to cross-curricular learning. Performances in this context are opportunities for children to demonstrate the degree and complexity of their learning by applying new learning to a real problem. The teacher uses several performances of understanding throughout the unit to gauge the progress of the class and of individuals. The first performance is a chance for children to show what they know already and what they can gather from collections, internet or library searches, focus exercises or questioning *without* formal teaching. The second performance gives children (in groups or individually) the space to articulate what they have learned from a period of focused teaching relevant to the foci identified. The final or 'culminating performance' results from an open-ended opportunity for groups or individuals to put their new knowledge into action by applying it to a new challenge. The 'performances' theme therefore combines an assessment strategy which is integral to the learning but which also provides structure to the unit.

A cross-curricular (PoU) unit requires first the planning of particular goals for each subject and then goals for creative expression. In the example below, music and history learning combine in an inter-disciplinary unit based on the Tudors. The idea of the Tudors was introduced in an activity funday run by a group of travelling actors/craftspeople/musicians who bring the 'Tudor experience' to schools. Because the unit is *inter*-disciplinary, the teacher will expect a degree of creative fusion between the knowledge and skills learned from two disparate subjects by the end. The culminating performance will involve the children being asked in groups of five to make a two-minute video on a Tudor theme with an appropriate soundtrack.

Creative expression might be graded as follows:

1 Awareness of links between ideas/materials/skills (e.g. the child knows that Tudors had different popular music from us).

2 Working with others on links between ideas/materials/skills (e.g. the child participates in a group talking about making some music for a Tudor video drama).

3 Independently suggesting links between ideas/materials/skills (e.g. the child suggests that the musicians wear Tudor clothes as well as the actors).

4 Making original links between ideas/materials/skills (e.g. the child bases an improvised tune and structure on an example of Dowland's lute music).

5 Successfully accomplishing a finished and original idea/product/process (e.g. the child directs the refinement and final performance of their original composition as background to their Tudor video).

The relevant subject skills and knowledge in music might be:

- to know that much Tudor music depended on two chords: chord I (tonic chord) and chord V (dominant)
- to know that Tudor music often used simple 'troubadour' drum rhythms as accompaniment
- to be able to describe the intended emotional impact of Tudor examples using appropriate music vocabulary
- to be able to recognize and apply chords I and V and troubadour drum rhythms to their own improvisations and compositions.

The relevant knowledge and skills for history might be:

- to know the dates of the Tudor period
- to describe distinctive features of Tudor life
- to know of and understand three different sources of evidence of the distinctive features of Tudor life
- to understand and be able to describe some reasons for major events in Tudor times.

A medium-term pro-forma for a Year 5 cross-curricular module of three weeks. The module is intended to develop history and music skills and knowledge in a cross-curricular context and assessed through performances of understanding.

Generative experience: *The visit of 'History Alive' theatre group for a Tudor activity day*

Subject 1: *History* Understanding Goals   Subject 2: *Music* Understanding Goals
- •   - •
- •   - •

Resources (what you will need to make this unit a success)
- •
- •
- •

(Continued)

(Continued)

SEQUENCE OF EVENTS	PERFORMANCES OF UNDERSTANDING (Plan how children will show the level of their understanding by applying their newly learned skills/knowledge to a new challenge)	ASSESSMENT (How will you know that children have (a) engaged, (b) sustained interest and (c) achieved new learning?)
Day or week 1 Introductory performance(s)	What do we know already? What do we want to know? What is the focus going to be? Using brainstorm, mind maps, Venn diagrams, lists, debates, internet, experts, collections, etc. e.g. *'everyone find twelve surprising facts about Tudor London'.* *What do you hear in this recorded music from the Tudor period?*	**Feedback:** Informal and oral, by peers and teachers, written or drawn reflections by students **Criteria:** Developed collaboratively by students and teacher
Day or week 2 Performance(s) resulting from the teaching of relevant new skills and knowledge	What skills and knowledge do you need to teach as a result of interest generated by the experience? In what ways can children show the new subject knowledge they have gained in each of two subjects? e.g. *musical improvisations and compositions in Tudor style.* *Three different interpretations of burning of Martyrs outside the city wall*	**Feedback:** Informal and oral, by peers, visitors, parents and teachers **Criteria:** Students complete a summary sheet about their learning
Day or week 3 Culminating performance(s)	How can children creatively combine the new subject skills in answering a new and independent problem or challenge which uses them? e.g. *make a two-minute Tudor video based on a true story and with appropriate soundtrack*	**Feedback:** Informal and oral, by peers and teachers, formal written evaluation by student groups and teacher. **Criteria:** Matched against relevant levels in national curriculum

Short-term planning

The lesson plan is a very personal thing though many schools and most ITE institutions provide standard formats to ensure coverage of all the complex demands of national curriculum strategies, cross-curricular strands and particular policy. I do not intend to offer a lesson plan format. Aside from the strictures of legislation and policy, daily or single lesson plan research and cross-curricular experience suggests just three reminders. Every lesson should have:

- small-scale experiences and challenges
- small achievable steps and noticeable progress
- small opportunities for performance and a sense of achievement.

Small-scale experiences and challenges

Focus exercises have been explained and exemplified fully in Chapter 3. Such exercises are intended to provide small-scale personal/sensory experience and engagement. Some will involve, some will seem boring or nonsensical, but experience in using them over a number of years shows that they are remarkably resilient means of capturing attention and also of demonstrating important principles (Dismore et al., 2008). Because the focus exercises listed are primarily sensory and open-ended, they are immediately cross-curricular in character and lend themselves to interpretation or extension in many directions. Their openness provides its own challenge.

Throughout every good lesson, a series of planned and unplanned challenges are also thrown out by the teacher – these add to pace and surprise but also work to refocus attention. Questioning has already been covered, but the quizzical look and questioning stance stimulates mirror neuron responses in most children.

Small achievable steps and noticeable progress

Throughout this book, I have reminded the reader that teaching of knowledge and skills is a required part of cross-curricular learning. If cross-curricular activity is poorly planned and not centred around teaching, the chances are that little deep learning will occur. Opportunistic approaches to cross-curricular learning depend upon significant stores of teacher knowledge and the ability to marshall it as the child/ren require. Assessment, differentiation and small and achievable steps of progression are easier to achieve with subjects approached in multi- or inter-disciplinary ways. These methods allow for more formal planning of the knowledge and skills to be introduced and these are the modes of cross-curricular teaching I would recommend novice teachers experiment with (see Chapter 2).

In any event, the sense that progress has been made, new knowledge learned, new skills applied is an important one for many children. The planning necessary for such feelings of achievement is argued by Ofsted to make the difference between good and failed creative teaching (Ofsted, 2010).

Small opportunities for performance and a sense of achievement

One of the unintended outcomes of the literacy and numeracy strategies is that children often feel they have not finished their work. The march of expectations means that children rarely get the chance to revisit and finish this incomplete work. Culminating performance of a low-key kind is particularly important to the success of cross-curricular work. A bringing together of learning at the end of each session clarifies what subject has been extended and specifically whether the understanding goals for that subject have been achieved. Even 40-minute lessons can have a structure of warm up–subject development–concluding performance, which provides the completed feel of the 'whole game' (Perkins, 2009).

Summary

The research cited in this book is as relevant to the planning of cross-curricular activity as to its delivery. Long-, medium- and short-term plans must take account of the observations and experience of teachers and those who research their work if they are to reach the majority of children. Similarly, the values stressed in Chapters 1, 2, 4, 7 and 8 should underpin planning at all levels well before, during and after the paperwork has been done. Some values lead to particular planning preoccupations: fairness and justice result in planning for inclusion and participation; individuality to the nurturing of creativity and progression; knowledge to a respect for the subject discipline; hope and faith perhaps to a desire to engender meaningful and shared experiences; community to the desire to foster good relationships; health to the espousal of outdoor learning; and values of care and kindness result in an abiding interest in safe and stimulating spaces for learning.

Key questions for discussion

- How can we help generate an atmosphere where conversations about children's learning are common?
- How can we minimize on the paperwork whilst maximizing the quality learning experience for the children?
- How can we ensure that understanding is expressed in visual, graphical, movement, artistic, creative, aural, numeric and interpersonal *as well as* linguistic ways?
- What is the advantage in planning in teams?

Further reading

Jeffrey, B. and Woods, P. (2003) *The Creative School*. London: Routledge.

Perkins, D. (2009) *Making Learning Whole: How Seven Principles of Teaching Can Transform Education*. New York: Jossey-Bass.

Rowley, C. and Cooper, H. (2009) *Cross-Curricular Teaching and Learning*. London: Sage.

Wineburg, S. and Grossman, P. (2000) *Interdisciplinary Curriculum: Challenges to Implementation*. New York: Teachers College Press.

CHAPTER 12

Key Issues for Debate

This chapter can be used to inform curriculum planning or professional/ personal development meetings. The issues and related questions are also useful starting points for ITE seminars and discussions. The subjects are designed to provoke debate which will impact upon ethos, management, planning, delivery, learning and personal experience in school.

Teachers do not have to choose between *either* subject disciplines *or* thematic methods, education policy and good pedagogy as *both* are essential (Alexander, 2010; Ofsted, 2009a, 2009b, 2010; Rose, 2009). At times, de-contextualized, didactic approaches are the best way to maintain a sense of challenge, introduce and develop certain subject skills, teach important facts and measure progression over a whole unit. Alongside cross-curricular modes of teaching and learning, equally creative instruction and coaching in skills and knowledge within the separated disciplines allow breadth and depth of learning experience. Sometimes a wholly cross-curricular approach seems the only way to address a theme. A sense of balance should be evident in all discussions aimed at finding an appropriate curriculum and pedagogy for today's children.

Cross-curricular methods have been argued to provide high degrees of motivation in children. However, motivation arises from many sources and children are inspired by different and unpredictable inputs. We need to generously allow for cultural and personal differences and avoid seeking one-size-fits-all solutions. Chapter 1 discussed children's responses to rapid and apparently inexorable change but, as Chapter 8 suggested, school learning should also offer the continuity and security of agreed values, aims and purposes.

Power and who holds it is also a live issue for schools. The UN convention on the Rights of the Child (UNICEF, 1989, website) issues a challenge to schools to share power with children. As children's voices are more frequently heard, schools are changing for the better, but such developments are tempered by unclear values, lack of confidence, over-centralized education policies, our 'litigation and surveillance culture' (BBC, 2002, website; Furedi, 2009), powerful and fickle news media, and what some have characterized as 'selfish capitalism' (James, 2009). Young people are rarely out of the news but rarely in it positively, yet the future of the planet depends upon their learning

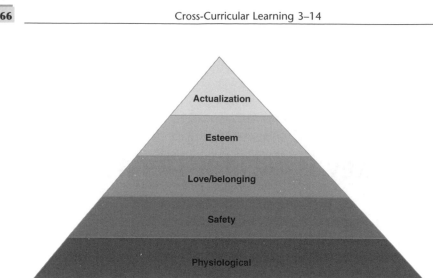

Figure 12.1 Maslow's hierarchy of needs. Does this apply today or is the picture more complex? (Maslow, 1943)

and relationship to concepts like: self, creativity, culture, society, the environment and globalization. What follows is a personal response to some of these issues; deliberately provocative, obviously open to question, but an attempt to mark out areas for productive debate in staffrooms, seminar groups and school councils.

Motivation

The motivation to learn must come first. As I visit classes in widely contrasting parts of the UK and the world, I feel increasingly confident to suggest that motivation is key to efficient, satisfying and lifelong learning. Indeed, research for the Organization for Economic Cooperation and Development (OECD) pinpoints motivation as the main factor in learning (OECD, 2003). Although devised in the first half of the last century, Maslow's notion of a hierarchy of needs remains an interesting model to describe various sources of motivation (Maslow, 1943).

The motivation of physical and economic well-being

To flourish, we need to feel physically secure. Observing classes of 7–16-year-olds in rapidly developing regions such as southern India, Indonesia or East Africa, I hear from children that they are motivated by a desire for a life economically more secure than that of their parents. In the developing countries of the world and the poorer sections of developed economies, physiological and economic security needs dominate. School learning for many is an instrumental activity providing the basic skills, knowledge and certificates to successfully compete for jobs in an increasingly tough and global jobs market. Schools in economically insecure areas may place more emphasis on the authority of the teacher, a didactic and subject-based approach to teaching, and learning generally more reliant upon memory and repetition. Education in the developing world is usually seen as a means of liberation from poverty. Whilst love, belonging, self-esteem and self-actualization appear abundantly present in the lives of the vast majority of those I observe, these attributes come largely from wider cultural and family contexts. In cultures which typically value community, spiritual interpretations, respect for elders and hard work, schools might appear to be places where peers are trusted, there is little bullying and children's sense of belonging is high.

Globalization, via the internet, satellite and cable TV, mobile phones and World Bank-sponsored curriculum revision, is now changing attitudes, educational practice and philosophy in many developing countries (James, 2009; Sharma, 2008). Education practice has become less polarized as global needs for creative solutions to economic and social problems have become more apparent (Craft et al., 2008). The powerful belief that education provides the way out of poverty and disadvantage remains but schools, in India for example (see Dorman and Scoffham, 2007; Scoffham, 2010), are increasingly considering the issues of environment, individuality and globalization that also concern their Western counterparts.

The motivation of psychological well-being

Rich countries continue to face significant degrees of child poverty (UNICEF, 2007, website) but in addition face the problems of affluence. Ask children aged between 11 and 15 in the UK or USA about school and aspects pertaining to their general well-being and the results may reflect the following figures from the World Health Organization (2008, website):

- 20 per cent of English 13-year-olds rate their health as 'poor' (compared to 23 per cent in the USA and only 7 per cent in Switzerland and Spain), and girls in each of 41 developed countries considered their health to be poorer than that of boys.
- Life satisfaction is considered 'high' for 87 per cent of English children at 13 (compared to 94 per cent in the Netherlands).
- 24 per cent of British boys and girls report having been drunk at least twice by the age of 13 (compared to 3 per cent of Norwegians and 5 per cent of US 13-year-olds).
- Only 62 per cent of Welsh 11-year-olds agree that their peers are 'kind and helpful' (compared with 48 per cent in the USA, 82 per cent in Scotland and 88 per cent in Macedonia).
- 40 per cent of 11-year-old boys in England (in the USA, 41 per cent) feel 'pressured by schoolwork' (compared with 8 per cent in the Netherlands).

- Only 32 per cent of English (in the USA, 25 per cent) children at 13 could say they 'liked school a lot' (compared with 58 per cent in Turkey) (WHO, 2008, website).

Such statistics suggest that significant numbers of children are unlikely to be motivated by economically centered approaches to education. Whilst the physiological, physical and security needs of children in developed countries may generally be more fulfilled than those of their Indian counterparts, the WHO report would suggest that children in richer countries may have greater deficits at Maslow's self-esteem, love and actualization levels. Psychologist Viktor Frankl noted half a century ago that the feeling of meaninglessness had become rife since the 1950s (Frankl, 1992). Such analyses could have wide educational implications. Perhaps government, and others directly impacting upon children's lives, should do significantly more to develop opportunities for self-actualization and meaning making as well as team building and social responsibility.

The construction of self-esteem, the redevelopment of community, support for family and an understanding of what it is to love, trust and belong may be fundamental to deep learning itself.

Questions for discussion:

- Do you think motivation is an important feature in learning? Give examples from your experience.
- Are there any specific kinds of activity which you have noticed motivate most children in your class/Year 7/Year R?
- What can we learn about motivation from observing children's play?
- How do we go about motivating the unmotivated child?
- What should government do to promote life satisfaction in children?
- What can we do?

Managing change

Schools have been subjected to 40 years of almost continual change. One year they are asked to make their curricula and teaching styles more creative and cross-curricular, the next to maintain a relentless focus on the basics. Many teachers feel comfortable with literacy and numeracy filling most mornings and the QCDA schemes of work for other subjects in the afternoon – for these teachers, creative approaches may seem too demanding. The guidance and schemes of work for National Curriculum subjects (QCA, 1998a, 2000) offered significant relief for many overloaded teachers after the introduction of literacy and numeracy strategies. But many have become unchallenged and bored by formulaic teaching methods. There is also evidence that teachers and student teachers have been professionally deskilled by being encouraged to depend too heavily on de-contextualized and externally prepared formulae (PWC, 2001; Smithers and Robinson, 2001, website), which makes contemplating more creative responses to the curriculum a daunting prospect. Teachers need professional and personal support if they are to help steer children successfully through a life of change.

Subjects have suffered from the changes of the last 20 years too. The first National Curriculum was quickly seen as too demanding, so the QCA produced schemes of work intended to support teachers. Just before the schemes were published, the ironically titled *Maintaining Breadth and Balance* told primary schools that they 'no longer had to teach the full programmes of study in the six foundation subjects' (QCA, 1998b: 3). The result was a loss of breadth, an upsetting of balance and a steady decline in time, thought and energy devoted to foundation subjects in primary schools. Inevitably, foundation subject standards suffered and training teachers noted significantly diminishing opportunities to observe practice in them (see Barnes, 2001; Rogers, 1999, 2003). These subjects increasingly suffer from lack of well-trained champions (for example, Ofsted, 2008 on geography in schools). Various official attempts have been made to address a situation where literacy and numeracy dominate school time and the foundation subjects – science, RE, ICT, PSHE and Citizenship – are squeezed into the remaining space. *Designing and Timetabling the Primary Curriculum* (QCA, 2002b) offered case study examples of how schools with differing aims fulfilled them though creative and sometimes cross-curricular approaches to the timetable. Ofsted in its turn has shown how primary and secondary schools have achieved excellence 'against the odds' (Ofsted, 2009a, 2009b) through new curriculum and organizational approaches or through creativity (Ofsted, 2010).

If teachers are to establish more creative curricula, then they must first feel that they are capable of being creative themselves. Lack of opportunity to invent their own lessons and schemes of work, or respond opportunistically to children's unplanned-for interests, have led some teachers to feel they are not creative (Cremin et al., 2009).

A climate of change presents new perspectives on transitions too. One such example in the UK is the difficult jump between Key Stages 2 and 3. Some imaginative schools in both key stages are developing a 'bridging curriculum', where primary and secondary school staff and children work together on a theme shared by Years 6 and 7 pupils (see Davies and McMahon, 2004, and case study 2 in Chapter 3). Shared themes, often focused around science (probably because of a secondary school's superior science resources), cushion the sometimes worrying shift between schools at 11 years but also serve to raise teaching and learning standards, ensure progression and enhance the status of learning over teaching.

Illustration 12.1   *How do we assess the confidence of this 12-year-old?*

Empowering and meaningful curricula can be constructed to suit community and specific subject strengths in the context of increasing school independence and social change. In Chapters 3, 4, 5 and 6, we read how writers across several disciplines addressed the issues of twenty-first-century change, but few looked to the curriculum for an answer. Yet a well-designed curriculum delivered by committed and community-conscious adults is a powerful force. The curriculum becomes even more effective in promoting positive social change when the child's voice is taken into account in forming it. Good relationships, good planning, a strong sense of personal/emotional relevance, authentic challenge and a recognition of the child's world will help children understand and engage with an otherwise bewildering world. As both back-up and guide in a caring society, such a curriculum can help children cope with multifarious categories of change now and in the future. To help children develop the skills, tenacity and self-motivation they will need to face unimaginable change, we need a curriculum to develop:

- a sense of personal, family and community meaning and belonging
- a heightened and positively framed sensitivity and care for the self, others and environment
- an ability to understand their own emotions and how to handle, harness and read them in the self and others
- a positive view of their ability to learn new things
- a positive view of others, valuing their diversity and uniqueness

- an appreciation of what their culture sees as beautiful, good, true and right

- a method of working which is cooperative, patient, fair and fulfilling

- a knowledge of the distinctive contributions of each subject discipline to understanding their world

- an understanding that a holistic view of experiences, emotions, places, things, patterns, processes and ideas requires the application of multiple disciplines and viewpoints

- a realization that they are creative beings, able to produce inventive and unique solutions to problems which confront them

- a confidence and accuracy with many technologies and in handling information from a wide variety of sources.

These could be argued to be required skills, regardless of what the future holds. They constitute a series of competences which can be seen as markers towards the (re?) establishment of a set of communally accepted values which might transcend change.

Questions for discussion:

- How can we adapt the curriculum in our school to take account of changing technologies?

- How can we support children in thinking about their role in the future?

- What kind of changes can we see happening around us, in our own area at the moment? How do they relate to more global issues?

- How can we counter the feeling that individuals are powerless in the face of change?

Power

Power relationships are changing in Western societies. The deference with which in former times we treated royalty, church, police, judiciary, the famous and the wealthy is constantly challenged by press, and often by individuals. Detailed awareness of rights and the possibility of litigation have come to characterize many aspects of daily life. Whilst huge power remains vested in politicians, newspaper magnates, senior civil servants, captains of industry, and even health and safety executives, power is also increasingly placed in the hands of many less powerful mortals using social networking sites. Transferring power to local, community levels has been central to coalition government education policy and also touched upon in discussions

Illustration 12.2   *Power reinterpreted from a different camera angle. Photo: Robert Jarvis*

concerning schools councils and children's participation. When pupils took control of information-gathering activities in the HEARTS project (Chapter 3, case study 7) their motivation, application and concentration increased. There are many arguments for the frequent shifting of power within a school setting (for example, Cheminais, 2008; Davies, 2000; Freire, 1994; Illich, 1971; Jeffrey and Woods, 2003; Ruddock and MacIntyre, 2007; Wrigley, 2005). Clearly, in many circumstances and for safety's sake, ultimate power may have to reside with adults, but there are plentiful opportunities in a school day where children can feel they have the power to influence things. In this regard, one teacher education student likened the effective teacher to 'a cunning dictator' who contrives to make a population feel they have freedom and power whilst actually retaining most for himself. But power sharing can be more genuine than this.

Cross-curricular practice often depends upon group work and self-directed activity, and in both cases children may need to be taught how to handle power. Modelling sessions in which children practise making decisions, taking a lead or dealing with disputes are invaluable just before the onset of genuine group problem solving. A class debate about the responsibilities of power need not be theoretical if this Personal, Social and Health Education (PSHE) and Citizenship theme is followed by a real class meeting to decide on the class theme or how to meet a particular challenge.

Illustration 12.3 *Children's response to the question, 'What can adults and children do together?' Courtesy of Scottish Children's Parliament*

Questions for discussion:

- How do we shift the locus of control whilst retaining responsibility for the health and safety of children?
- What are the health and safety implications of shifting power towards children?
- How do we give children the impression of choice whilst we continue to make decisions about curriculum content?
- What differences have new technologies made to children's sense of power and control?

Creativity

Cross-curricular learning and creativity go hand in hand; this is recognized by the QCA (2002a, 2005, website) and Ofsted (2010) and in the practice of thousands of teachers. Mixing a group of children and two subject perspectives together to make sense of a single event, theme or object should be a recipe for unusual insights, original questions, unique perspectives and valued products. There are almost endless possibilities in the mix because, as we have seen, each child brings to any situation his or her own set of memories, links and associations, and each of these link in a different way to his or her understanding of the subjects involved. As I have made clear, the teaching of distinct bodies of subject knowledge and skills is irreplaceable. The robustness and rigidity of this disciplined understanding can in many ways be a good provoker of creativity. 'Structure ignites spontaneity', says Nachmanovitch, who continues in a musical context:

> In ragas, or solo jazz play, sounds are limited to a restricted sphere, within which a gigantic range of inventiveness opens up. If you have all the colours available, you are sometimes almost too free. With one dimension constrained, play becomes freer in other dimensions. (Nachmanovitch, 1990: 85)

Creativity is not a matter of blindly letting go or weakly allowing 'free expression'. The NACCCE report made it very clear that in its view sustained creative achievement 'involves knowledge of the field in question and skills in the media concerned ... [and] recognise[s] the mutual dependence of freedom and control at the heart of the creative process' (NACCCE, 1999, para. 49). More recent Ofsted guidance has stressed the vital factors of good planning, high degrees of teacher knowledge and frequent evaluation in successful creative learning (Ofsted, 2010).

 Creativity is not situated in a single area of the brain or found in a single set of experiences. Creativity may be stimulated by the accidental coming together of thoughts, materials or people, and cross-curricular approaches will make such accidents more likely. As Boden suggests:

> Creativity is best construed not as a single power which you either have or do not, but as multidimensional. Creative processes involve different mental functions, combinations of skills and personality attributes ... they involve special purposes for familiar mental operations and the more efficient use of our ordinary abilities, not something profoundly different. (Boden, 1990: 250)

Creative acts are judged so by acceptance by a particular field of judges, and this applies, as Pope says, 'at every level from considering Nobel Prize nominations to the scribbles of four year olds' (Pope, 2005: 68). But whilst Csikszentmihalyi generally speaks of creativity within one domain of understanding, Pope reminds us that much of the most startling and influential creativity goes on in the margins *between* domains, in interdisciplinary or cross-cultural exchanges which result in hybrid forms. Such exchanges happen in nature of course, but in human cultures some of the most creative forms have come at the overlap of cultures; think of medieval Venice, ninth-century Spain, Moghul India, jazz in the southern states of the USA, or the fusions of ancient cultures in Ptolomy's Egypt.

 Thematic work may provoke opportunities for the overlap of ideas in a school setting too. Creative solutions to a well-defined brief from the teacher might involve a mathematical sequence applied to a musical challenge, a geographical process described using a dance, scientific understandings like the movement of water created through painting or a technological problem solved through reference to an historical solution.

My own research (Cremin et al., 2009) has suggested the importance of teachers recognizing and naming creative acts amongst children as they work on such projects.

One class of eight-year-olds was designing and constructing a handbag which was to be filled with objects which showed what their head teacher, Ms Masters, was interested in. Their teacher consistently identified original responses in the children:
  'Talking to other people helped Linda have more ideas didn't it?'

Sarah: 'Jordan has just written what *he* likes.' [to put in his model of Ms Masters' bag]
Teacher: 'Is that what you think he thinks? I think he's got very good reasons for drawing a Dalek *as well* as liking them himself.'
          'What is that telling us about Ms Masters?'
          'That's a really good idea, Taylor, combining two ideas in one.'
          'Who would like to come up and share just a little bit of what they are doing?'
          'Raise your hand if you have thought of anything new or different today.'
          (Barnes, 2005c)

My co-researchers and I have shown that establishing a creative frame of mind both in teachers and children, is a key aspect of promoting creative thinking and creative activity. A background atmosphere where creativity is frequently (and precisely) honoured has distinct and positive effects on the children's view of their own and others' creativity. The children had little problem in naming aspects of their teacher's creativity and spoke confidently of their own. Being aware of one's own creativity is good for confidence but also seems to be related to a sense of well-being, prolongs concentration and promotes warm, positive relationships and is associated with an enhanced sense of meaning (Barnes et al., 2008; Pope, 2005).

Questions for discussion:

- How can we promote creativity in the adults in our school?
- How can we sustain the sense of growth in our own learning?
- How could we gain more job satisfaction?
- How can we create the conditions in which these things are likely to be the experience of children too?

Behaviour

Controlling behaviour has always been a key issue for teachers. Some are concerned that group work, increased autonomy, 'pupil voice' and activity

Illustration 12.4   *After finding out about wind direction and air pressure, these 13- and 14-year-olds send messages to a 'marooned' artist in the middle of the English channel as part of a Creative Partnerships initiative. Courtesy of Creative Partnerships Kent*

outside the classroom will provoke poor conduct. It is difficult to counter this perception unless the teaching teachers do is carefully planned, resourced and implemented. In the HEARTS project (Chapter 3, case study 7), most ITE students expected behaviour challenges amongst their 12-year-olds, but after two full days of the project over 80 per cent remarked upon the good conduct of the children in this child-led setting. Additionally, almost 50 per cent of the student teachers used the words 'enthusiastic', 'collaborative', 'relaxed' and 'new ideas' to describe their feelings about the behaviour of the children. More than 70 per cent used the words 'enjoyed' or 'engaged' to describe children's attitude to learning in this context. Planning and helping children find personal relevance was crucial to the success of this cross-curricular activity, just as it is for *any* school activity, but I would further argue that involvement in cross-curricular and creative activities has been responsible many times for *producing* good behaviour. In the case of the HEARTS project, finding relevance did not involve identifying direct links with children's everyday lives, but discovering tiny aspects of an unfamiliar environment which connected in one way or another to the lives of every individual. For one it was fossils, another a fairy story, another an angry friend and yet another a film, but for each, that link had a kind of personal existential significance – a recognizable part of their autobiographical self.

Just as productive group work needs teaching, so does behaviour; it is not always 'caught' as we might hope. Neither do specific subjects like music (see Gove, 2010a, website) necessarily improve behaviour, but high expectations and clear, simple ground rules for safe, caring responses do work for many

Illustration 12.5   *These six-year-olds are discovering personal links to a medieval castle by meaning making their own descriptive and atmospheric music whilst on their visit*

children. Identifying, describing and praising specific examples of 'good' behaviour as it occurs, keeps children aware of these expectations.

Added to general subject planning and specific learning objectives, one of the most powerful motivators to increased self-control is success at something which is perceived as truly challenging. The teacher or team should therefore plan and work to generate enthusiasm through authentic challenge targeted just a little *beyond* the current grasp of individuals.

Questions for discussion:

- Is behaviour best improved by rules or a stimulating curriculum?
- How can we help children become aware of and responsible for their own behaviour?
- How can we positively involve family, community and child in discussions about behaviour?

The global dimension

We have become very aware of the global dimension in our lives. The global financial crisis of 2008/9, the disruption caused by the Icelandic volcano of 2010, the catastrophic oil spill in the Gulf of Mexico, the implications of continuing wars in Afghanistan and Iraq and tensions between the West and Iran or North Korea have ensured that we all recognize our interdependence. It is difficult to ignore the impact of pandemics, global technologies, global terrorism, the global economy, global climate change and global pollution. Yet despite guidance from the Development Education Association (for example, DEA, 2001), the global plays too small a role in our programmes of study, schemes of work or school prospectuses. Government periodically reminds us of the importance of the global dimension (DfES, 2004d, website) in an attempt to broker partnerships between schools across the globe. But such centralized advice often comes with economic 'strings' attached – notice the UK government's three economy-driven aims:

1 Equipping children for life in a global society and work in a global economy.

2 Engaging international partners to achieve their goals and ours.

3 Maximizing the contribution of education to overseas trade and inward investment. (DfES, 2004)

UK schools partnerships with schools across the world need to be conscious of the dangers of unequal and neo-colonialist outcome. The global can play a big part in the kind of thematic activity already outlined in this book, but partnerships should strive to be equal. The global dimension does not have to be as overtly British-economy serving as the government's three aims. Neither do they need to involve charitable giving which instantly changes power relationships. Global connections between schools can be used to develop a more sensitive and informed understanding of cultural differences and common issues facing all people.

One school on the Kent coast established a link with a primary school in Tanzania and their link forms the core of thematic work for several weeks of combined geography, PSHE/Citizenship and English work. Children write letters with real questions they know will be answered, and they research and present comprehensive details about the actual locality of their partner school: its weather statistics, its population, maps of the village, plans of the farms and detail about daily life of a few actual families. This year they worked with a teacher who had visited the area. In groups of five, they took on family roles and used the plans of six fragmented and steeply sited farms to discuss what the

(Continued)

(Continued)

family could do with £50 given by the local church organization for improvements. They were able to check out what actually happened in subsequent letters, but this activity gave the children a remarkably deep and lasting insight into the issues facing $^4/_5$ of the world's population. (Glen Sharp)

Illustration 12.6   *This village child in south India has access to the rest of the world through the internet*

Questions for discussion:

- What global links do we already have?
- How can we make the global significant to the children in our school?
- How can the global be made an integrator in our curriculum?

Litigation and 'the surveillance culture'

Advice on school policy and legislation regarding safety on school visits is contained on the government's Teachernet website (DfES, 2005a, website). It reflects the increasing concern for children's safety after a number of well-publicized and very tragic accidents involving children on school visits. The fear of litigation and the extra paperwork involved in detailed 'risk assessments' along with the requirement of particular ratios of adults to children and the need for individual parental permission, has resulted in an understandable reduction of school visits. *None of the requirements are unnecessary – all are the result of carefully considered and responsible practice and none should be disregarded.* However, schools which continue to make fieldwork a major priority have found that establishing such procedures as:

- clear and uniform school-based guidelines
- adequate and school-provided preparation time
- accessible and easily understood paperwork
- the advice of experienced practitioners
- the preparation of individual 'class visit packs' containing essential medication, mobile phone, first aid kit and permission slips

significantly lessens the load on teachers.

The parliamentary Education and Skills Committee appeared in full agreement that education outside the classroom is a valuable and motivating thing in itself: 'Outdoor learning supports academic achievement ... as well as development of "soft skills" and social skills particularly in hard to reach children ... neither the DfES nor Local Authorities have done enough to publicize the benefits of education outside the classroom ...' (HC, 2005: 3). The same committee agreed that the bureaucracy associated with school visits is a major problem but found no evidence that school visits are inherently risky. The committee recommended a 'Manifesto for Outdoor Learning' (DFES, 2005c, website) with structures and a personality to champion outdoor learning across all curriculum areas. It also recommended that unions currently advising their members not to go on school trips reconsider their position.

Related to the lack of trust inherent in the development of a litigation culture has been the gradual rise of surveillance activities in our schools as well as our high streets. Whilst I understand schools choosing closed-circuit television (CCTV) to lessen public perceptions of increased risk to children, the recent development of stringent curriculum surveillance can have negative and unforeseen effects on teaching and learning quality. As ordinary teachers are increasingly observed by heads, curriculum coordinators, parents, governors and inspectors, they are likely to choose the 'safest' and least disruptive options for their teaching. They are less likely to take the risks explored throughout this book. Cross-curricular teaching *is* risky; sometimes a well-prepared topic does not catch the imagination as hoped for. Group work, open-ended questions and situations, or creative lessons will often be nosier and appear less controlled than a highly structured and inflexible 'off-the-shelf lesson'. But I have argued that this risky, noisy, exciting and unpredictable education is vital to the healthy future of our individuals and our society.

Questions for discussion:

- What kind of curriculum/lessons best build positive attitudes to lifelong learning?
- What kind of curriculum/lessons help children develop transferable skills for use in a variety of future circumstances?
- What kind of curriculum/lessons assist children in forming positive views of themselves?
- What kind of curriculum/lessons teach social and emotionally intelligent skills necessary for work in teams in later life?
- What kind of curriculum/lessons help children learn independence, understand how to use initiative, cultivate flexibility, rehearse prioritizing and discover their own creativity?
- What kind of curriculum/lessons can prepare children for an uncertain future of inevitable and yet unimaginable change?

The changing role of the school

Well before the publication of the US's *No Child Left Behind* (NCLB) (USDE, 2002, website) education policy, or the UK's *Every Child Matters (ECM)* (DfES, 2004a, website), it was clear that the nature of schools was fast changing. Children's Centres or Community Learning Centres, and closer relationships between children's medical, social and educational services are being established throughout the UK, the rest of Europe and the USA. Many schools are already effectively operating variations of the 8.00 a.m. to 6.00 p.m. day with breakfast clubs, after-school clubs and the like. Many new primary and secondary academies are making community links a priority. Since ECM, the pace of change has quickened. In the UK, Directors of Children's Services and coordinated local authority responsibility for all aspects of childhood mean that each school has to consider a widening of its role in the community. Alongside these changes, contradictory but economically driven moves appear to threaten the very communities ECM and NCLB wish to sustain.

School closures continue because of falling rolls or low numbers, thus removing some schools from the heart of small and fragile communities. The administration of primary health care and social services continue to suffer from the inexorable pressures to economize by being organized in bigger but less locally accountable units. Finally, increasing poverty and an increasing gap between the haves and the have-nots in the developed world, but especially affecting the lives of young people in the UK, add to the list of social, health and educational problems confronting them.

Information and communication technology now makes it possible for each child to have a separate and isolated education. Education can

Illustration 12.7   *Infant children's plans for their school entrance realized by a team of architects who worked with them. Courtesy of Creative Partnerships Kent*

conceivably be totally individualized. The BBC attempted to deliver 50 per cent of the National Curriculum to 5–16-year-olds over the heads of teachers in an 'interactive dialogue directly with learners', but this project failed partly because of competition laws. Wholesale digital education is possible, but is it right? Against the burgeoning communications, technological and political background, schools will inevitably become more complex organizations with multiple functions beyond the simple passing on of knowledge. Schools will be increasingly charged with developing independence as well as community, self-direction and moral behaviour. With so many demands, an old-fashioned timetable or traditional curriculum may be totally unfit for purpose, which is why organizations like the Curriculum Foundation (2010, website) and the RSA (see Chapter 3, case study 3) are offering alternatives.

There are warning signs that teachers will bear the brunt of many of these new initiatives. To ensure that children continue to get the best from their teachers, teachers themselves need to be more fully aware of the unique, precious and professional knowledge they possess. The knowledge they gain is not possessed by any other professionals, and it should not be underestimated, neglected or watered down. Neither should teachers feel trapped into propping up systems and approaches they know from experience do not work. Human beings are social and cultured animals – we only consider ourselves mentally well when we are generally happy with the relationships we form with others. Whilst society continues to see education as a social, communal, culture-driven affair, teachers will be the key adults in children's lives after their carers. At their best, teachers are made distinctive by the insights they accumulate about young people's learning. At its best, teachers' contribution to the well-being of each individual and of society can be expressed in the following statements:

1 Teachers are the only professionals who serve their clients *en masse.* They understand and use many different methods of presenting information so as to match different styles of learning within a single class. They know simultaneously how to engage children from a wide range of backgrounds.

2 Teachers know how to organize activities in groups so as to ensure social, emotional and personal development at the same time as intellectual development.

3 Teachers know how to control large groups of young people without fear, how to motivate them without bribery, how to excite them without losing control, how to take risks without danger and how to praise without lying.

4 Teachers understand the importance of motivation in learning and the variety of ways of persuading children that they want to learn.

5 Teachers understand about simultaneously stretching the most and the least able child in the same class *and know that those two children may be interchangeable in different learning situations.*

6 Teachers are unique in knowing, understanding and in many ways representing the whole range of sub-cultures within the communities they serve. They know how to arrange educational experiences so that at one and the same time they generate meaningful learning *and* avoid offence to both the most liberal and most conservative members of society. They know and understand how different extremes of society feel about things that matter to them.

7 Teachers experience daily the close relationship between physical and mental well-being and learning. They see the multitude of ways family break-up, a house move, the loss of a friend or an eraser can affect a child's learning. They also regularly witness the impact of deprivation or wealth.

8 Teachers are at the front line of applying government policy to generate change in society and the economy through the curriculum, yet they are rarely directly consulted.

Teachers rapidly become experts in children's learning and the kind of curriculum which motivates them. They need to be carefully listened to in building the new approach to the curriculum required for a world of children's

Figure 12.2 Shared values of community, creativity and care encompassing a curriculum founded on a balance between individual and group, the disciplines and environment, will result in greater chances of individual well-being for both teacher and child

centres, new technologies, new definitions of family, globalization, new challenges and very old moral dilemmas. No other professional has the teacher's wealth of research knowledge of how to make links between the disciplines, manage children in groups, how to fire an individual's imagination, how to rebuild a child's self-esteem and how to construct an environment which promotes in them the desire to learn. Both the child's and the teacher's well-being depend on balance of attention to the disciplines, the group, the individual and the environment for learning. Good teachers have been balancing these factors forever. With these and many more unique and undeniable qualities, it is amazing that teachers continue to be so maligned in the press, threatened by inspection, replaced by under-qualified assistants and put upon by politicians. In the changing world of the school, teachers' unique and professional range of skills and knowledge must be fully and sensitively utilized. Ask teachers about the curriculum which will best serve today's children for now and their future, and I believe the majority will respond with a variant of the creative and cross-curriculum.

References

Abbs, P. (2003) *Against the Flow*. London: Routledge.

Adey, P. and Shayer, M. (1994) *Really Raising Standards*. London: Routledge.

Ainscow, M., Booth, T. and Dyson, A. (2006) *Improving Schools, Developing Inclusion*. London: Routledge.

Ajegbo, K. (2007) *Diversity and Citizenship*. Nottingham: DfES.

Alexander, R. (1998) Basics, cores and choices: towards a new primary curriculum, *Education 3–13*, vol. 26, no. 2, pp. 60–9.

Alexander, R. (2010) *Children, Their World, Their Education: The Report of the Cambridge Primary Review*. London: Routledge.

Alexander, R., Rose, A. and Woodhead, C. (1992) *Curriculum Organisation and Classroom Practice in Primary Schools: A Discussion Paper*. London: DES.

Alexander, T. (2001) *Citizenship Schools: A Practical Guide to Education for Citizenship and Personal Development*. London: Campaign for Learning/UNICEF.

Alexander, T. and Potter, J. (eds) (2005) *Education for a Change: Transforming the Way We Teach our Children*. London: Routledge-Falmer.

Andrade, H. and Perkins, D. (1998) Learnable intelligence and intelligent learning, in R. Sternberg and W. Williams (eds), *Intelligence Instruction and Assessment: Theory into Practice*. Mahwah, NJ: Erlbaum.

Antidote (2003) *The Emotional Literacy Handbook*. London: David Fulton.

Arnsten, A. and Li, B. (2005) Neurobiology of executive functions: catecholamine influences in prefrontal cortical functions, *Biological Psychiatry*, vol. 57, no. 11, pp. 1377–84.

Arthur, J. and Cremin, T. (2010) *Learning to Teach in the Primary School*, 2nd edition. London: Routledge.

Attingham Trust (2004) *Opening Doors: Learning in the Historic Environment*. London: Attingham Trust.

Austin, R. (2007) *Letting the Outside In: Developing Teaching and Learning Beyond the Early Years Classroom*. Stoke on Trent: Trentham Books.

Bandura, A. (1994) Self-efficacy, in V.S. Ramachaudran (ed.), *Encyclopedia of Human Behaviour*, vol. 4, pp. 71–81. New York: Academic Press.

Barnes, J. (1994) The city planners of St Peters, *Remnants*, Journal of English Heritage Education Service, no. 24, Autumn, pp. 1–4.

Barnes, J. (2001) Creativity and composition in music, in C. Philpott and C. Plummeridge (eds), *Issues in Music Education*. London: Routledge.

Barnes, J. (2005a) On your mind, *Nursery World*, vol. 105, no. 3965, pp. 12–13.

Barnes, J. (2005b) Strangely familiar: authentic experience, teacher education and a thought provoking environment, *Improving Schools*, vol. 8, no. 2, pp. 199–206.

Barnes, J. (2005c) Case study notes, 28 November.

Barnes, J. (2005d) Case study notes, 14 December.

Barnes, J. (2005e) You could see it on their faces: the importance of provoking smiles in schools, *Health Education*, vol. 105, no. 5, pp. 392–400.

Barnes, J. (2006) Strangely familiar: cross curricular and creative thinking in teacher education, paper presented at International Conference on Imagination in Education, Vancouver, July.

Barnes, J. (2009) The integration of music with other subject disciplines, particularly other art forms, in J. Evans and C. Philpott (eds), *A Practical Guide to Music in the Secondary School*. London: Routledge.

Barnes, J. (2010a) The integration of music with other subject disciplines, particularly other art forms, in C. Philpott and Evans (eds), *A Practical Guide to Music in the Secondary School*. London: Routledge.

Barnes, J. (2010b) The Generate Project: curricular and pedagogical inspiration from parents working with their children, *Improving Schools*, vol. 13, no. 2, pp. 143–57.

Barnes, J. (2011) Unpublished PhD thesis, *What Sustains a Life in Education?* Canterbury Christ Church University.

Barnes, J. and Hancox, G. (2004) Young, gifted and human: a report from the National Gifted and Talented Summer Academy, *Improving Schools*, vol. 7, no. 1, pp. 11–21.

Barnes, J. and Shirley, I. (2005) Strangely familiar: promoting creativity in initial teacher education, paper presented at British Educational Research Association (BERA) conference, 16 September.

Barnes, J. and Shirley, I. (2007) Strangely familiar: cross-curricular and creative thinking in teacher education, *Improving Schools*, vol. 10. no. 2, pp. 289–306.

Barnes, J., Hope, G. and Scoffham, S. (2008) A conversation about creative teaching and learning, in A. Craft, T. Cremin and P. Burnard (eds), *Creative Learning 3–11 and How we Document it*. Stoke on Trent: Trentham Books.

Baron, R. and Byrne, D. (2004) *Social Psychology*, 10th edition. London: Allyn and Bacon.

Bell, D. (2004) The value and importance of geography, *Primary Geographer*, vol. 56, pp. 4–5.

Bentley, T. (2006) Towards a self creating society, presentation at 'This Learning Life' conference, Bristol, 21 April.

Bernstein, B. (1971) *Class, Codes and Control*, vol. 1. London: Paladin.

Bernstein, B. (1996) *Pedagogy, Symbolic Control and Identity*. Lanham, MD: Rowman and Littlefield.

Black, P. and Wiliam, D. (1998) *Inside the Black Box*. Slough: NFER/Nelson.

Blacking, J. (1974) *How Musical is Man?* Washington: University of Washington Press.

Blake, W. (1789 [1967]) *Songs of Innocence and Experience*. London: Oxford University Press.

Blakemore, S. and Frith, U. (2006) *The Learning Brain: Lessons for Education*. Oxford: Blackwell.

Blythe, T. (ed.) (1997) *The Teaching for Understanding Guide*. New York: Jossey-Bass.

Boden, M. (1990) *The Creative Mind: Myths and Mechanisms*. London: Abacus.

Boix-Mansilla, V., Gardner, H. and Miller, W. (2000) On disciplinary lenses and inter-disciplinary work, in S. Wineburg and P. Grossman (eds), *Interdisciplinary Curriculum: Challenges to Implementation*. New York: Teachers College Press.

Booth, T. (2003) Inclusion and exclusion in the city, concepts and contexts, in P. Potts (ed.), *Inclusion in the City: Selection, Schooling and Community*. London: Routledge.

Booth, T. and Ainscow, M. (2002) *Index for Inclusion: Developing Learning and Participation in Schools*. Bristol: Centre for Studies on Inclusive Education.

Bourdieu, P. (1984) *Distinction: A Social Critique of the Judgment of Taste*, trans. Richard Nice. Harvard: Harvard University Press.

Bowlby, J. (1988) *A Secure Base: Clinical Applications of Attachment Theory*. London: Routledge.

Bowlby, J. (1997) *Attachment and Loss: Vol. 1: Attachment*, revised edition. London: Pimlico.

Bransford, J., Brown, A. and Cooking, R. (1999) *How People Learn: Brain, Mind, Experience and School*. Stanford, CA: National Research Council.

Brice Heath, S. and Wolf, S. (2004) *Visual Learning in the Community School*. London: Arts Council.

Brice Heath, S. and Wolf, S. (2005) Focus in creative learning: drawing on art for language development, *Literacy*, vol. 39, no. 1, pp. 38–45.

Bruner, J. (1960) *The Process of Education*. Cambridge, MA: Harvard University Press.

Bruner, J. (1968) *Towards a Theory of Instruction*. New York: Norton.

Bruner, J. (1976) *Man: A Course of Study*.

Bruner, J. (1996) *The Culture of Education*. Cambridge, MA: Harvard University Press.

Bruner, J. (2003) Some specifications for a space to house a Reggio preschool, in G. Ceppi and M. Zini (eds), *Children, Spaces, Relation: Metaproject for an Environment for Young Children*. Milan: Reggio Children and Domus Academy Research Center.

Bruner, J. and Haste, H. (1987) *Making Sense: The Child's Construction of the World*. New York: Methuen.

Burke, C. and Grosvenor, I. (2003) *The School I'd Like: Children and Young People's Reflections on an Education for the 21st Century*. London: Routledge.

Buzan, T. (2002) *How to Mind Map*. London: Thorsons.

Callaghan, J. (1976) Towards a national debate (The full text of the speech by Prime Minister James Callaghan, at a foundation stone-laying ceremony at Ruskin College, Oxford, on 18 October 1976), *The Guardian*, available at http://education.guardian.co.uk/thegreatdebate/story/0,9860,574645,00.html

Catling, S. (2004) Primary student teachers' world map knowledge, in S. Catling and F. Martin (eds), *Researching Primary Geography*. London: Register of Research in Primary Geography.

Catling, S. (2005) Children's personal geographies and the English primary school geography curriculum, *Children's Geographies*, vol. 3, no. 3, pp. 325–44.

Catling, S. (2010) Organising and managing learning outside the classroom, in J. Arthur and T. Cremin (eds), *Learning to Teach in the Primary School*, 2nd edition. London: Routledge.

Catling, S. and Willey, T. (2009) *Teaching Primary Geography*. Exeter: Learning Matters.

Cheminais, R. (2008) *Engaging Pupil Voice to Ensure that Every Child Matters: A Practical Guide*. London: David Fulton.

Clark, S. (2008) *Active Learning through Formative Assessment*. London: Hodder.

Claxton, G. (1998) *Hare Brain, Tortoise Mind*. London: Fourth Estate.

Claxton, G. (2003) *Building Learning Power*. London: TLO.

Collishaw, S., Maughan, B., Goodman, R. and Pickles, A. (2004) Time trends in adolescent mental health, *Journal of Child Psychology and Psychiatry*, vol. 45, no. 8. p. 1350.

Comenius, J. (1967) *The Great Didactic*. London: Russell and Russell.

Costa, A. (ed.) (1991) *Developing Minds: A Resource Book for Teaching Thinking*, vol. 1. Alexandra, VA: Association for Supervision and Curriculum Development.

Craft, A. (2000) *Creativity across the Primary Curriculum*. London: Routledge.

Craft, A. (2005) *Creativity in Schools: Tensions and Dilemmas*. London: Routledge.

Craft, A., Gardner, H. and Claxton, G. (2008) *Creativity, Wisdom and Trusteeship: Exploring the Role of Education*. Thousand Oaks, CA: Corwin Press.

Creative Partnerships Kent (2005) *Footnotes to an Idea*. London: Creative Partnerships/ Arts Council.

Cremin, T. and Barnes, J. (2010) Creativity in the curriculum, in J. Arthur and T. Cremin (eds), *Learning to Teach in the Primary School*, 2nd edition. London: Routledge.

Cremin, T., Barnes, J. and Scoffham, S. (2009) *Creative Teaching for Tomorrow: Fostering a Creative State of Mind*. Margate: Future Creative.

Critchley, H. (2003) Emotion and its disorders, *British Medical Bulletin*, vol. 65, pp. 35–47.

Csikszentmihalyi, M. (1997) *Creativity: Flow and the Psychology of Discovery and Invention*. New York: HarperCollins.

Csikszentmihalyi, M. (2002) *Flow: The Classic Work on How to Achieve Happiness*. New York: Ebury Press.

Csikszentmihalyi, M. (2003) *Good Business*. New York: Hodder and Stoughton.

Damasio, A. (1994) *Descartes' Error*. London: HarperCollins.

Damasio, A. (2000) *The Feeling of What Happens: Body, Emotion and the Making of Consciousness*. London: Heinemann.

Damasio, A. (2003) *Looking for Spinoza: Joy, Sorrow and the Feeling Brain*. Orlando, FL: Harcourt.

Damasio, A. and Immordino-Yang, M. (2007) We feel therefore we learn: the relevance of affective and social neuroscience to education, *Brain, Mind and Education*, vol. 1, no. 1, pp. 3–10.

Darder, A. (2002) *Reinventing Paulo Freire: A Pedagogy of Love*. Oxford: Westview.

Davey, C., Burke, T. and Shaw, C. (2010) *Children's Participation in Decision-making: A Children's Views Report*. London: National Children's Bureau.

David , T. (1999) *Teaching Young Children*. London: Paul Chapman Publishing.

David, T. (2001) Curriculum in the early years, in G. Pugh (ed.), *Contemporary Issues in the Early Years*, 3rd edition. London: Paul Chapman Publishing.

Davidson, R., Daren, C. and Kalin, N. (2000) Emotion, plasticity, context and regulation: perspectives from affective neuroscience, *Psychological Bulletin*, vol. 126, no. 6, pp. 890–906.

Davies, D. and McMahon, K. (2004) A smooth trajectory: developing continuity and progression between primary and secondary science education through a jointly planned projectiles project, *International Journal of Science Education*, vol. 26, pp. 1009–21.

Davies, N. (2000) *The School Report: Why Britain's Schools are Failing*. London: Vintage.

Dawkins, R. (2003) *A Devil's Chaplin: Selected Essays*. London: Phoenix.

De Bono, E. (1999) *Six Thinking Hats*. New York: Black Bay.

De Boo, M. (ed.) (2004) *The Early Years Handbook: Support for Practitioners in the Foundation Stage*. Sheffield: Geographical Association.

Department for Children, Schools and Families (DCSF)/Qualifications and Curriculum Development Agency (QCDA) (2010) *The National Curriculum Primary Handbook*. Coventry: Qualifications and Curriculum Development Agency.

Department for Culture, Media and Sport (DCMS)/English Heritage (2000) *The Power of Place: The Future of the Historic Environment*. London: Stationery Office.

Department of Economic Affairs (DEA) (2001) *Global Perspectives in Education*. London: DEA.

Department for Education and Employment (DfEE) (1998) *The National Literacy Strategy*. London: DfEE.

Department for Education and Employment (DfEE) (1999) *The National Numeracy Strategy*. London: DfEE.

Department for Education and Employment/Qualifications and Curriculum Authority (DfEE/QCA) (1999) *The National Curriculum Handbook for Primary Teachers in England*. London: DfEE.

Department of Education and Science (DES) (1967) *Children and their Primary Schools: A Report of the Central Advisory Council for Education (England)* (Plowden Report). London: HMSO.

Department of Education and Science (DES) (1989) *The National Curriculum for England and Wales*. London: HMSO.

Department for Education and Skills (DfES) (2003) *Developing Children's Social, Emotional and Behavioural Skills: Guidance*. London: DfES.

Department for Education and Skills (DfES) (2004) *Putting the World into World Class Education: An International Strategy for Educations, Skills and Children's Services*. London: DfES.

Department for Education and Skills/Qualifications and Curriculum Authority (DfES/QCA) (1999) *Curriculum Guidance for the Foundation Stage*. London: HMSO.

Department for Education and Skills/Qualifications and Curriculum Authority (DfES/QCA) (2003) *Speaking, Listening, Learning: Working with Children in Key Stages 1 and 2*. London: DfES.

Department of Health/Department for Education and Skills (DoH/DfES) (2005) *National Healthy Schools Status: Guide for Schools*. London: DoH/DfES.

Department of Health and Social Security (DHSS) (2004) *Promoting Emotional Health and Wellbeing, Through the National Healthy Schools Standard*. London: DHSS.

Deutscher, G. (2006) *The Unfolding of Language: An Evolutionary Tour of Mankind's Greatest Invention*. New York: Owl Books.

Deutscher, G. (2010) *Through the Language Glass: How Words Colour Your World*. London: Arrow Books.

Dewey, J. (1897) My pedagogic creed, *The School Journal*, vol. 54, no. 3, pp. 77–80.

Diener, E. and Seligman, M. (2002) Very happy people, *Psychological Science*, vol. 13, pp. 81–4.

Dismore, H., Barnes, J. and Scoffham, S. (2008) *Space to Reflect*. London: Creative Partnerships.

Dorman, P. and Scoffham, S. (2007) Multiple perspectives, profound understandings, *Primary Geographer*, no. 64, pp. 31–3.

Dunn, R., Dunn, K. and Price, G.E. (1984) *Learning Style Inventory*. Lawrence, KS: Price Systems.

Eaude, T. (2008) *Children's Spiritual, Moral, Social and Cultural Development*, 2nd edition. Exeter: Learning Matters.

Ekman, P. (2004) *Emotions Revealed: Understanding Faces and Feelings*. London: Phoenix.

English Heritage/Durbin, G., Morris, S. and Wilkinson, S. (1990) *Learning from Objects*. London: English Heritage.

English Heritage/Barnes, J. (1999) *A Teachers Guide to Design/Technology and the Historic Environment*. London: English Heritage.

Entwistle, N. (2000) Promoting deep learning through teaching and assessment: conceptual frameworks and educational contexts, paper presented at Teaching and Learning Research Programme (TLRP) conference, Leicester, 11 November.

Evans, J. and Philpott, C. (2009) *A Practical Guide to Music and the Secondary School.* London: Routledge.

Feldman, D. (1976) The child as craftsman, *Phi Delta Kappan*, vol. 58, no.1, pp. 143–9.

Fisher, R. (1999) *Head Start: How to Develop your Child's Mind.* London: Souvenir Press.

Fisher, R. (2008) *Teaching Thinking: Philosophical Enquiry in the Classroom.* London: Continuum.

Fisher, R. and Williams, M. (2004) *Unlocking Creativity: Teaching across the Curriculum.* London: David Fulton.

Frankl, V. (1992) *Man's Search for Meaning.* London: Rider.

Fraser-Smith, N., Lesperance, F. and Talajic, M. (1995) The impact of negative emotions on prognosis following myocardial infarction: is it more than depression? *Health Psychology*, vol. 14, pp. 388–98.

Frederickson, B. (2003) The value of positive emotions, *American Scientist*, vol. 91, pp. 300–5.

Fredrickson, B. (2004) The broaden and build theory of positive emotions, *Philosophical Transactions of the Royal Society: Biological Sciences*, vol. 359, no. 1449, pp. 1367–77.

Fredrickson, B. (2009) *Positivity.* New York: Crown.

Fredrickson, B. and Branigan, C. (2005) Positive emotions broaden the scope of attention and thought–action repertoires, *Cognition and Emotion*, vol. 19, no. 3, pp. 313–32.

Fredrickson, B. and Tugade, M. (2004) Resilient individuals use positive emotions to bounce back from negative experiences, *Journal of Personality and Social Psychology*, vol. 80, no. 2, pp. 326–33.

Freire, P. (1994) *The Pedagogy of Hope: Reliving the Pedagogy of the Oppressed.* New York: Continuum.

Froebel, F. (1826) *Die Menschenerziehung (On the Education of Man).* Leipzig: Weinbrach.

Furedi, F. (2009) *Wasted: Why Education isn't Educating.* London: Continuum.

Gardner, H. (1993) *Frames of Mind: The Theory of Multiple Intelligences*, 2nd edition. London: Fontana.

Gardner, H. (1999a) *The Disciplined Mind: What All Students Should Understand.* New York: Simon and Schuster.

Gardner, H. (1999b) *Intelligence Reframed: Multiple Intelligence for the 21st Century.* New York: Basic Books.

Gardner, H. (2004) *Changing Minds: The Art and Science of Changing our Own and Other People's Minds.* Boston, MA: Harvard Business School.

Gardner, H., Csikszentmihalyi, M. and Damon, W. (2000) *Good Work: When Ethics and Excellence Meet.* New York: Basic Books.

Garrett, A., Carrion, V., Pageler, N., Menon, V., Mackenzie, K., Saltzman, K. and Reiss, A. (2002) fMRI response to facial expression in adolescent PTSD, paper presented at the 49th Annual Meeting of the American Academy of Child and Adolescent Psychiatry, San Francisco, CA, 22–27 October.

Geake, J. (2009) *The Brain at School: Educational Neuroscience in the Classroom.* Maidenhead: Open University Press.

Giedd, J., Blumenthal, J., Jeffries, N., Castellanos, F., Liu, H., Zijdenbos, A., Paus, T., Evans, A. and Rapoport, J. (1999) Brain development during childhood and adolescence: a longitudinal MRI study, *Nature Neuroscience*, vol. 10, pp. 861–3.

Gipps, C. and MacGilchrist, B. (1999) Primary school learners, in P. Mortimore (ed.), *Understanding Pedagogy and its Impact on Learning*. London: Paul Chapman.

Glazzard, J., Chadwick, D., Webster, A. and Percival, J. (2010) *Assessment for Learning in the Early Years Foundation Stage*. London: Sage.

Gogtay, N., Giedd, J., Hayaski, K., Greenstein, D., Vaituzis, C., Hugent, T., Herman, D., Clasen, L., Toga, A., Rapoport, J. and Thompson, P. (2004) Dynamic mapping of human cortical development during childhood through early adulthood, *Proceedings of the National Academy of Sciences of the USA*, vol. 101, no. 21, pp. 8174–9.

Goldstein, L. (1997) *Teaching with Love: A Feminist Approach to Early Childhood Education*. New York: Peter Lang.

Goldstein, L. and Lake, V. (2000) Love, love, and more love for children: exploring pre-service teachers' understandings of caring, *Teaching and Teacher Education*, vol. 16, no. 7, pp. 861–72.

Goleman, D. (1996) *Emotional Intelligence*. London: Bloomsbury.

Goleman, D. (ed.) (1997) *Healing Emotions*. Boston, MA: Shambhala.

Goleman, D. (1999) *Working with Emotional Intelligence*. London: Bloomsbury.

Goleman, D. (2006) *Social Intelligence: The New Science of Human Relationships*. New York: Arrow.

Goouch, K. (2010) *Towards Excellence in Early Years Education: Exploring Narratives of Experience*. London: Routledge.

Goswami, U. and Bryant, P. (2007) Children's Cognitive Development and Learning, *Primary Review Research Briefings 2/1*. Cambridge: University of Cambridge Faculty of Education.

Grainger, T., Barnes, J. and Scoffham, S. (2004) A creative cocktail: creative teaching in ITE, *Journal of Education in Teaching (JET)*, vol. 30, no. 3, pp. 243–53.

Greenfield, S. (2003) *Tomorrow's People*. London: Penguin.

Greenfield, S. (2009) *ID: The Quest for Meaning in the 21st Century*. London: Sceptre.

Greenhalgh, P. (1994) *Emotional Growth and Learning*. London: Routledge.

Gruzelier, J. (2003) Enhancing music performance through brain rhythm training, *Music Forum* (journal of the Music Council of Australia), October, pp. 34–5.

Guardian, The (2006) Alzheimer's drug could be widely sold to make everyone brainier, 27 January, p. 11.

Halpin, P. (2003) *Hope and Education*. London: Routledge.

Hanko, G. (1999) *Increasing Competence through Collaborative Problem Solving*. London: David Fulton.

Harland, J., Kinder, K., Lord, P., Stott, A., Schagen, I. and Haynes, J. (2000) *Arts Education in Secondary Schools: Effects and Effectiveness*. Slough: NFER.

Hayes, D. (2003) *Planning Teaching and Class Management in Primary Schools*. London: David Fulton.

Hayes, D. and Ecclestone, C. (2008) *The Dangerous Rise of Therapeutic Education*. London: Routledge.

Hicks, D. (2001) *Citizenship for the Future: A Practical Classroom Guide*. Godalming: World Wide Fund for Nature.

Hicks, D. (2006) *Lessons for the Future: The Missing Dimension in Education*. London: Routledge.

Higgins, S., Baumfield, V. and Leat, D. (2003) *Thinking Through Primary Teaching*. Cambridge: Kington.

Hirsch, E. (1999) *The Schools We Need: And Why We Don't Have Them*. New York: Anchor.

HM Government (HMG) (2004) *Children Act 2004*. London: Stationery Office.

HMG (2006) *Education and Inspections Act*. London: Stationery Office.

House of Commons Education and Skills Committee (HC) (2005) *Education Outside the Classroom: Second Report of Session 2004–2005*. London: Stationery Office.

House of Commons Education and Skills Standing Committee (HC) (2007) *Creative Partnerships and the Curriculum*. London: Stationery Office.

House of Commons (HC) (2008) *Creative Partnerships and the Curriculum: Government Response to the Eleventh Report from the Education and Skills Committee*. London: Stationery Office.

Howard-Jones, P. (2010) *Introducing Neuroeducational Research*. Abingdon: Routledge.

Howard-Jones, P. and Pickering, S. (2005*) Collaborative Frameworks for Neuroscience and Education: Scoping Paper*. Bristol: TLRP- ESRC.

Huppert, F., Baylis, N. and Keverne, B. (2005) *The Science of Well-being*. Oxford: Oxford University Press.

Illich, I. (1971) *Deschooling Society*. London: Calder and Boyars.

Isen, A. (2002) A role for neuropsychology in understanding the facilitating influence of positive affect on social behaviour and cognitive processes, in C. Snyder and S. Lopez (eds), *Handbook of Positive Psychology*. New York: Oxford University Press.

Jacobs, H. (2004) *Interdisciplinary Curriculum, Design and Implementation*. Heatherton, Victoria: Hawker Brownlow Education.

James, M. and Pollard, A. (2008) Learning and teaching in primary schools: insights from TLRP, *Primary Review Research Briefings 2/4*. Cambridge: University of Cambridge, Faculty of Education.

James, O. (2008) *The Selfish Capitalist: Origins of Affluenza*. London: Vermilion.

James, O. (2009) *Britain on the Couch: How Keeping up with the Joneses has Depressed us since 1950*. London: Vermilion.

Jeffrey, B. and Woods, P. (2003) *The Creative School*. London: Routledge.

Jensen, E. (1995) *Brain Based Learning*. Del Mar, CA: Eric Jensen.

Jensen, E. (2000*) Music with Brain in Mind*. San Diego, CA: The Brain Store.

John-Steiner, V. (2006) *Creative Collaboration*. Oxford: Oxford University Press.

John-Steiner, V., Panovsky, C. and Smith, L. (eds) (2008) *Sociocultural Approaches to Language and Literacy: An Interactionist Perspective*. Cambridge: Cambridge University Press.

Jones, P. (1995) Contradictions and unanswered questions in the Genie case: a fresh look at the linguistic evidence, *Language and Communication*, vol. 15, no. 3, pp. 261–80.

Justlin, P. and Sloboda, J. (2009) *Music and Emotion*. Cambridge: Cambridge University Press.

Kawachi, I., Sparrow, D., Vokonas, P. and Weiss, S. (1994) Symptoms of anxiety and risk of coronary heart disease, *Circulation*, vol. 89, pp. 1992–7.

Kerry, T. (ed.) (2010) *Cross-Curricular Teaching in the Primary School*. London: Routledge.

Keverne, B. (2005) Understanding well-being in the evolutionary context of brain development, in F. Huppert, N. Baylis and B. Keverne (eds), *The Science of Well-being*. Cambridge: Cambridge University Press.

Khul, P. (2002) *Born to Learn: Language, Reading and the Brain of the Child*, North West Region, USA, Idaho, Early Learning Summit, 9–10 June.

Kirby, P., Lanyon, F. and Synelaw, R. (2003) *Building a Culture of Participation*. London: DfES.

Koestler, A. (1964) *The Act of Creation*. London: Penguin Arkana.

Laevers, F. (ed.) (1994a) *Defining and Assessing Quality in Early Childhood Education*. Leuven: Leuven University Press.

Laevers, F. (1994b) *The Leuven Involvement Scale for Young Children, LIS-YC, Manual*. Leuven: Centre for Experiential Education.

Lave, J. and Wenger, E. (1991) *Situated Learning: Legitimate Peripheral Participation*. Cambridge: Cambridge University Press.

Layard, R. (2005) *Happiness*. London: Penguin.

Layard, R. (2006) *The Depression Report: A New Deal for Depression and Anxiety Disorders*. London: Centre for Economic Performance.

Layard, R. and Dunn, C. (2009) *A Good Childhood*. London: Penguin.

LeDoux, J. (1999) *The Emotional Brain*. London: Phoenix.

LeDoux, J. (2002) *The Synaptic Self*. New York: Viking.

Lee, A., Ogle, W. and Sapolsky, R. (2002) Stress and depression: possible links to neuron death in the hippocampus, *Bipolar Disorders*, vol. 4, no. 2, p. 117.

Luna, B. and Sweeney, J. (2004) The emergence of collaborative brain function: fMRI studies of the development of response inhibition, *Annals of the New York Academy of Science*, vol. 1021, no. 1, pp. 296–309.

Maguire, E., Gadian, D., Johnsrude, I., Good, C., Ashburner, J., Frackowiak, R. and Frith, C. (2000) Navigation-related structural change in the hippocampi of taxi drivers, *Proceedings of the National Academy of Sciences*, vol. 97, no. 8, pp. 4398–403.

Marks, M. and Shah, H. (2005) A well-being manifesto for a flourishing society, in Huppert, F., Baylis, N. and Keverne, B. *The Science of Well-being*. Oxford: Oxford University Press.

Marton, F. and Booth, S. (1997) *Learning and Awareness*. Mahwah. NJ: Lawrence Erlbaum Associates.

Marton, F. and Saljo, R. (1976) On qualitative differences in learning: I – outcome and process, *British Journal of Educational Technology*, vol. 46, pp. 115–27.

Maslow, A. (1943) A theory of human motivation, *Psychological Review*, vol. 50, pp. 370–96.

Matheson, D. and Grosvenor, I. (eds) (1999) *An Introduction to the Study of Education*. London: David Fulton.

Maynard, T. (2007) Forest schools in Great Britain: an initial exploration, *Contemporary Issues in Early Childhood*, vol. 8, no. 4, pp. 320–31.

Mithen, S. (2005) *The Singing Neanderthals: The Origins of Music, Language, Mind and Body*. London: Phoenix.

McCauley, C. and Rose, W. (2010) *Child Well-being: Understanding Children's Lives*. London: Kingsley.

McCrea, R. (2005) Personal email communication 25/10/2005.

Morris, D. (2004) *The Nature of Happiness*. London: Little Books.

Morris, E. (2005) *Developing Emotionally Literate Staff: A Practical Guide*. London: Paul Chapman Publishing.

Morris, E. and Scott, C. (2002) *Whole School Emotional Literacy Indicator*. Frampton on Severn: School of Emotional Literacy Press.

Mortimore, P. (ed.) (1999) *Understanding Pedagogy and its Impact on Learning*. London: Paul Chapman Publishing.

Moseley, J. (1996) *Quality Circle Time in the Primary School*. Wisbech: LDA.

Murray, J. (2007) TV violence: research and controversy, in N. Pecora, J. Murray and E. Wartella (eds) *Children and Television: Fifty Years of Research*. Mahwah, NJ: Erlbaum.

National Advisory Council on Creative and Cultural Education (NACCCE) (1999) *All Our Futures: Creativity, Culture and Education*. London: DfEE.

Nachmanovitch, S. (1990) *Free Play: Improvisation in Life and Art*. New York: Penguin Putnam.

Noddings, N. (2003) *Happiness and Education*. Cambridge: Cambridge University Press.

Office for Standards in Education (Ofsted) (1998) *Maintaining Breadth and Balance*. London: Ofsted.

Office for Standards in Education (Ofsted) (2002) *The Curriculum in Successful Primary Schools*. London: Ofsted.

Office for Standards in Education (Ofsted) (2004) *A New Relationship with Schools: Improving Performance through School Self-Evaluation*. Nottingham: DfES Publications.

Office for Standards in Education (Ofsted) (2008) *Geography in Schools: Changing Practice*. London: Crown.

Office for Standards in Education (Ofsted) (2009a) *12 Outstanding Secondary Schools – Excelling Against the Odds*. London: Ofsted.

Office for Standards in Education (Ofsted) (2009b) *20 Outstanding Primary Schools – Excelling Against the Odds*. London: Ofsted.

Office for Standards in Education (Ofsted) (2010) *Learning: Creative Approaches that Raise Standards*. London: Ofsted.

Organization for Economic Cooperation and Development (OECD) (2003) *Learners for life: Student Approaches to Learning*. Paris: OECD Publications.

Overy, K. (1998) Can music really improve the mind? *Psychology of Music*, vol. 26, pp. 97–9.

Page, J. (2000) *Reframing the Early Childhood Curriculum: Educational Imperatives for the Future*. London: Routledge.

Pahl, R. (2000) *On Friendship*. Cambridge: Polity Press.

Pantev, C., Oostenveld, R., Engelien, A., Ross, B., Roberts, L. and Hoke, M. (1998) Increased auditory cortical representation in musicians, *Nature*, vol. 392, pp. 811–14.

Perkins, D. (1992) *Smart Schools*. New York: Free Press.

Perkins, D. (1995) *Outsmarting IQ: The Emerging Science of Learnable Intelligence*. New York: Free Press.

Perkins, D. (2002) *The Eureka Effect: The Art and Logic of Breakthrough Thinking*. New York: Norton.

Perkins, D. (2006) Whole game learning, presentation at 'This Learning Life' conference, University of Bristol, 20 April.

Perkins, D. (2009) *Making Learning Whole: How Seven Principles of Teaching can Transform Education*. San Francisco: Jossey-Bass.

Piaget, J. (1954) *The Construction of Reality in the Child*, trans. M. Cook. New York: Basic Books.

Pinker, S. (1994) *The Language Instinct: The New Science of Language and Mind*. New York: Penguin Science.

Pinker, S. (2002) *The Blank Slate*. London: Penguin.

Plato (1955) *The Republic*, trans. D. Lee. London: Penguin Classics.

Plato (1970) *The Laws*, trans. T. Saunders. London: Penguin Classics.

Pollard, A. (1990) *Towards a Sociology of Learning in Primary School*. London: Rinehart and Winston.

Pollard, A. (1996) *The Social World of Children's Learning*. London: Cassell.

Pollard, A. (2008) *Reflective Teaching: Evidence-informed Professional Practice*, 3rd edition. London: Continuum.

Pollard, A. (ed.) (2010) *Professionalism and Pedagogy: A Contemporary Opportunity: A Commentary by TLRP and GTCE*. London: TLRP.

Pope, R. (2005) *Creativity: History, Theory, Practice*. London: Routledge.

Popenici, S. (2006) Imagine the future: role models and schools' captured imagination, paper presented at the International Conference on Imagination and Education, Vancouver, July.

Popper, K. (1978) Three worlds, paper presented at the Tanner Lecture on Human Values, University of Michigan, 7 April.

Potter, J. (2002) *Active Citizenship in Schools: A Good Practice Guide to Developing Whole School Policy*. London: Kogan Page.

Potts, P. (ed.) (2003) *Inclusion in the City: Selection, Schooling and Community*. London: Routledge.

Powell, S. and Barnes, J. (2008) *Evaluation of the TRACK Project*. Report to Future Creative (formerly Creative Partnerships). Margate: Future Creative.

PriceWaterhouseCoopers (PWC) (2001) *Teacher Workload Study*. London: DfES.

Qualifications and Curriculum Authority (QCA) (1998a) *A Scheme of Work for Key Stages 1 and 2: Geography, History, Design Technology, Physical Education*. London: QCA.

Qualifications and Curriculum Authority (QCA) (1998b) *Maintaining Breadth and Balance*. London: QCA.

QCA (2000) *A Scheme of Work for Key Stages 1 and 2: Art and Design, Music*. London: QCA.

QCA (2002a) *Citizenship at Key Stages 1–4*, 1 January QCA/02/944. London: QCA.

QCA (2002b) *Designing and Timetabling the Primary Curriculum*. London: QCA.

QCDA (2010) *The National Curriculum Primary Handbook*. London: QCDA.

Raffo, C., Dyson, A., Gunter, H., Hall, D., Jones, L. and Kalambouka, A. (eds) (2010) *Education and Poverty in Affluent Countries*. Abingdon: Routledge.

Rhen, J. (1995) Deep and surface approaches to learning: an introduction, *National Teaching and Learning Forum*, vol. 5, no. 1, pp. 1–3.

Richhart, R. (2002) *Intellectual Character: Why It Is, Why It Matters and How to Get It*. New York: Jossey-Bass.

Riddle, J. (2009) *Engaging the Eye Generation: Visual Literacy Strategies for the K-5 Classroom*. Portland. OR: Stenhouse.

Riley, P. (2006) To stir with love: imagination, attachment and teacher behaviour, paper delivered at the International Conference on Imagination in Education, Vancouver, July.

Roberts, P. (2006) *Nurturing Creativity in Young People: A Report to Government to Inform Future Policy*. London: DCMS.

Robertson, I. (1999) *Mind Sculpture*. London: Bantam.

Robertson, I. (2002) *The Mind's Eye*. London: Bantam.

Robinson, K. (2001) *Out of Our Minds*. London: Capstone.

Robinson, K. and Aronica, L. (2010) *The Element: How Finding Your Passion Changes Everything*. London: Penguin.

Rogers, R. (1999) *The Disappearing Arts*. London: RSA/Gulbenkian.

Rogers, R. (2003) *Time for the Arts?* London: RSA.

Rogoff, B. (2003) *The Cultural Nature of Human Development*. New York: Oxford University Press.

Rose, J. (2008) *Independent Review of the Primary Curriculum: Interim Report*. London: DCSF.

Rose, J. (2009) *Independent Review of the Primary Curriculum*. London: DCSF.

Roth, M. (2000) The metamorphosis of Columbus, in S. Wineburg and P. Grossman (eds), *Interdisciplinary Curriculum: Challenges to Implementation*. New York: Teachers College Press.

Rowley, C. and Cooper, H. (2009) *Cross-Curricular Teaching and Learning*. London: Sage.

Royal Society of Arts (RSA) (2003) *Opening Minds: Project Handbook*. London: RSA.

Ruddock, J. and MacIntyre, D. (2007) *Improving Learning through Consulting Pupils*. London: Routledge.

Ryff, C. (1989) Happiness is everything, or is it? Explorations on the meaning of psychological well-being, *Journal of Personality and Social Psychology*, vol. 57, no. 6, pp. 1081–9.

Salovey, P. and Sluyter, D. (1997) *Emotional Development and Emotional Intelligence*. New York: Basic Books.

Saron, C. and Davidson, R.J. (1997) The brain and emotions, in D. Goleman (ed.), *Healing Emotions*. Boston, MA: Shambhala.

School Curriculum and Assessment Authority (SCAA) (1997) *The Arts and the Curriculum*. London: SCAA.

Scoffham, S. (ed.) (2010) *Primary Geography Handbook*. Sheffield: Geographical Association.

Scoffham, S. and Barnes, J. (2009) Transformational experiences and deep learning: the impact of an intercultural study visit to India on UK initial teacher education students, *Journal of Education for Teaching*, vol. 35, no. 3, pp. 257–70.

Scottish Executive (2004) *A Curriculum for Excellence*. Edinburgh: Scottish Executive.

Scottish Office of Education (SOED) (1993) *National Guidelines 5–14: Environmental Studies*. Edinburgh: SOED.

Seligman, M. (2004) *Authentic Happiness*. New York: Basic Books.

Seltzer, K. and Bentley, T. (1999) *The Creative Age: Knowledge and Skills for the New Economy*. London: Demos.

Sharp, P. (2001) *Nurturing Emotional Literacy*. London: David Fulton.

Sharma, N. (2008) *Makiguchi and Ghandi: Their Educational Relevance for the Twenty-first Century*. Plymouth: University Press of America.

Shayer, M. and Adey, P. (2002) *Learning Intelligence: Cognitive Acceleration Across the Curriculum from 5 to 15 years*. Buckingham: Open University Press.

Shepard, L. (1992) What policy makers who mandate tests should know about the new psychology of intellectual ability and learning, in B. Gifford and M. O'Conner (eds), *Changing Assessments: Alternative Views of Aptitude, Achievement and Instruction*. London: Kluwer.

Shepherd, L. (1991) Psychometricians' beliefs about learning, *Education Researcher*, vol. 20, no. 8, pp. 2–16.

Shirley, I. (2007) Exploring the great outdoors, in R. Austin (ed.) (2007) *Letting the Outside In: Developing Teaching and Learning Beyond the Early Years Classroom*. Stoke on Trent: Trentham.

Silber, K. (1965) *Pestalozzi: The Man and his Work*. London: Routledge.

Slaughter, R. (1996) Mapping the future: creating a structural overview of the next 20 years, *Journal of Futures Studies*, vol. 1, no. 1, pp. 5–26.

Smith, A. and Call, N. (2000) *The Alps Approach: Accelerated Learning in Primary Schools*. Stafford: Network Educational Press.

Smith, F., Hardman, F., Wall, K. and Mroz, M. (2004) Interactive whole class teaching in the national literacy and numeracy strategies, *British Educational Research Journal*, vol. 30, no. 3, pp. 395–411.

Steiner, R. (1919) *Education: An Introductory Reader*. London: Rudolf Steiner Press.

Sternberg, R. (1997a) *Thinking Styles*. Cambridge: Cambridge University Press.

Sternberg, R. (1997b) *Successful Intelligence*. New York: Plume.

Sternberg, R. (2002) Teaching students to be wise and not just smart, keynote lecture delivered at the 10th International Conference on Thinking, Harrogate, 16 June.

Sternberg, R. (2003) *Wisdom, Intelligence and Creativity Synthesised*. Cambridge: Cambridge University Press.

Sternberg, R. (2008) *The New Psychology of Love*. New York: Yale University Press.

Sternberg, R. and Williams, W. (eds) (1998) *Intelligence, Instruction and Assessment*. Mahwah. NJ: Lawrence Erlbaum Associates.

Stone-Wiske, M. (ed.) (1998) *Teaching for Understanding*. San Francisco, CA: Jossey-Bass.

Swanwick, K. (1994) *Musical Knowledge: Intuition, Analysis and Music Education*. London: Routledge.

Swanwick, K. (1999) *Teaching Music Musically*. London: Routledge.

Teacher Training Agency (TTA) (2003) *Qualifying to Teach: Handbook of Guidance*. London: TTA.

TES (Times Educational Supplement) 28/05/10.

Theroux, L. (2006) *The Call of the Weird*. London: Pan.

Thompson, P.M., Giedd, J.N., Woods, R.P., MacDonald, D., Evans, A.C. and Toga, A.W. (2000) Growth patterns in the developing brain detected by using continuum mechanical tensor maps, *Nature*, vol. 404, pp. 190–3.

UK Board of Education (1931) *The Primary School* (Hadow Report). London: HMSO.

UNICEF (2007) Child poverty in perspective: an overview of child well-being in rich countries, *Innocenti Report Card 7, 2007. UNICEF* Innocenti Research Centre.

Vygotsky, L. (1962) *Thought and Language*. New York: Wiley.

Vygotsky, L. (1978) *Mind in Society: The Development of Higher Psychological Processes*, Cambridge, MA: Harvard University Press.

Warnock, M. (1996) Foreword, in M. Bennathan and M. Boxall, *Effective Intervention in Primary Schools*. London: David Fulton.

Weare, K. and Gray, G. (2003) *What Works in Developing Children's Emotional and Social Competence and Well Being?* Norwich: HMSO.

Wenger, E. (1998) *Communities of Practice: Learning, Meaning and Identity*. Cambridge: Cambridge University Press.

Wenger, E. (1999) *Communities of Practice: Learning, Meaning and Identity*. Cambridge: Cambridge University Press.

White, J. (2002) *The Child's Mind*. London: Routledge.

Wilkinson, R. (2005) *The Impact of Inequality*. London: Routledge.

Wilson, A. (ed.) (2005) *Creativity in the Primary Classroom*. Exeter: Learning Matters.

Wilson, V., Durrant, J., Stow, W., Barnes, J. and Gershon, J. (2010) *Virtuous Triangles for Curriculum Innovation and Pupil Participation: Supporting School-based Action Research*

Through Local Authority and HEI Collaboration, BERA conference, University of Warwick, 3 September.

Wineburg, S. and Grossman, P. (eds) (2000) *Interdisciplinary Curriculum: Challenges to Implementation*. New York: Teachers College Press.

Wrigley, T. (2005) *Schools of Hope: A New Agenda for School Improvement*, reprinted edn. Stoke-on-Trent: Trentham Books.

Wyse, D. and Rowson, P. (2008) *The Really Useful Creativity Book*. London: Routledge.

Yates, K., Taylor, H., Drotar, D., Wade, S., Klein, S., Stancin, T. and Schatschneider, C. (1997) Pre-injury family environment as a determinate of recovery from traumatic brain injuries in school aged children, *Journal of the International Neurophysiological Society*, vol. 3, pp. 617–30.

Young Foundation (2010) *The State of Happiness*. London: Young Foundation.

Websites

A New Direction (AND) (2010) www.anewdirection.org.uk/ (accessed July 2010).

Baird, A. and Fugelsang, J. (2004) The emergence of consequential thought: evidence from neuroscience, *Philosophical Transactions of the Royal Society*, published online November, http://royalsocietypublishing.org/journals (accessed July 2010).

Barnado's (2010) www.barnados.org.uk

Bawden, A. (2006) On social cohesion, *Guardian* article, www.guardian.co.uk/society/2006/oct/05/comment.politics (accessed August 2010).

BBC (2002) Reith Lecture www.bbc.co.uk/radio4/reith2002/

BBC News website (2010) http://news.bbc.co.uk/1/hi/education/10121931.stm (accessed July 2010).

BBC Trust (2008) www.bbc.co.uk/bbctrust/assets/files/pdf/regulatory_framework/service_licences/service_reviews/childrens/childrens_review.pdf (accessed July 2010).

Bread for the world (2010) www.bread.org/hunger/global (accessed July 2010).

Byron (2008) www.dcsf.gov.uk/byronreview/pdfs/Final%20Report%20Bookmarked.pdf (accessed July 2010).

CABE (2010) www.cabe.org.UK/education

Childline (2010) Children's charity, www.childline.org.uk/Pages/Home.aspx (accessed August 2010).

Childnet International (2010) www.childnet-int.org1

Children's Commissioner (2010) www.childrenscommissioner.gov.uk (accessed 20 July 2010).

Children's Use of the Internet (2006) http://internet-filter-review.toptenreviews.com (accessed August 2010).

Clarke, S. (2001) Assessment for learning in a Gillingham partnership, www.teaching-resource.co.uk/teachers/afl.htm (accessed August 2010).

Claxton, G. (2006) Building learning power, www.buildinglearningpower.co.uk (accessed August 2010).

Common Curriculum (1991) www.deni.gov.uk/index/pre-school-education-pg.htm

Creativity, Culture and Education (2010) www.creativitycultureeducation.org (accessed September 2010).

Csikszentmihalyi, M. (2004) Lecture on flow theory, www.ted.com/talks/mihaly_csik-szentmihalyi_on_flow.html (accessed August 2010).

Curriculum Foundation (2010) www.curriculumfoundation.org/ (accessed July 2010).

Department for Children, Schools and Families (DCSF) (2010) Every Child Matters, www.dcsf.gov.uk/everychildmatters/ (accessed July 2010).

Department of Culture Media and Sport (DCMS) (2008) The Cultural Offer, http://webarchive.nationalarchives.gov.uk/+/ www.culture.gov.uk/Reference_library/Press_notices/archive_2008/dcms009_08.htm (accessed July 2010).

Department for Education and Skills (DfES) (2002) Governors' reports and school prospectuses, http://eduwight.iow.gov.uk/governor/clerks_corner/images/GovernorsAnnualReport&SchoolProspectus%28PRIMARY%29-May2002.pdf (accessed August 2010).

DfES (2004a) *Every Child Matters: Change for Children in Schools*, http://publications.education.gov.uk/eOrderingDownload/DFES-1089-200MIG748.pdf (accessed 2 August 2010).

DfES (2004b) *Learning and Teaching in the Primary School*, www.standards.dfes.gov.uk/numeracy/publications/targeted_support/learn_teach_primary/pc_learnteach034404_improve.pdf (accessed 7 June 2006).

DfES (2004c) *Excellence and Enjoyment*, primary education strategy, www.standards.dfes.gov.uk/primary/publications/literacy/63553/pns_excell_enjoy037703v2.pdf (accessed August 2010).

DfES (2004d) Global Gateway website, www.globalgateway.org.uk/ (accessed July 2010).

DfES (2005a) Teachernet website, www.teachernet.com/ (accessed August 2010).

DfES (2005b) Social, emotional and behavioural skills, www.teachernet.gov.uk/whole-school/sen/datatypes/Behaviour_emotionalldevelopment/ (accessed August 2010).

DfES (2005c) Manifesto for outdoor learning www.publications.Parliment.uk/pa/cm200405/cmselect/cmeduski/120/12009.htm

DfES (2006a) The standards site section on teachers as researchers, www.tda.gov.uk/teachers/continuingprofessionaldevelopment/epd/epd_methods/classroom_based_research.aspx?keywords=teachers+as+researchers (accessed July 2010).

DfES (2006b) Creative learning journey, www.creativelearningjourney.org.uk/ (accessed July 2010).

DfES (2006c) 'Global Gateway' links with schools across the world, www.globalgateway.org.uk/ (accessed July 2010).

DfES (2006d) Learning Outside the Classroom Manifesto, www.lotc.org.uk/getmedia/fe5e8f73-a53c-4310-84af-c5e8c3b32435/Manifesto.aspx (accessed July 2010).

DfES/OFSTED (2004) Indicators of a school's contribution to well-being, p. 25, http://webcache.googleusercontent.com/search?q=cache:oIH-TQpPrScJ:www.ofsted.gov.uk/content/download/7431/75706/file/Indicators%2520of%2520a%2520schools%2520contribution%2520to%2520well-being%2520-%2520by%2520hand.doc (accessed August 2010).

Department of Education (DoE) (2010) www.education.gov.uk/curriculum (accessed July 2010).

Department of Health (DoH) (2005) National Healthy Schools Standard, www.teachernet.gov.uk/management/atoz/n/nhss/ (accessed July 2010).

DH/DfES (2005) *National Healthy Schools Status: Guide for Schools*, www.saled.org/what-we-offer/Schools/resources/schools-every-child-matters/be-healthy (accessed August 2010).

Djuric, Z., Bird, C., Furumoto-Dawson, A., Raucher, G., Ruffin, M., Stowe, R., Tucker, K. and Masi, C. (2008) Biomarkers of psychological stress in Health Disparities Research, www. ncbi.nlm.nih.gov/pmc/articles/PMC2841407/

Eco Schools project (2010) www.eco-schools.org.uk/ (accessed July 2010).

Engaging Places website (2010) http://www.engagingplaces.org.uk/network/art68390 (accessed July 2010).

Forest Schools (2010) www.forestschools.com/ (accessed July 2010).

Frontline (2002) Article/video on the teenage brain, www.pbs.org/wgbh/pages/frontline/shows/teenbrain/view/ (accessed August 2010).

Global gateway (2006) www.globalgateway.org/ (accessed July 2010); www.primary
review.org.uk/Downloads/Int_Reps/4.Children_development-learning/Primary_
Review_2-1a_briefing_Cognitive_development_learning_071214.pdf

Gove, M. (2010a) www.michaelgove.com (accessed July 2010).

Gove, M. (2010b) www.education.gov.uk/inthenews/pressnotices/oo649251education-se.

Guardian (2006) http://image.guardian.co.uk/sys-files/Education/documents/2006/07/17/
NCHrep ort.pdf (accessed July 2010).

HM Government (2005) Higher Standards, Better Schools for All, www.publications.
parliament.uk/pa/cm/200506/cmselect/cmeduski/633/633.pdf

HM Government advice on health and safety (2010) www.teachernet.gov.uk/whole-
school/healthandsafety/visits/ (accessed August 2010).

Hoffer, E. (2006) Wikipedia website, en.wikipedia.org/wiki/Eric_Hoffer (accessed 10
August 2006).

International Primary Curriculum (IPC) (2006) www.internationalprimarycurriculum.
com/ (accessed July 2010).

Layard, R. (2006) Report on depression, http://cep.lse.ac.uk/textonly/research/mental-
health/DEPRESSION_REPORT_LAYARD2.pdf (accessed July 2010).

MACOS (2010) www.macosonline.org

Marks, T. and Shah, H. (2004) A well-being manifesto, www.neweconomics.org/sites/
neweconomics.org/files/A_Well-Being_Manifesto_for_a_Flourishing_Society.pdf
(accessed August 2010).

Morris, E. (2006) www.emotionalintelligence.co.uk/appliedei.htm (accessed August
2010).

National Literacy Trust (2005) www.literacytrust.org.uk/Database/stats/readchild.
html#Young (accessed 28 August 2005).

New Horizons (1991) www.newhorizons.org/future/creating_the_future/crfut_perkins.
html

NFER (2007) HEARTS project evaluation, www.nfer.ac.uk/nfer/publications/HEA01/
HEA01.pdf (accessed July 2010).

NSPCC (2009) www.nspccannualreview.org.uk/ (accessed July 2010).

Ofsted (2002) *The Curriculum in Successful Primary Schools*, www.ofsted.gov.uk/publications/
index.cfm?fuseaction=pubs.displayfile&id=303&type=pdf (accessed 8 June 2006).

Ofsted (2003) Expecting the unexpected, www.ofsted.gov.uk/.../Expecting%20the%20
unexpected%20(PDF%20format).pdf (accessed August 2010).

Ofsted (2008) Geography in Schools: changing practice, www.ofstedgov.co.uk/Ofsted-
home/Publications-and-research/Browse-all-by/Education/Curriculum/Geography/
Primary/Geography-in-schools-changing-practice/%28language%29/eng-GB
(accessed July 2010).

One Org (2005) International campaign to make poverty history, www.makepoverty-
history.org (accessed August 2010).

Pediatrics (2002) http://pediatrics.aappublications.org/cgi/content/full/109/6/1028
(accessed 12 June 2006).

Pew International (2008) http://people-press.org/report/444/news-media (accessed
July 2010).

Pew Internet and American Life project (2005) http://www.pewinternet.org/Reports/2001/
Teenage-Life-Online/Part-2/1-Family.aspx?r=1 (accessed July 2010).

Project Zero (2006) http://pzweb.harvard.edu/ (accessed August 2010).

Puttnam, D. (2009) www.wearethepeoplemovie.com/ (accessed July 2010).

QCA (2003) Respect for all: reflecting cultural diversity through the curriculum, http://webarchive.nationalarchives.gov.uk/20090902230247/qcda.gov.uk/6753.aspx (accessed July 2010).

QCA (2005) *Creativity: Find It, Promote It* (video May 2005) and website, www. ncaction. org.uk/creativity/index.htm (accessed 23 March 2006).

QCDA (2007) Secondary Curriculum, http://curriculum.qcda.gov.uk/key-stages-3-and-4/index.aspx (accessed July 2010).

QCDA (2010) *The National Curriculum Primary Handbook*, http://orderline.qcda.gov.uk/gempdf/184962383X.PDF (accessed July 2010).

Reggio Emilia (2006) http://zerosei.comune.re.it/inter/index.htm (accessed July 2010).

Room 13 Scotland (2005) www.room13scotland.com/index.php (accessed July 2010).

Rousseau, J. (1762) Translation of *Emile ou de l'education*, www.ilt.columbia.edu/pedagogies/rousseau/index.html (accessed July 2010).

RSA (2005) RSA's Global Challenges, by J. Glenn, August, www.thersa.org/projects

RSA (2010) http://comment.rsablogs.org.uk/2010/10/14/rsa-animate-changing-education-paradigms/ (accessed November 2010).

Sanchez, E. and Gruber, H. (2005) *Rhythm Is It* [film], www.rhythmisit.com/en/php/index_noflash.php (accessed July 2010).

School Councils (2005) www.schoolcouncils.org/ (accessed August 2010).

Sing up (2010) www.singup.org

Smithers, A. and Robinson, P. (2001) *Teachers Leaving*, Centre for Employment Research University of Liverpool, report. London: NUT. Available at: www.education.gov.uk/research/data/uploadfiles/rr430.pdf (accessed August 2010).

Social and Emotional Aspects of Learning (SEAL) (2006) http://nationalstrategies.standards.dcsf.gov.uk/node/65859 (accessed August 2010).

Statistics on television-watching and young people (2005) www.ukfilmcouncil.org.uk/statistics/yearbook/?y=2004&c=9&skip=1 (accessed 11 August 2005).

Stephen Lawrence Inquiry (1999) Macpherson Report, www.archive.official-documents.co.uk/document/cm42/4262/4262.htm (accessed August 2010).

Storyline (2010) www.storyline-scotland.com/whatisstoryline.html (accessed July 2010).

Teacher Development Agency (TDA) (2008) www.tda.gov.uk/upload/resources/pdf/p/professional_standards_2008.pdf (accessed August 2010).

Techeye (2010) www.techeye.net/internet/children-find-social-networking-more-important-than-family (accessed July 2010).

TES (2005) www.tes.co.uk/article.aspx?storycode=2084657

Times Educational Supplement (TES) (2010) Gove on education, 28 May, www.tes.co.uk/article.aspx?storycode=6045168 (accessed July 2010).

UK Film Council (2004) www.ukfilmcouncil.org.uk/information/statistics/yearbook/?y=2004&c=9&skip=1 (accessed 10 August 2006).

UN (2000) United Nation's millennium goals, www.un.org/millenniumgoals/ (accessed July 2010).

UN (2006) Schools website 'Cyberschoolbus', www.un.org/cyberschoolbus/briefing/labour/index.htm (accessed July 2010).

UNICEF (1989) *Convention on the Rights of the Child*, www.unicef.org/crc/ (accessed July 2010).

UNICEF (2005) Children living in poverty: a review of child poverty definitions, measurements and policies, www.unicef.org/policyanalysis/files/child_poverty_final_draft_4_05 (accessed August 2010).

UNICEF (2007) *Child Poverty in Rich Countries*, www.unicef.org/media/files/ChildPoverty
  Report.pdf (accessed July 2010).
UNICEF (2009) www.unicef.org.uk/press/news_detail_full_story.asp?news_id=1300
  (accessed July 2010).
USDE (2002) No Child Left Behind policy, www2.ed.gov/admins/lead/account/
  nclbreference/index.html (accessed July 2010).
WHO (2004) Health behaviour in school aged children study, international report
  2001/2002, www.euro.who.int/__data/assets/pdf_file/0008/110231/e82923.pdf
  (accessed July 2010).
WHO (2008) Inequalities in young people's health report, www.euro.who.int/__data/
  assets/pdf_file/0005/53852/E91416.pdf (accessed July 2010).
Youth Music (2010) www.youthmusic.org.uk/musicispower/index.html

Index

CHILDREN'S RIGHTS IN PRACTICE

Edited by **Phil Jones** *University of Leeds* and
Gary Walker *Leeds Metropolitan University*

Considering the rights of the child is now central
to all fields involving children and to good multi-
agency working. This book offers an explanation of the theoretical issues and the key policy
developments that are crucial to all professions,
and helps the reader to understand children's
rights in relation to their role in working with children and young people. Looking at education,
health, social care and welfare, it bridges the gap
between policy and practice for children from Birth
to 19 years. Chapters cover:
- the child's right to play
- youth justice, children's rights and the voice of the child
- ethical dilemmas in different contexts
- involvement, participation and decision making
- safeguarding and child protection, social justice and exclusion.

This book helps the reader understand what constitutes good practice, whilst
considering the advantages and tensions involved in working across disciplines
to implement children's rights against a complex legislative and social policy
backdrop.

April 2011 • 256 pages
Cloth (978-1-84920-379-1) • £65.00
Paper (978-1-84920-380-7) • £22.99

ALSO FROM SAGE

DIVERSITY, EQUALITY AND ACHIEVEMENT IN EDUCATION

Gianna Knowles and **Vini Lander** both at *University of Chichester*

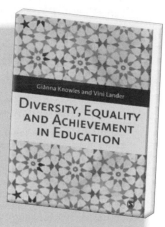

Most classrooms contain children from a variety of backgrounds, where home culture, religious beliefs and the family's economic situation all impact on achievement. This needs to be recognised by teachers in order to establish fair, respectful, trusting and constructive relationships with children and their families, which will allow every child to reach their full potential.

This book looks at real issues that affect teachers in the classroom, and examines a variety of influences affecting child development. It provides you with the theoretical and practical information you need to ensure you understand the complex factors which affect the children in your care, and it encourages good, thoughtful teaching. Dealing with some of the less widely addressed aspects of diversity and inclusion, the book considers:

- children who are asylum seekers
- the notion of 'pupil voice'
- what diversity and equality mean in practice
- gender and achievement
- looked-after children
- social class
- disability
- ethnicity and whiteness

This book is essential reading for any education student looking at diversity and inclusion, and for teachers in role looking for advice on how to meet the professional standards.

February 2011 • 192 pages
Cloth (978-1-84920-600-6) • £65.00
Paper (978-1-84920-601-3) • £21.99

ALSO FROM SAGE

CONTEMPORARY ISSUES IN LEARNING AND TEACHING

Edited by **Margery McMahon**, **Christine Forde** and **Margaret Martin** all at *University of Glasgow*

Contemporary Issues in Learning and Teaching looks at current issues across the three key areas of policy, learning and practice. It will help you to think critically on your Education course, and to make connections between the processes of learning and the practicalities of teaching. The book addresses key issues in primary, secondary and special education, and includes examples from all four countries of the UK.

The contributors reflect on current thinking and policy surrounding learning and teaching, and what it means to be a teacher today. Looking at the practice of teaching in a wider context allows you to explore some of the issues you will face, and the evolving expectations of your role in a policy-led environment. The book focuses on core areas of debate including:

- education across different contexts and settings
- teaching in an inclusive environment
- Continuing Professional Development (CPD) for practitioners

Each chapter follows the same accessible format. They contain case studies and vignettes providing examples and scenarios for discussion; introduction and summary boxes listing key issues and concepts explored in the chapter; key questions for discussion reflection; and further reading.

This essential text will be ideal for undergraduate and postgraduate courses, including BEd//BA degrees, initial teacher-training courses, and Masters in Education programmes.

All editors and contributors are based in the Faculty of Education at Glasgow University, UK.

November 2010 • 232 pages
Cloth (978-1-84920-127-8) • £65.00
Paper (978-1-84920-128-5) • £21.99

ALSO FROM SAGE

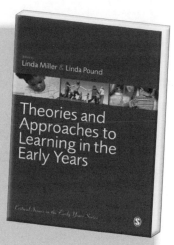

978-1-84860-616-6

978-1-84920-030-1

978-1-84920-114-8

978-1-84860-713-2 978-1-84920-076-9 978-1-84920-126-1 978-1-84920-078-3

Find out more about these titles and our wide range
of books for education students and practitioners at
www.sagepub.co.uk/education

EXCITING EDUCATION TEXTS FROM SAGE